D0771971

BEYOND GOOD AND EVIL

FRIEDRICH NIETZSCHE was born near Leipzig in 1844, the son of a Lutheran clergyman. He attended the famous Pforta School, then went to university at Bonn and at Leipzig, where he studied philology and read Schopenhauer. When he was only twenty-four he was appointed to the chair of classical philology at Basle University; he stayed there until his health forced him into retirement in 1879. While at Basle he made and broke his friendship with Wagner, participated as an ambulance orderly in the Franco-Prussian War, and published *The Birth of Tragedy* (1872), *Untimely Meditations* (1873–6) and the first part of *Human, All Too Human* (1878; two supplements entitled *Assorted Opinions and Maxims* and *The Wanderer and his Shadow* followed in 1879 and 1880 respectively). From 1880 until his final collapse in 1889, except for brief interludes, he divorced himself from everyday life and, supported by his university pension, he lived mainly in France, Italy and Switzerland. *The Dawn* appeared in 1881 followed by *The Gay Science* in the autumn of 1882. *Thus Spoke Zarathustra* was written between 1883 and 1885, and his last completed books were *Ecce Homo*, an autobiography, and *Nietzsche contra Wagner*. He became insane in 1889 and remained in a condition of mental and physical paralysis until his death in 1900.

R. J. HOLLINGDALE translated eleven of Nietzsche's books and published two books about him; he also translated works by, among others, Schopenhauer, Goethe, E. T. A. Hoffman, Lichtenberg and Theodor Fontane, many of these for Penguin Classics. He was the honorary president of the British Nietzsche Society. R. J. Hollingdale died in 2001. In its obituary *The Times* described him as 'Britain's foremost postwar Nietzsche specialist' and the *Guardian* paid tribute to his 'inspired gift for German translation'. Richard Gott wrote that he 'brought fresh generations – through fluent and intelligent translation – to read and relish Nietzsche's inestimable thought'.

Professor Richard Schacht, Executive Director of the North American Nietzsche Society, said that 'Hollingdale and Walter Kaufmann, his sometime collaborator, deserve much of the credit for Nietzsche's rehabilitation during the third quarter of the twentieth century. It is hard to imagine what Nietzsche's fate in the English-speaking world would have been without them. All of us in Nietzsche studies today are in Hollingdale's debt.'

MICHAEL TANNER was educated in the RAF and at Cambridge University, where he was a Lecturer in Philosophy until 1997 and is a Fellow of Corpus Christi College. He is equally interested in philosophy, music and literature, his particular areas being Friedrich Nietzsche and Richard Wagner. He has written for many journals, contributed 'The Total Work of Art' to *The Wagner Companion*, and is the author of *Nietzsche* (1995) and *Wagner* (1996).

FRIEDRICH NIETZSCHE

Beyond Good and Evil

PRELUDE TO A PHILOSOPHY
OF THE FUTURE

TRANSLATED BY
R. J. Hollingdale

WITH AN INTRODUCTION BY
Michael Tanner

PENGUIN BOOKS

PENGUIN BOOKS

Published by the Penguin Group
Penguin Books Ltd, 80 Strand, London, WC2R ORL, England
Penguin Putnam Inc., 375 Hudson Street, New York, New York 10014, USA
Penguin Books Australia Ltd, 250 Camberwell Road, Camberwell, Victoria 3124, Australia
Penguin Books Canada Ltd, 10 Alcorn Avenue, Toronto, Ontario, Canada M4V 3B2
Penguin Books India (P) Ltd, 11 Community Centre, Panchsheel Park, New Delhi – 110 017, India
Penguin Books (NZ) Ltd, Cnr Rosedale and Airborne Roads, Albany, Auckland, New Zealand
Penguin Books (South Africa) (Pty) Ltd, 24 Sturdee Avenue, Rosebank 2196, South Africa

Penguin Books Ltd, Registered Offices: 80 Strand, London, WC2R ORL, England

www.penguin.com

This translation first published 1973
Reprinted with revisions and a new introduction 1990
Reprinted with new further reading and chronology, 2003

056

Translation, translator's note and commentary copyright © R. J. Hollingdale, 1973, 1990
Introduction copyright © Michael Tanner, 1990
All rights reserved

Set in Garamond Monophoto

Printed and bound in Great Britain by Clays Ltd, Elcograf S.p.A.

ISBN-13: 978–0–140–44923–5

www.greenpenguin.co.uk

CONTENTS

INTRODUCTION

Beyond Good and Evil is one of the greatest books by a very great thinker, and like all such books it is very difficult, all the more so for not seeming to be. It was the first book that Nietzsche wrote after what he considered to be his master-piece, *Thus Spoke Zarathustra*. That had been for him a great creative effort, and he never wavered in his view that it contained all the most important things he had to say. Perhaps it was, none the less, a suspicion that he had not been so entirely successful in it as he had hoped that led him to claim that all the books he wrote subsequently, at least up to *Twilight of the Idols* (1888), were commentaries on or expansions of it. When he sent the great historian Jacob Burckhardt a copy of *Beyond Good and Evil* (henceforth *BGE*) he wrote in the accompanying letter: 'Please read this book (although it says the same things as my *Zarathustra*, but differently, very differently).' If he hadn't said so, one would hardly have guessed it; and though he did say so, I'm inclined to disagree. Nietzsche was always obsessed with there being a pattern to his life and works, and it is entirely characteristic of him that his last completed work, the wonderfully bizarre so-called autobiography *Ecce Homo*, should have been devoted to estab-lishing what that pattern was, mainly through tracing the course of his literary productivity in the most tendentious way. But since he was also obsessed with teasing his readers, I rather feel that, both in the letter to Burckhardt and in *Ecce Homo*, Nietzsche was poking fun, and am inclined to resist his claim about *BGE*.

2

The most obvious difference between *Thus Spoke Zarathustra* and *BGE* is that in the former we have a narrative, though a tenuous one, that Zarathustra communicates through parables, exemplary encounters with a wide variety of people and even animals, and through sermons addressed to mankind but often insisting on the necessity of man's being replaced by the Superman. In *BGE*, by contrast, Nietzsche is very much concerned with addressing his contemporaries, in his favourite role of an 'untimely man', telling them things about themselves that he is sure they would rather not hear. 'There is not a single good-natured word in the entire book,' he says in the chapter devoted to *BGE* in *Ecce Homo*, wilfully forgetting considerable tracts of it that express as powerfully as anything he ever wrote his tormented love for mankind. He also stresses in *Ecce Homo* that, while *Zarathustra* had been his great work of affirmation, after it he had to do what he had often sworn that he wouldn't: namely, say 'No' as emphatically as possible. On 1 January 1882 he had taken a set of New Year's resolutions, and had recorded them at the beginning of Part Four of *The Gay Science*: 'I do not want to wage war against what is ugly, I do not want to accuse; I do not even want to accuse those who accuse. *Looking away* shall be my only negation. And all in all and on the whole: some day I wish only to be a Yes-sayer.' That day never came – in fact receded further and further as he went on writing for a non-existent public. 'From now on,' he writes of *BGE* in *Ecce Homo*, 'all my writings are fish-hooks: perhaps I understand fishing as well as anyone? . . . If nothing got *caught* I am not to blame. *There were no fish* . . .' And the less he was taken notice of, the more critical, the more No-saying he became towards his non-readers. The subtitle of *Thus Spoke Zarathustra* is 'A Book for Everyone and No One'. It turned out to be, at least in his lifetime, for the latter only. Since it was clear that the world wasn't ready for Zarathustra's messages, ardently devoted to proclaiming how life was to be made worth living, Nietzsche turned more confidently than he had before, even in the great series of books which preceded *Zarathustra*, to diagnosing the reasons for the worthlessness of contemporary existence – both his and ours. Again in *Ecce Homo* he writes of *BGE* that it was 'in all essentials a *critique of modernity*, the modern sciences, the modern arts, not even excluding modern politics'. But its objects of attack are still wider than this suggests. For Nietzsche attacks modernity by analysing the perennial tendencies that it manifests. In giving a critique of modernity, he is simultaneously producing an account of decadence – a term to which he was addicted, though oddly enough not in *BGE*, where he employs the possibly more drastic word 'degeneration'.

3

From *The Birth of Tragedy* onwards Nietzsche had produced a series of ever-deepening accounts of the ways in which cultures lose their creative drive and become decadent, and the great positive vision of *Zarathustra* had put him, he felt, in the strongest position for reinforcing these accounts. The first great culture with which he had been concerned was that of what he called 'the tragic age of the Greeks', which for him comprised the pre-Socratic philosophers and the first two of the great tragedians, Aeschylus and Sophocles. They had had the courage to recognize the fundamentally terrible nature of existence and yet still to affirm it, and furthermore not in moral terms – conveyed by such phrases as 'We become better through suffering' and assorted similar claptrap – but purely as an aesthetic phenomenon. Such tragic heroism was short-lived, thanks to the arrival on the scene of Euripides and his philosophical counterpart Socrates. These two villains, according to Nietzsche, contrived the suicide of tragic drama through their purveying of optimistic rationalism: in teaching that virtue is knowledge, and that we therefore err through ignorance alone, they deprived their culture of its greatest insight, that the more we know about reality the more frightful we realize that it is; and thus they inaugurated the period of decadence. The situation went from bad to worse, in Nietzsche's view. For what in Socrates was merely a belief that reasoning could lead us to virtue-inducing wisdom became in the hands of his perversely brilliant pupil Plato a completely worked-out system, which, whatever its author may have thought about it (and Plato was in many ways the most pessimistic of philosophers), was regarded by Nietzsche as the hideous perfection of optimism in its positing of a world more real than this one, a world immune to change, and thus to decay and death. As usual when he is tackling his arch-enemies, Nietzsche feels highly ambivalent towards Plato: appalled by his system, but reluctantly admiring of the élan and cunning with which he devised it. Furthermore, however decadent Socrates and his philosophical progeny may have been, they represent the decadence of something magnificent, and thus reflect, however distortedly, one of mankind's supreme moments.

4

Meanwhile, a little to the east of Greece, another drama was being played out. The relationship of the Jews to their god was not of a kind to induce in them a tragic vision of existence, but it was of a kind that Nietzsche could admire, and several passages in *BGE* celebrate it. But while he seems always to have felt that there was nothing inevitable in the movement of decline from the tragic Greeks to their successors (in other words that with better luck the latter could have maintained, perhaps even have extended, the tragic insights of the former), it was inherent in Judaism that it should lead to its own overthrow in the most disastrous way. Constantly on the look-out for a Messiah, the Jews finally got one; and though they denied that he was the genuine article, he acquired enough of a following to conquer the civilized world, at any rate the western part of it. Yet Christianity – in Nietzsche's analysis, a grotesque distortion of Christ's own vision – is inherently decadent ('Platonism for "the people"', as he curtly puts it in the preface to *BGE*), and what we are now witnessing, as well as being participants in, is the decadence of decadence. Platonism proper had been glamorous; now we are confronted with mere squalor on every front, and it is the unsavoury task of the man who is spelling out the 'Prelude to a Philosophy of the Future' (the subtitle of *BGE*) to unmask

Christianity, for which purpose, among others, he finds it essential to don a mask himself. Nietzsche's favourite activity – there can be no doubt about it – was celebration. But when he realized how little there was to celebrate in the world around him, and how much to be nauseated by, he brought a gusto to his demolitions that makes them marvellously exhilarating.

5

This may all seem to be rather distant from the experience of reading *BGE*, at least with respect to the first two parts, 'On the Prejudices of Philosophers' and 'The Free Spirit'. But in fact the prejudices of philosophers turn out to be ones that we all share. Or perhaps it is fairer to say that Nietzsche regards us all, insofar as we subscribe to a system of values, as being philosophers. Nietzsche immediately raises a series of questions concerning values that we hold so deeply that we are not aware of having them as values at all. '*What* really is it in us that wants "the truth"?' he asks, thereby immediately establishing a distance between himself and other philosophers. He is, as so often, interested in asking a question prior to any it would normally occur to us to ask. As philosophers, that is as 'lovers of wisdom', how could we want anything other than the truth? We could hardly go out consciously looking for untruth. As it stands, this first question seems provokingly silly, and it is only when we realize that with it Nietzsche is launching on a *series* of questions that we are made to feel genuinely uneasy. To want truth and begin searching for it we need to have confidence in our capacity to find it; to recognize it when we encounter it. What gives us this confidence? It is, Nietzsche claims in Section 2, '*the faith in antithetical values*' that is the 'fundamental faith of the metaphysicians'. We operate, in the most natural way, with a series of opposites, of which truth–falsity is the most obvious and fundamental. Indeed, it is hard to see how we could avoid working in this way, and one might feel inclined to ask Nietzsche, before he succeeds in dazzling us with a series of increasingly alarming doubts, whether *he* doesn't operate within this dichotomy too. And it very soon turns out that he does. The original query is, to a large extent, one of those effects which Nietzsche the melodramatist of the inner life is betrayed into making when he lapses from his role as 'the first tragic philosopher'. The issues that he is most valuably concerned with in these heady opening sections are all closely related to the first one, but not identical with it. His real anxieties have to do with our readiness to take as truths things that for him manifestly aren't, thereby displaying the lack of refinement in our sense of truth. In addition, he is irritated by the dogmatism that insists that between the poles of truth–falsity, good–bad, and so on, there can be no fruitful connections. And, perhaps crucially, he claims (and here I quote the whole of Section 4):

> The falseness of a judgement is to us not necessarily an objection to a judgement: it is here that our new language perhaps sounds strangest. The question is to what extent it is life-advancing, life-preserving, species-preserving, perhaps even species-breeding; and our fundamental tendency is to assert that the falsest judgements (to which synthetic judgements *a priori* belong) are the most indispensable to us, that without granting as true the fictions of logic, without measuring reality against the purely invented world of the unconditional and self-identical, without a continual falsification of the world by means of numbers, mankind could not live – that to renounce false judgements would be to renounce life, would be to deny life. To recognize untruth as a condition of life: that, to be sure, means to resist customary value-sentiments in a dangerous fashion; and a philosophy which ventures to do so places itself, by that act alone, beyond good and evil.

This remarkable passage, besides being perplexing, may very well be true. To make it clearer it is necessary to run the risk that besets all commentators on Nietzsche – that of seeming to be painfully prosaic. However, to offer my interpretation: Nietzsche is not claiming that we do, or should, embrace judgements that we know to be false – it is not even clear that such a suggestion makes sense. His point is rather that many of the judgements to which we subscribe most firmly may in fact be false, but that it is better that we should not discover this, or that it *may* be better. We should, that is, be very careful about where our philosophers are leading us. Actually he would have made his point more effectively if he had spoken of scientists rather than of philosophers, for the latter have not been notably successful in uncovering any concrete truths, palatable or the reverse, at any stage in the history of the subject. But the search for truth at any cost, though it is inspired by a philosophy, *has* been carried through with terrifying success by scientists; admittedly more so in the century since Nietzsche wrote that passage than in all preceding times. It may well be the case that it is more important that a judgement be 'life-advancing, life-preserving', etc., than that it be true. But one can't decide to believe in something because it ministers to life, though one thinks that it is false, simply because one can't *decide* to believe. Nietzsche is aware of this, to the extent that he has a 'Hands off!' attitude towards knowledge-seekers. As he puts it in the preface to the second edition of *The Gay Science*, written later in the year that *BGE* was published: '"Is it true that God is present everywhere?" a little girl asked her mother; "I think that's indecent" – a hint for philosophers! One should have more respect for the bashfulness with which nature has hidden behind riddles and iridescent uncertainties.' But surely Nietzsche would again have done better to speak of scientists – the secrets of nature seem to be safe from philosophers. It must be the case that he was so concerned with the drive to truth, which philosophers ceaselessly boast of possessing to a supreme degree, that he overlooked what ought to have been for him their gratifying failure-rate. Or, more sympathetically to him, one might say it was the whole nexus of science-inspired-by-philosophy-inspired-by-religion that really concerned him. For, as he had argued in *The Gay Science* and was to argue again at greater length in *The Genealogy of Morals*, it was the self-destructive urge of Christianity, intent on exploring to its furthest recesses the glory of God's world, that led to the discovery that explanations of natural phenomena could continue indefinitely without ever needing to call on divine assistance.

6

But this makes it sound as if Nietzsche regretted the erosion of Christian belief and value by advancing science, whereas if there is one widely held view about him that is true, it is that he was passionately anti-Christian. So if there is one good thing about Christianity, mustn't this be its inherent tendency to autodestruct? This is where Nietzsche's passion for intellectual cleanliness asserts itself. For although we think of Christianity as primarily a religion, it is, like all systems of religious belief, based on a set of views about the way things are, in other words a metaphysic. And as soon as he hears that word, Nietzsche pounces. He puts his case in Section 6, which begins:

> It has gradually become clear to me what every great philosophy has hitherto been: a confession on the part of its author and a kind of involuntary and unconscious memoir; moreover, that the moral (or immoral) intentions in every philosophy have every time constituted the real germ of life out of which the entire plant has grown. To explain how a philosopher's most remote metaphysical assertions have actually been arrived at, it is always well (and wise) to ask oneself first: what morality does this (does *he* –) aim at? I accordingly do not believe a 'drive to knowledge' to be the father of philosophy, but that another drive has, here as elsewhere, only employed knowledge (and false knowledge!) as a tool.

So, in the course of four pages, Nietzsche has performed a *volte face*. Having called into question the value of the urge to knowledge, he now denies that it ever is the basic urge, for we always pursue knowledge, so-called, in the interests of supporting a moral order, which is a dressed-up version of how we want things to be, or how we want them to be forced to be. It would be absurd to say that Nietzsche deplores this basic drive of ours – it is the 'will to power' in action, and everything is will to power. What he finds intolerable is the lack of intellectual hygiene that is universal among philosophers; the way they 'pose as having discovered and attained their real opinions through the self-evolution of a cold, pure, divinely unperturbed dialectic ... while what happens at bottom is that a prejudice, a notion, an "inspiration", generally a desire of the heart sifted and made abstract, is defended by them with reasons sought after the event' (Section 5). He immediately goes on to instance Kant and Spinoza, who are certainly two flagrant examples of what he has just claimed.

7

While we may readily agree that philosophers in their claims to be following the argument wherever it leads are being disingenuous in so obvious a way as to border on the banal, we might also ask of Nietzsche how he would like them to behave now in order to redeem their predecessors' delinquency. The search for truth is a dubious enterprise, it seems, both because it isn't clear that it's a good idea for us to try to live with it, and because the very notion of finding truth is in itself suspect. But he has no sooner made these points than he arraigns philosophers for *not* really searching for truth, but for presenting as truth what they want to be the case! Is he merely asking that they should be more honest with themselves and their public? Hardly, for he attacks them, so far as their conclusions go, for inventing worlds that put this one to shame. But why is that in itself wrong, if their inventions are magnificent when judged by, perhaps, aesthetic criteria or by the enrichment of life that they – the invented worlds – have made possible? There is no simple answer to that question, for the best of reasons. Many of Nietzsche's commentators have taken him to task for what they see as crucial vacillations. Yet it is impossible for a person who feels these issues as deeply as he does not to be torn – Nietzsche's characteristic condition. He is far too honest to deny the enormous allure of what in the end seems to him harmful; so ruthless with himself, indeed, that he has constantly to fight off a kind of paralysis in the face of the huge diversity of phenomena that he feels forcing themselves on his attention. 'In the philosopher,' he writes in Section 6, '... there is

nothing whatever impersonal.' Most philosophers would vehemently deny that, and claim that on the contrary they were at
least aiming at the wholly impersonal. In this they are deluded,
however, and Nietzsche provides them with an object lesson
in bringing the whole of one's personality into one's work,
which he does so blatantly that no one could be under any
false impressions about it.

Thus we often find him praising lightheartedness: urging
us not to burrow but to remain at the surfaces of things,
practising a kind of ideal frivolity. But no less often he
exhorts us to stop at nothing in order to find out what is
really the case, especially in that most treacherous area, the
human heart. In urging both these ideals on us, he is acknow-
ledging something of the utmost importance about human
beings that anyone acquainted with the greatest art recognizes:
the juxtaposition of unblinking recognition of the frightfulness
of life with a stubborn determination not to be subdued by it,
which must often mean that even the greatest artists turn their
backs on the things they have seen, and insist on carrying on
in spite of them, while those who achieve the supreme heights
perform the further feat of converting that 'in spite of' into
'because of'. It is Nietzsche's ultimate task, throughout all his
work, to justify that transition, to see that it is not a mere
sleight of argument or act of self-betrayal. In the end, what he
accuses philosophers of is cheapness and over-simplification.
In Section 9 he taunts the Stoics for perpetrating just such a
'noble' trick:

> You want to *live* 'according to nature'? O you noble Stoics,
> what fraudulent words! Think of a being such as nature is,
> prodigal beyond measure, indifferent beyond measure, without
> aims or intentions, without mercy or justice, at once fruitful and
> barren and uncertain; think of indifference itself as a power –
> how *could* you live according to such indifference? To live – is
> that not precisely wanting to be other than this nature? Is living
> not valuating, preferring, being unjust, being limited, wanting
> to be different? And even if your imperative 'live according to
> nature' meant at bottom the same thing as 'live according to
> life' – how could you *not* do that?

Nietzsche takes the Stoics to task because they provide a particularly clear example of the dishonesty and trickery that he finds pervasive in philosophy. Their avowed ideal of finding out what nature is and then submitting to it, with the idea of the nobility of such an enterprise being smuggled in along the way, is mere humbug. In the first place, they tailor nature to suit their purposes, making it into a much less intimidating affair than it really is, ignoring its cruelty and wastefulness. Secondly, since nature is simply everything that there is, the idea of submitting to it rather than fighting it turns out to be boastful nonsense, an empty flourish to keep up their spirits. Nature is already in a state of ceaseless combat, one part against all others – this is an idea which Nietzsche first propounded in *The Birth of Tragedy*, and which he never abandoned, though he often modified his formulations of it. In contrast to the 'resignationism' of the Stoics (to use a term with which he abused Schopenhauer in his 'Attempt at a Self-Criticism', the introduction to the third edition of *The Birth of Tragedy*, written in 1886, shortly after *BGE*), Nietzsche posits living as choosing – that is the force of 'Is living not valuating, preferring, being unjust?', etc. The answer to that question, an answer so obvious that Nietzsche doesn't deign to give it, is of course 'Yes'.

8

Anyone who knows the central teachings of *Zarathustra*, or at least of the eponymous central figure in that work, may begin wondering at this point what is going on. Indeed, anyone who knows any of Nietzsche's writings may find his attack on the Stoics odd. For the Superman, whose coming is proclaimed in *Zarathustra*, and the tragic Greeks, whose courage is celebrated in *The Birth of Tragedy*, are characterized by, among other things, their unflinching capacity to say 'Yes' to whatever comes their way. And one of the other most celebrated teachings of *Zarathustra* is the 'eternal recurrence' of all things; it is, indeed, the test of Supermanship that one should live without regret, converting every 'Thus it happened' into

'Thus I willed it'. One could be forgiven, surely, for thinking that there wasn't a significant difference between that and the scornful description Nietzsche gives of 'living according to nature'. And the fact that *BGE*, allegedly a work that says the same things as *Zarathustra*, contains not a single mention of the Superman, and only one of the eternal recurrence, might lead one to think that Nietzsche had changed his mind, as usual without announcing the fact. Yet that one reference to the eternal recurrence is a very emphatic one. It occurs in Section 56, where Nietzsche writes of

> the ideal of the most exuberant, most living and most world-affirming man, who has not only learned to get on and treat with all that was and is but who wants to have it again *as it was and is* to all eternity, insatiably calling out *da capo* not only to himself but to the whole piece and play, and not only to a play but fundamentally to him who needs precisely this play – and who makes it necessary.

Granted that exuberance isn't in the Stoic repertoire, and that the Stoics stressed coping with rather than affirming the world, the critique of them in Section 9 does seem, if valid, to apply equally to this ideal that Nietzsche celebrates a mere forty pages further into the book.

The resolution of this problem lies in the fact that, though Nietzsche is most famous for his sharp, emphatic dichotomies, such as the one between Apollo and Dionysus, or between master and slave moralities, he is actually (as he isn't hesitant to claim) at least as much a connoisseur of nuances. In particular, his broad distinctions tend to draw attention away from his fine ones. For instance, and with especial relevance to this context, he is often concerned with attitudes that appear to resemble one another, even to be identical, but between which he sees all the difference. And he is cunning enough to leave the hard work of sorting them out to his readers, while he elaborately explains distinctions where confusion is unlikely. This is one of the crucial respects in which he 'wears a mask' – something he advocates with great warmth in *BGE*, more than in any of his other books.

So, to take the case under discussion: both the Stoic and Superman assume an attitude of acceptance (to use the most neutral word available) towards life. But the grounds on which they found their attitudes are fundamentally different, and so their attitudes are essentially different too. The Stoic, in Nietzsche's account of him, examines the world and realizes that it is futile to attempt to interfere with its predetermined course. The Stoic maintains that his values are imposed on him by the world, that having scrutinized the world there is only one possible attitude to take and in this respect he is no different from other philosophers: as Nietzsche writes later in Section 9, 'this is an old and never-ending story: what formerly happened with the Stoics still happens today as soon as a philosophy begins to believe in itself'. And he expresses this attitude in terms so vague that in a way he can't be faulted; hence Nietzsche's jeering 'how could you *not* do that?'.

Nietzsche's basic methodological point against such philosophical carryings-on is that they put the cart before the horse. There is not, because there can't be, any value-free scrutinizing of the world followed by either the acceptance of a value scheme that the world forces on one, or the adoption of a set of values based on a decision taken after surveying the way things are. That is the central point of Nietzsche's much celebrated and equally much misunderstood doctrine of perspectivism.

Nietzsche's claim that we create values has, then, in the first place, a logical force. It is a mistake to think that values are forced upon us by the nature of things, and in that sense, at least, he would be dubbed by contemporary philosophers a subjectivist. It is also, therefore, an ontological claim: values do not exist in the fabric of the world, are not out there to be discovered by us. Sometimes he is so keen to make this point, and to stress that all our apprehensions of the world are value-laden, that he says that there can be no facts, only interpretations. In other words, we should realize the extent to which our drives and desires colour all our dealings with what we like to think of as a reality existing entirely independently of us, which we can neutrally investigate. The truth of this very wide claim – or challenge, even – doesn't concern me here. What *is* significant is Nietzsche's stance: though it is perfectly correct to call Nietzsche a subjectivist, this term does not convey the same meaning as it does when applied to those philosophers who maintain that there is a fact–value distinction and that it is entirely up to us to determine what our values should be, whatever the facts are. That kind of subjectivism, often called in anglophone philosophical circles 'anti-naturalism', is impossible for Nietzsche, simply because he refuses to grant that it makes sense to talk of facts as opposed to values. So, in Nietzsche's view, we inevitably do create values, whether we want to or not. If we fail to see that, we are not only confused about the nature of our relationship to the world, but we also are likely to take a specific attitude to the world that is damaging and that makes us smaller.

It is in this perception that Nietzsche becomes truly original, indeed epoch-making. There had been plenty of subjectivists before him, just as there have been plenty since. But they have nearly all been at pains to insist that locating the source of value in the valuer rather than in the valued makes absolutely no difference to the actual values that they hold; or they have been plunged into gloom by the thought that nothing is 'really' good or bad, so that in some way moral differences are not nearly as important as they seem to be (Bertrand Russell was an acute sufferer from this complaint). Nietzsche is the first philosopher to exult in the fact (yes, there *are* facts, and this is one of the most important, since it is a fact about values) that value is not something that we discover, but something that we invent. At the same time, he is acutely aware of the extent to which values are heavily dependent on one kind of fact – the nature of those doing the valuing. And he is just as aware of the extent to which the individual valuers are liable to derive their values from the culture of which each of them is a member, and to think that because they feel values to be imposed on them, it is the world in general that is doing the imposing, and not the group of which they are members.

Hence Nietzsche's overriding concern, in *BGE* as in everything else he wrote, with the typology of cultures. His sense of the extreme difficulty of going against the grain of one's culture is the source of his deepest anguish, for he knew both the necessity of distancing himself from his own wretchedly decadent culture, and the risks that were inherent in effecting the separation. He knew, for instance, that if he didn't practise hyperbole his voice would be unlikely to be heard at all, and that if he did he would be likely to be shrugged off as a mere ranter. He also suspected, and more than suspected, that in providing a recipe for the overcoming of decadence he would have to envisage a kind of man, or Superman, who carried self-sufficiency to a degree which virtually meant total exile from society. To create and maintain values of a kind that Nietzsche could approve in the face of the contemporary world would require an act of will so prodigious that the person who could perform it would have to be allocated to a new species. Though the Superman remains a fascinating concept, which deserves a much fuller investigation than I can give it here or than is the fashion among commentators to give it, Nietzsche's subsequent published works do seem to indicate that Nietzsche himself remained deeply unsure of his success in characterizing this ideal figure, and that he returned, in *BGE* in the first instance, to seeing whether there was any chance for great men to emerge from within society, though to qualify they would have to transcend and violate the values of their society, even more than great men by definition always do. I think that it is for this reason that the concepts of '*master morality*' and '*slave morality*' are introduced in Section 260 of *BGE*, thereby developing an opposition that Nietzsche had first adumbrated seven years before in Section 45 of *Human, All Too Human*, but had not worked out further in the intervening books.

9

One of the characteristics of a master morality is that those who participate in it are aware of their role as creators of value. Though they differ in many other vital respects from

slave moralists, their consciousness that they are responsible
for the values by which they live already gives them cause
for rejoicing – they are, one might say, self-important in the
best sense of that term (a sense it normally lacks, indicating
to what degree we ourselves are slave or herd moralists).
Nietzsche writes in Section 260:

> The noble type of man feels *himself* to be the determiner of
> values, he does not need to be approved of, he judges 'what
> harms me is harmful in itself', he knows himself to be that
> which in general first accords honour to things, he *creates values*.
> Everything he knows to be part of himself, he honours: such a
> morality is self-glorification. In the foreground stands the feeling
> of plenitude, of power which seeks to overflow, the happiness
> of high tension, the consciousness of a wealth which would like
> to give away and bestow . . .

Such a passage arouses at least mixed feelings, if not wholly
hostile ones. We are so permeated by the idea that morality is
not a matter of self-glorification, of overflowing power, nor of
the subsequent characterizations of hardness and 'a mild contempt for and caution against sympathy and the "warm
heart"'; we are so wedded to seeing 'the mark of the moral
precisely in pity or in acting for others or in *désinteréssement*'
that we find it hard to take such concepts seriously at all.
Moreover, the way in which they have been misused by
ideological thugs makes it still more difficult. But if one
considers them in their context – that is, if one reads *BGE*
carefully and repeatedly, and doesn't regard it as a work that
combines brilliant aphorisms with a repulsive general view of
things – it becomes clear that Nietzsche is attempting to
formulate the conditions under which we may hope to recover
a conception of greatness, above all of that kind of greatness
which we associate with creativity, at least before that term
was so debased by pop psychologists and educational theorists.
According to Nietzsche, our attitude towards greatness is, in
general, in a state of hopeless confusion. We tend to be
grateful for its manifestations while often being appalled at
the behaviour of the people who were responsible for them.

We indulge in orgies of moral recrimination against those who have done most to enhance our culture, who have given us a very large part of our sense of what makes life worth living. We wish that those who have contributed most to our artistic heritage, our increased knowledge, our political and social arrangements, where those can be prized, had been 'better' men than their biographies, more often than not, show them to have been. The thought that if a great man had *been* different from what he was, he wouldn't have *done* what he did is rapidly dismissed as special pleading. At the same time, we tend to take pleasure in the notion that great men are, in various ways, human, all too human. It is part of our fear and anxiety in the face of greatness; one might say we take revenge on the greatness of men's works by studying their lives, prying into them with an intensity of scrutiny from which no one would emerge unscathed.

10

Those last sentences are a crude summary of some of what Nietzsche has to say about how slave moralists regard master moralists. He is preoccupied with the way in which those who are used to obeying regard those who are used to commanding, which he believes can be equated with the relationship between those who regard values as imposed, external and universal in their application and those who regard values as coming from within, created by those who are powerful enough for the task, and who delight in their sense of being different from others. In an especially acute passage in Section 199 he writes:

> The strange narrowness of human evolution, its hesitations, its delays, its frequent retrogressions and rotations, are due to the fact that the herd instinct of obedience has been inherited best and at the expense of the art of commanding. If we think of this instinct taken to its ultimate extravagance there would be no commanders or independent men at all; or, if they existed, they would suffer from a bad conscience and in order to be able to command would have to practise a deceit upon themselves: the

deceit, that is, that they too were only obeying. This state of things actually exists in Europe today: I call it the moral hypocrisy of the commanders. They know no way of defending themselves against their bad conscience other than to pose as executors of more ancient or higher commands (commands of ancestors, of the constitution, of justice, of the law or even of God), or even to borrow herd maxims from the herd's way of thinking and appear as 'the first servant of the people' for example, or as 'instruments of the common good'.

Nietzsche doesn't need to present any argument in favour of those observations; they are manifestly true, and constitute a devastating *reductio ad absurdum* of contemporary morality. Moreover, they help us to understand why Nietzsche regards even the great men of the nineteenth century with suspicion, with the signal exceptions of Napoleon and Goethe, the two men who emphatically didn't think of themselves as acting in obedience to laws from beyond or outside. That is why Nietzsche jubilantly ends Section 209 with:

One should at last have a sufficiently profound comprehension of Napoleon's astonishment when he caught sight of Goethe: it betrays what had for centuries been thought was meant by the 'German spirit'. '*Voilà un homme!*' – which is to say: 'but that is a *man*! And I had expected only a German!'

Typically, in making his point, Nietzsche distractingly localizes it by jibing at the Germans, a recurrent tendency in his later writings. One needn't be concerned about this; he took his fellow-countrymen as highly advanced examples of slave morality, partly because of their delight in obeying the commands of the Reich – their delight that there *was* a Reich to obey – and partly because he saw Kantian morality as a quintessentially German phenomenon: that morality which insisted that one acts morally only if one acts according to the dictates of the 'categorical imperative', a law founded in reason alone and equally applicable to all rational beings. It must be granted that between them, Bismarck's Reich and Kant's ethics were seen by Nietzsche as providing a very handy mnemonic. Adherence to both of them results in the total legalization of life, so to speak, the situation in which most people feel happiest, so long as obedience to the laws carries with it the promise of happiness. In such a context art is seen as a relief from the serious things in life, and artistic greatness is consequently diminished and 'safe': the great artist is reduced to the level of a great sportsman.

For Nietzsche, however, art was the epitome of seriousness, and artistic greatness of a kind where the greatest risks are run. Though in his later writings he often seems to slight the supreme importance that he had allotted to art in *The Birth of Tragedy*, the insistence with which he returns to it, and especially his inability to forgive Richard Wagner either for betraying his genius or for being a fake genius in the first place (Nietzsche can never quite make up his mind which), show that it remained for him what it had always been: the peak of human activity, above all the realm in which man can celebrate existence most completely. And celebration, comprehensive in its spirit but not indiscriminate in what it celebrates, is a leading indication of master morality – another reason why Goethe takes an increasingly central place in Nietzsche's later writings: Goethe the joyous pagan, the contemptuous anti-Christian, the equally tireless investigator of nature and composer of magnificent lyric poetry.

II

There seems to be a vast gap in Nietzsche's argument, as I have been selectively expounding it. For if the chief task of art is to celebrate, and there is at least some intimate connection between the impressiveness of the celebration and the value of that which is celebrated, what of the glories of Christian art? Christianity is the slave morality *par excellence*, and yet it is the inspiration – to take one of its most spectacular manifestations – behind the Sanctus of the Mass in B minor, where Bach celebrates as no one ever has before or since. But though Nietzsche is horrified by Christian morality, his attitude towards the Deity Himself is much more complex, which is made clear in what is probably the most famous passage in all his writings – the madman's proclamation that God is dead in Section 125 of *The Gay Science*. The man is regarded as mad precisely because he makes such a fuss about God's death, which seems to be a matter of indifference to the people in the marketplace. Nietzsche is of course the madman, and everything he produced after this proclamation is written in its shadow. It is taken for granted, therefore, in *BGE* that God's death is a *fait accompli*, and that, without God, the only possibility of greatness is in its *creation*. 'He who does not find greatness in God *finds* it nowhere,' Nietzsche says in a notebook; 'he must either deny it or create it.' *Zarathustra* is Nietzsche's major attempt to indicate how it might be created; *BGE* is in large part an exploration of how greatness is rendered impossible if we continue in the habits of thought instilled by two millennia of Christianity while abandoning the presupposition of the whole enterprise: God. Bach found greatness in God, and had no doubts about the truths of his religion. To return to the beginning of *BGE*: 'The falseness of a judgement is to us not necessarily an objection . . . the question is to what extent it is life-advancing, life-preserving . . .' But now we know that Bach's judgement was false, and that all our perspectives need to be altered. Indeed, no one, I think, can read *BGE* seriously without at least having an impressive number of his perspectives altered.

Michael Tanner

FURTHER READING

David B. Allison, *Reading the New Nietzsche* (2001)

MaudeMarie Clark, *Nietzsche on Truth and Morality* (1990)

R. J. Hollingdale, *Nietzsche: The Man and His Philosophy* (1965; 1999)

Brian Leiter, *Nietzsche on Morality* (2002)

Bernd Magnus and Kathleen Higgins (eds.), *The Cambridge Companion to Nietzsche* (1996)

Alexander Nehemas, *Nietzsche: Life as Literature* (1985)

F. Nietzsche, *Daybreak: Thoughts on the Prejudices of Morality*, trans. R. J. Hollingdale, introduction by M. Tanner (1982)

——, *Dithyrambs of Dionysus*, trans. with introduction and notes R. J. Hollingdale (1984; 2001)

——, *Untimely Meditations*, trans. R. J. Hollingdale, introduction by J. P. Stern (1983)

John Richardson and Brian Leiter (eds.), *Nietzsche* (2001)

Rudiger Safranski, *Nietzsche: A Philosophical Biography*, trans. Shelley Frisch (2002)

Henry Staten, *Nietzsche's Voice* (1990)

Tracy Strong, *Friedrich Nietzsche and the Politics of Transfiguration* (1988)

TRANSLATOR'S NOTE

Like all his books from *Human, All Too Human* onwards, *Beyond Good and Evil* got off to a very slow start. It was written in the summer of 1885 and the winter of 1885–6, with additions during the spring of 1886, printed during June and July, and published in August under the imprint of C. G. Naumann, of Leipzig. It was the immediate successor of *Zarathustra*, the first two parts of which had been published in 1883, and the third in 1884, by Ernst Schmeitzner, Chemnitz (now Karl-Marx-Stadt); all three volumes had sold very badly, and the fourth part, which should have appeared in 1885, was spared similar embarrassment by being merely privately printed in forty copies. Nietzsche blamed Schmeitzner for this lack of success, and when *Beyond Good and Evil* was ready he decided on the experiment of becoming his own publisher: he bore the expense of printing the book and Naumann distributed it. His ambition was modest enough: he hoped to cover his costs by selling 300 copies; but by June 1887 only 114 had been sold, and this time Schmeitzner could *not* be blamed. The results were, in fact, precisely what they had been since *Human, All Too Human* appeared in 1878 and only 170 copies were sold in its first year: his books went unread. He saw no further edition of *Beyond Good and Evil*, but in the 1890s there were three editions ('91, '93, '94) and in the present century it has never been out of print. The standard edition, established by the *Gesamtausgabe in Grossoktav* (1894ff), differs from the first edition of 1886 only in the most trifling respects.

R. J. Hollingdale

BEYOND GOOD AND EVIL

Prelude to a Philosophy of the Future

Preface

Supposing truth to be a woman – what? is the suspicion not well founded that all philosophers, when they have been dogmatists, have had little understanding of women? that the gruesome earnestness, the clumsy importunity with which they have hitherto been in the habit of approaching truth have been inept and improper means for winning a wench? Certainly she has not let herself be won – and today every kind of dogmatism stands sad and discouraged. *If* it continues to stand at all! For there are scoffers who assert it has fallen down, that dogmatism lies on the floor, more, that dogmatism is at its last gasp. To speak seriously, there are good grounds for hoping that all dogmatizing in philosophy, the solemn air of finality it has given itself notwithstanding, may none the less have been no more than a noble childishness and tyronism; and the time is perhaps very close at hand when it will be grasped in case after case *what* has been sufficient to furnish the foundation-stone for such sublime and unconditional philosophers' edifices as the dogmatists have hitherto been constructing – some popular superstition or other from time immemorial (such as the soul superstition which, as the subject-and-ego superstition, has not yet ceased to do mischief even today), perhaps some play on words, a grammatical seduction, or an audacious generalization on the basis of very narrow, very personal, very human, all too human facts. Let us hope that dogmatic philosophy was only a promise across millennia: as, in a still earlier age, was astrology, in the service of which more labour, money, ingenuity and patience has perhaps been expended than for any real science hitherto – we owe to it and to its 'supra-terrestrial' claims the grand style of architecture in Asia and Egypt. It seems that, in order to inscribe themselves in the hearts of humanity with eternal demands, all great things have first to wander the earth as monstrous and fear-inspiring grotesques: dogmatic philosophy, the doctrine of the Vedanta in Asia and Platonism in Europe for example, was a grotesque of this kind. Let us not be ungrateful to it, even though it certainly has to be admitted that the worst, most wearisomely protracted and most dangerous of all errors hitherto has been a dogmatist's error, namely Plato's invention of pure spirit and the good in itself. But now, when that has been overcome, when Europe breathes again after this nightmare and can enjoy at any rate a healthier – sleep, we *whose task is wakefulness itself* have inherited all the strength which has been cultivated by the struggle against this error. To be sure, to speak of spirit and the good as Plato did meant standing truth on her head and denying *perspective* itself, the basic condition of all life; indeed, one may ask as a physician: 'how could such a malady attack this loveliest product of antiquity, Plato? did the wicked Socrates corrupt him after all? could Socrates have been a corrupter of youth after all? and have deserved his hemlock?' – But the struggle against Plato, or, to express it more plainly and for 'the people', the struggle against the Christian-ecclesiastical pressure of millennia – for Christianity is Platonism for 'the people' – has created in Europe a magnificent tension of the spirit such as has never existed on earth before: with so tense a bow one can now shoot for the most distant targets. European man feels this tension as a state of distress, to be sure; and there have already been two grand attempts to relax the bow, once by means of Jesuitism, the second time by means of democratic enlightenment – which latter may in fact, with the aid of freedom of the press and the reading of newspapers, achieve a state of affairs in which the spirit would no longer so easily feel itself to be a 'need'! (The Germans invented gun-powder – all credit to them! But they evened the score again – they invented the press.) But we who are neither Jesuits nor democrats, nor even sufficiently German, we *good Europeans* and free, *very* free spirits – we have it still, the whole need of the spirit and the whole tension of its bow! And perhaps also the arrow, the task and, who knows? the *target* . . .

Sils-Maria, Upper Engadine.
June 1885

32

Part One: On the Prejudices of Philosophers

I

The will to truth, which is still going to tempt us to many a hazardous enterprise; that celebrated veracity of which all philosophers have hitherto spoken with reverence: what questions this will to truth has already set before us! What strange, wicked, questionable questions! It is already a long story – yet does it not seem as if it has only just begun? Is it any wonder we should at last grow distrustful, lose our patience, turn impatiently away? That this sphinx should teach us too to ask questions? *Who* really is it that here questions us? *What* really is it in us that wants 'the truth'? – We did indeed pause for a long time before the question of the origin of this will – until finally we came to a complete halt before an even more fundamental question. We asked after the *value* of this will. Granted we want truth: *why not rather* untruth? And uncertainty? Even ignorance? – The problem of the value of truth stepped before us – or was it we who stepped before this problem? Which of us is Oedipus here? Which of us sphinx? It is, it seems, a rendezvous of questions and question-marks. – And, would you believe it, it has finally almost come to seem to us that this problem has never before been posed – that we have been the first to see it, to fix our eye on it, to *hazard* it? For there is a hazard in it and perhaps there exists no greater hazard.

2

'How *could* something originate in its antithesis? Truth in error, for example? Or will to truth in will to deception? Or the unselfish act in self-interest? Or the pure radiant gaze of the sage in covetousness? Such origination is impossible; he who dreams of it is a fool, indeed worse than a fool; the things of the highest value must have another origin *of their own* – they cannot be derivable from this transitory, seductive, deceptive, mean little world, from this confusion of desire and illusion! In the womb of being, rather, in the intransitory, in the hidden god, in the "thing in itself" – *that* is where their cause must lie and nowhere else!' – This mode of judgement constitutes the typical prejudice by which metaphysicians of all ages can be recognized; this mode of evaluation stands in the background of all their logical procedures; it is on account of this their 'faith' that they concern themselves with their 'knowledge', with something that is at last solemnly baptized 'the truth'. The fundamental faith of the metaphysicians is *the faith in antithetical values*. It has not occurred to even the most cautious of them to pause and doubt here on the threshold, where however it was most needful they should: even if they *had* vowed to themselves '*de omnibus dubitandum*'. For it may be doubted, firstly whether there exist any antitheses at all, and secondly whether these popular evaluations and value-antitheses, on which the metaphysicians have set their seal, are not perhaps merely foreground valuations, merely provisional perspectives, perhaps moreover the perspectives of a hole-and-corner, perhaps from below, as it were frog-perspectives, to borrow an expression employed by painters. With all the value that may adhere to the true, the genuine, the selfless, it could be possible that a higher and more fundamental value for all life might have to be ascribed to appearance, to the will to deception, to selfishness and to appetite. It might even be possible that *what* constitutes the value of those good and honoured things resides precisely in their being artfully related, knotted and crocheted to these wicked, apparently antithetical things, perhaps even in their being essentially identical with them. Perhaps! – But who is willing to concern himself with such dangerous perhapses! For that we have to await the arrival of a new species of philosopher, one which possesses tastes and inclinations opposite to and different from those of its predecessors – philosophers of the dangerous 'perhaps' in every sense. – And to speak in all seriousness: I see such new philosophers arising.

3

Having kept a close eye on philosophers and read between their lines for a sufficient length of time, I tell myself: the greater part of conscious thinking must still be counted among the instinctive activities, and this is so even in the case of philosophical thinking; we have to learn differently here as we have learned differently in regard to heredity and the 'innate'. Just as the act of being born plays no part in the procedure and progress of heredity, so 'being conscious' is in no decisive sense the *opposite* of the instinctive – most of a philosopher's conscious thinking is secretly directed and compelled into definite channels by his instincts. Behind all logic too and its appa. nt autonomy there stand evaluations, in plainer terms physiological demands for the preservation of a certain species of life. For example, that the definite shall be of greater value than the indefinite, appearance of less value than 'truth': but such valuations as these could, their regulatory importance for *us* notwithstanding, be no more than foreground valuations, a certain species of *niaiserie* which may be necessary precisely for the preservation of beings such as us. Assuming, that is to say, that it is not precisely man who is the 'measure of things' . . .

4

The falseness of a judgement is to us not necessarily an objection to a judgement: it is here that our new language perhaps sounds strangest. The question is to what extent it is life-advancing, life-preserving, species-preserving, perhaps even species-breeding; and our fundamental tendency is to assert that the falsest judgements (to which synthetic judgements *a priori* belong) are the most indispensable to us, that without granting as true the fictions of logic, without measuring reality against the purely invented world of the unconditional and self-identical, without a continual falsification of the world by means of numbers, mankind could not live – that to renounce false judgements would be to renounce life, would be to deny life. To recognize untruth as a condition of life: that, to be sure, means to resist customary value-sentiments in a dangerous fashion; and a philosophy which ventures to do so places itself, by that act alone, beyond good and evil.

5

What makes one regard philosophers half mistrustfully and half mockingly is not that one again and again detects how innocent they are – how often and how easily they fall into error and go astray, in short their childishness and childlikeness – but that they display altogether insufficient honesty, while making a mighty and virtuous noise as soon as the problem of truthfulness is even remotely touched on. They pose as having discovered and attained their real opinions through the self-evolution of a cold, pure, divinely unperturbed dialectic (in contrast to the mystics of every rank, who are more honest and more stupid than they – these speak of 'inspiration'): while what happens at bottom is that a prejudice, a notion, an 'inspiration', generally a desire of the heart sifted and made abstract, is defended by them with reasons sought after the event – they are one and all advocates who do not want to be regarded as such, and for the most part no better than cunning pleaders for their prejudices, which they baptize 'truths' – and *very* far from possessing the courage of the conscience which admits this fact to itself, very far from possessing the good taste of the courage which publishes this fact, whether to warn a foe or a friend or out of high spirits and in order to mock itself. The tartuffery, as stiff as it is virtuous, of old Kant as he lures us along the dialectical bypaths which lead, more correctly, mislead, to his 'categorical imperative' – this spectacle makes us smile, we who are fastidious and find no little amusement in observing the subtle tricks of old moralists and moral-preachers. Not to speak of that hocus-pocus of mathematical form in which, as if in iron, Spinoza encased and masked his philosophy – 'the

love of *his* wisdom', to render that word fairly and squarely –
so as to strike terror into the heart of any assailant who
should dare to glance at that invincible maiden and Pallas
Athene – how much personal timidity and vulnerability this
masquerade of a sick recluse betrays!

6

It has gradually become clear to me what every great philosophy has hitherto been: a confession on the part of its author
and a kind of involuntary and unconscious memoir; moreover,
that the moral (or immoral) intentions in every philosophy
have every time constituted the real germ of life out of which
the entire plant has grown. To explain how a philosopher's
most remote metaphysical assertions have actually been arrived
at, it is always well (and wise) to ask oneself first: what
morality does this (does *he* –) aim at? I accordingly do not
believe a 'drive to knowledge' to be the father of philosophy,
but that another drive has, here as elsewhere, only employed
knowledge (and false knowledge!) as a tool. But anyone who
looks at the basic drives of mankind to see to what extent
they may in precisely this connection have come into play as
inspirational spirits (or demons and kobolds –) will discover
that they have all at some time or other practised philosophy
– and that each one of them would be only too glad to present
itself as the ultimate goal of existence and as the legitimate
master of all the other drives. For every drive is tyrannical:
and it is as *such* that it tries to philosophize. – In the case
of scholars, to be sure, in the case of really scientific men,
things may be different – 'better', if you will – there may really
exist something like a drive to knowledge there, some little
independent clockwork which, when wound up, works
bravely on *without* any of the scholar's other drives playing
any essential part. The scholar's real 'interests' therefore generally lie in quite another direction, perhaps in his family or in
making money or in politics; it is, indeed, almost a matter of
indifference whether his little machine is set up in this region
of science or that, whether the 'promising' young worker

makes himself into a good philologist or a specialist in fungus or a chemist – he is not *characterized* by becoming this or that. In the philosopher, on the contrary, there is nothing whatever impersonal; and, above all, his morality bears decided and decisive testimony to *who he is* – that is to say, to the order of rank the innermost drives of his nature stand in relative to one another.

7

How malicious philosophers can be! I know of nothing more venomous than the joke Epicurus allowed himself to make against Plato and the Platonists: he called them *Dionysiokolakes*. The literal and foreground meaning of this word is 'flatterers of Dionysus', that is to say, tyrants' hangers-on and lickspittles; in addition, however, it is as much as to say 'they are all *actors*, there is nothing genuine about them' (for *Dionysiokolax* was a popular term for an actor). And the latter meaning is really the piece of malice that Epicurus discharged at Plato: he was annoyed by the grandiose manner, the *mise en scène* of which Plato and his pupils were masters – of which Epicurus was not a master! He, the old schoolteacher from Samos who sat hidden in his little garden at Athens and wrote three hundred books – who knows, perhaps out of rage at Plato and ambitious envy of him? – It took a century for Greece to find out who this garden god Epicurus had been. – Did it find out? –

8

In every philosophy there is a point at which the philosopher's 'conviction' appears on the scene: or, to put it in the words of an ancient Mystery:

> *adventavit asinus,*
> *pulcher et fortissimus.*

9

You want to *live* 'according to nature'? O you noble Stoics, what fraudulent words! Think of a being such as nature is, prodigal beyond measure, indifferent beyond measure, without aims or intentions, without mercy or justice, at once fruitful and barren and uncertain; think of indifference itself as a power – how *could* you live according to such indifference? To live – is that not precisely wanting to be other than this nature? Is living not valuating, preferring, being unjust, being limited, wanting to be different? And even if your imperative 'live according to nature' meant at bottom the same thing as 'live according to life' – how could you *not* do that? Why make a principle of what you yourselves are and must be? – The truth of it is, however, quite different: while you rapturously pose as deriving the canon of your law from nature, you want something quite the reverse of that, you strange actors and self-deceivers! Your pride wants to prescribe your morality, your ideal, to nature, yes to nature itself, and incorporate them in it; you demand that nature should be nature 'according to the Stoa' and would like to make all existence exist only after your own image – as a tremendous eternal glorification and universalization of Stoicism! All your love of truth notwithstanding, you have compelled yourselves for so long and with such persistence and hypnotic rigidity to view nature *falsely*, namely Stoically, you are no longer capable of viewing it in any other way – and some abysmal arrogance infects you at last with the Bedlamite hope that, *because* you know how to tyrannize over yourselves – Stoicism is self-tyranny – nature too can be tyrannized over: for is the Stoic not a *piece* of nature? . . . But this is an old and never-ending story: what formerly happened with the Stoics still happens today as soon as a philosophy begins to believe in itself. It always creates the world in its own image, it cannot do otherwise; philosophy is this tyrannical drive itself, the most spiritual will to power, to 'creation of the world', to *causa prima*.

The zeal and subtlety, I might even say slyness, with which the problem 'of the real and apparent world' is set upon all over Europe today makes one think hard and prick up one's ears; and anyone who hears in the background only a 'will to truth' and nothing more, certainly does not enjoy the best of hearing. In rare and isolated cases such a will to truth, some extravagant and adventurous courage, a metaphysician's ambition to maintain a forlorn position, may actually play a part and finally prefer a handful of 'certainty' to a whole cartful of beautiful possibilities; there may even exist puritanical fanatics of conscience who would rather lie down and die on a sure nothing than on an uncertain something. But this is nihilism and the sign of a despairing, mortally weary soul, however brave the bearing of such a virtue may appear. In the case of stronger, livelier thinkers who are still thirsty for life, however, it seems to be different: when they take sides *against* appearance and speak even of 'perspective' with an arrogant disdain, when they rank the credibility of their own body about as low as the credibility of the ocular evidence which says 'the earth stands still', and thus with apparent good humour let slip their firmest possession (for what is believed in more firmly today than the body?) – who knows whether they are not at bottom trying to win back something that was formerly an even *firmer* possession, some part or other of the old domain of the faith of former times, perhaps 'the immortal soul', perhaps 'the old God', in short ideas by which one could live better, that is to say more vigorously and joyfully, than by 'modern ideas'? There is *distrust* of these modern ideas in this outlook, there is disbelief in all that has been constructed yesterday and today; there is perhaps in addition a little boredom and mockery which can no longer endure the bric-à-brac of concepts of the most various origin such as so-called positivism brings to the market today; the disgust of a more fastidious taste at the village-fair motleyness and patchiness of all these reality-philosophasters in whom there is nothing new or genuine except this motleyness. In this, it seems to me, we ought to acknowledge that these sceptical anti-realists and knowledge-microscopists of today are in the right: the instinct which makes them recoil from *modern* reality stands unrefuted – what do we care about the retrograde bypaths they choose! The essential thing about them is *not* that they want to go 'back', but that they want to – get *away*. A little strength, soaring, courage, artistic power *more*, and they would want to go *up and away* – and not back! –

11

It seems to me that there is today an effort going on every-where to distract attention from the actual influence exercised on German philosophy by Kant and, in particular, prudently to gloss over the value he set upon himself. Kant was first and foremost proud of his table of categories; with this table in his hand he said: 'This is the hardest thing that could ever be undertaken on behalf of metaphysics.' – But let us under-stand this 'could be'! He was proud of having *discovered* a new faculty in man, the faculty of synthetic judgements *a priori*. Granted he deceived himself in this: the evolution and rapid burgeoning of German philosophy none the less depended on this pride of his and on the eager rivalry of the whole younger generation to discover, if possible, something of which to be still prouder – and in any event 'new faculties'! – But let us stop and reflect: it is time we did so. Kant asked himself: how are synthetic judgements *a priori possible*? – and what, really, did he answer? *By means of a faculty*: but unfortunately not in a few words, but so circumspectly, venerably, and with such an expenditure of German profundity and flourishes that the comical *niaiserie allemande* involved in such an answer was overlooked. People even lost their heads altogether on account of this new faculty, and the rejoicing reached its climax when Kant went on further to discover a moral faculty in man – for at that time the Germans were still moral and by no means practitioners of *Realpolitik*. – The honeymoon time of German philosophy arrived; and the young theologians of the College of Tübingen went straightway off into the bushes – all in

search of 'faculties'. And what did they not find – in that innocent, rich, still youthful era of the German spirit, to which the
malicious fairy, romanticism, piped and sang, in those days
when one was not yet able to distinguish between 'finding'
and 'inventing'! They found above all a faculty for the 'supra-
sensible': Schelling baptized it intellectual intuition, and therewith satisfied the most heartfelt longings of his Germans, which
longings were fundamentally pious. One can do no greater
wrong to this whole high-spirited and enthusiastic movement,
which was really youthfulness however boldly it disguised itself
in hoary and senile concepts, than to take it seriously and, an
even worse injustice, to treat it with moral indignation; it is
enough to say that one grew older – and the dream disappeared.
A time came when one rubbed one's eyes: one is still rubbing
them today. One had been dreaming: and the first and foremost of the dreamers was – old Kant. 'By means of a faculty' –
he had said, or at least meant. But is that – an answer? An
explanation? Or is it not rather merely a repetition of the question? How does opium induce sleep? 'By means of a faculty',
namely the *virtus dormitiva* – replies the doctor in Molière,

> *quia est in eo virtus dormitiva,*
> *cujus est natura sensus assoupire.*

But answers like that belong in comedy, and it is high time
to replace the Kantian question 'how are synthetic judgements
a priori possible?' with another question: 'why is belief in such
judgements *necessary*?' – that is to say, it is time to grasp that,
for the purpose of preserving beings such as ourselves, such
judgements must be *believed* to be true; although they might of
course still be *false* judgements! Or more clearly, crudely and
basically: synthetic judgements *a priori* should not 'be possible'
at all: we have no right to them, in our mouths they are
nothing but false judgements. But belief in their truth is, of
course, necessary as foreground belief and ocular evidence
belonging to the perspective optics of life. – Finally, in
considering the enormous influence 'German philosophy' – I
hope you understand its right to inverted commas? – has
exercised throughout Europe, one cannot doubt that a certain

virtus dormitiva has played a part in it: the noble idlers, the virtuous, the mystics, the artists, the three-quarter Christians and the political obscurantists of all nations were delighted to possess, thanks to German philosophy, an antidote to the still overwhelming sensualism which had overflowed out of the previous century into this, in short – *'sensus assoupire'* . . .

I2

As for materialistic atomism, it is one of the best-refuted things there are; and perhaps no scholar in Europe is still so unscholarly today as to accord it serious significance except for handy everyday use (as an abbreviated means of expression) – thanks above all to the Pole Boscovich who, together with the Pole Copernicus, has been the greatest and most triumphant opponent of ocular evidence hitherto. For while Copernicus persuaded us to believe, contrary to all the senses, that the earth does *not* stand firm, Boscovich taught us to abjure belief in the last thing of earth that 'stood firm', belief in 'substance', in 'matter', in the earth-residuum and particle atom: it was the greatest triumph over the senses hitherto achieved on earth. – One must, however, go still further and also declare war, a remorseless war of the knife, on the 'atomistic need' which, like that more famous 'metaphysical need', still goes on living a dangerous after-life in regions where no one suspects it – one must also first of all finish off that other and more fateful atomism which Christianity has taught best and longest, the *soul atomism*. Let this expression be allowed to designate that belief which regards the soul as being something indestructible, eternal, indivisible, as a monad, as an *atomon*: *this* belief ought to be ejected from science! Between ourselves, it is not at all necessary by that same act to get rid of 'the soul' itself and thus forgo one of the oldest and most venerable of hypotheses: as is often the way with clumsy naturalists, who can hardly touch 'the soul' without losing it. But the road to new forms and refinements of the soul-hypothesis stands open: and such conceptions as 'mortal soul' and 'soul as multiplicity of the subject' and 'soul

as social structure of the drives and emotions' want henceforth
to possess civic rights in science. To be sure, when the *new*
psychologist puts an end to the superstition which has hitherto
flourished around the soul-idea with almost tropical luxuri-
ance, he has as it were thrust himself out into a new wilderness
and a new mistrust – it may be that the older psychologists
had a merrier and more comfortable time of it – : ultimately,
however, he sees that, by precisely that act, he has also
condemned himself to *inventing* the new – and, who knows?
perhaps to *finding* it. –

13

Physiologists should think again before postulating the drive
to self-preservation as the cardinal drive in an organic being.
A living thing desires above all to *vent* its strength – life as
such is will to power – : self-preservation is only one of the
indirect and most frequent *consequences* of it. – In short, here as
everywhere, beware of *superfluous* teleological principles! –
such as is the drive to self-preservation (we owe it to Spinoza's
inconsistency). For this is a requirement of method, which has
essentially to be economy of principles.

14

It is perhaps just dawning on five or six minds that physics
too is only an interpretation and arrangement of the world
(according to our own requirements, if I may say so!) and *not*
an explanation of the world: but in so far as it is founded on
belief in the senses it passes for more than that and must
continue to do so for a long time to come. It has the eyes and
the hands on its side, it has ocular evidence and palpability on
its side: and this has the effect of fascinating, persuading,
convincing an age with fundamentally plebeian tastes – for it
instinctively follows the canon of eternal, popular sensualism.
What is obvious, what has been 'explained'? Only that which
can be seen and felt – thus far has every problem to be
scrutinized. Obversely: it was precisely in opposition to palpa-

bility that the charm of the Platonic mode of thinking, which was a *noble* mode of thinking, consisted – on the part of men who perhaps rejoiced in even stronger and more exacting senses than our contemporaries possess, but who knew how to experience a greater triumph in mastering them: which they did by means of pale, cold, grey conceptual nets thrown over the motley whirl of the senses – the mob of the senses, as Plato called them. This overcoming and interpretation of the world in the manner of Plato involved a kind of *enjoyment* different from that which the physicists of today offer us, or from that offered us by the Darwinists and anti-teleologists among the labourers in physiology, with their principle of the 'smallest possible effort' and the greatest possible stupidity. 'Where man has nothing more to see or grasp he has nothing more to do' – that is certainly a different imperative from the Platonic, but for an uncouth industrious race of machinists and bridge-builders of the future, which has nothing but *course* work to get through, it may well be the right one.

15

If one is to pursue physiology with a good conscience one is compelled to insist that the organs of sense are *not* phenomena in the sense of idealist philosophy: for if they were they could not be causes! Sensualism therefore is at least a regulative hypothesis, certainly a heuristic principle. – What? and others even go so far as to say that the external world is the work of our organs? But then our body, as a piece of this external world, would be the work of our organs! But then our organs themselves would be – the work of our organs! This, it seems to me, is a complete *reductio ad absurdum*, supposing that the concept *causa sui* is something altogether absurd. Consequently the external world is *not* the work of our organs – ?

16

There are still harmless self-observers who believe 'immediate certainties' exist, for example 'I think' or, as was

Schopenhauer's superstition, 'I will': as though knowledge here got hold of its object pure and naked, as 'thing in itself', and no falsification occurred either on the side of the subject or on that of the object. But I shall reiterate a hundred times that 'immediate certainty', like 'absolute knowledge' and 'thing in itself', contains a *contradictio in adjecto*: we really ought to get free from the seduction of words! Let the people believe that knowledge is total knowledge, but the philosopher must say to himself: when I analyse the event expressed in the sentence 'I think', I acquire a series of rash assertions which are difficult, perhaps impossible, to prove – for example, that it is *I* who think, that it has to be something at all which thinks, that thinking is an activity and operation on the part of an entity thought of as a cause, that an 'I' exists, finally that what is designated by 'thinking' has already been determined – that I *know* what thinking is. For if I had not already decided that matter within myself, by what standard could I determine that what is happening is not perhaps 'willing' or 'feeling'? Enough: this 'I think' presupposes that I *compare* my present state with other known states of myself in order to determine what it is: on account of this retrospective connection with other 'knowledge' at any rate it possesses no immediate certainty for me. – In place of that 'immediate certainty' in which the people may believe in the present case, the philosopher acquires in this way a series of metaphysical questions, true questions of conscience for the intellect, namely: 'Whence do I take the concept thinking? Why do I believe in cause and effect? What gives me the right to speak of an "I", and even of an "I" as cause, and finally of an "I" as cause of thought?' Whoever feels able to answer these metaphysical questions straight away with an appeal to a sort of *intuitive* knowledge, as he does who says: 'I think, and know that this at least is true, actual and certain' – will find a philosopher today ready with a smile and two question-marks. 'My dear sir,' the philosopher will perhaps give him to understand, 'it is improbable you are not mistaken: but why do you want the truth at all?' –

17

As for the superstitions of the logicians, I shall never tire of underlining a concise little fact which these superstitious people are loath to admit – namely, that a thought comes when 'it' wants, not when 'I' want; so that it is a *falsification* of the facts to say: the subject 'I' is the condition of the predicate 'think'. *It* thinks: but that this 'it' is precisely that famous old 'I' is, to put it mildly, only an assumption, an assertion, above all not an 'immediate certainty'. For even with this 'it thinks' one has already gone too far: this 'it' already contains an *interpretation* of the event and does not belong to the event itself. The inference here is in accordance with the habit of grammar: 'thinking is an activity, to every activity pertains one who acts, consequently – '. It was more or less in accordance with the same scheme that the older atomism sought, in addition to the 'force' which acts, that little lump of matter in which it resides, out of which it acts, the atom; more rigorous minds at last learned to get along without this 'residuum of earth', and perhaps we and the logicians as well will one day accustom ourselves to getting along without that little 'it' (which is what the honest old 'I' has evaporated into).

18

It is certainly not the least charm of a theory that it is refutable: it is with precisely this charm that it entices subtler minds. It seems that the hundred times refuted theory of 'free will' owes its continued existence to this charm alone – : again and again there comes along someone who feels he is strong enough to refute it.

19

Philosophers are given to speaking of the will as if it were the best-known thing in the world; Schopenhauer, indeed, would have us understand that the will alone is truly known to us, known completely, known without deduction or addition. But it seems to me that in this case too Schopenhauer has done only what philosophers in general are given to doing: that he has taken up a *popular prejudice* and exaggerated it. Willing seems to me to be above all something *complicated*, something that is a unity only as a word – and it is precisely in this *one* word that the popular prejudice resides which has overborne the always inadequate caution of the philosophers. Let us therefore be more cautious for once, let us be 'unphilosophical' – let us say: in all willing there is, first of all, a plurality of sensations, namely the sensation of the condition we *leave*, the sensation of the condition towards which we *go*, the sensation of this 'leaving' and 'going' itself, and then also an accompanying muscular sensation which, even without our putting 'arms and legs' in motion, comes into play through a kind of habit as soon as we 'will'. As feelings, and indeed many varieties of feeling, can therefore be recognized as an ingredient of will, so, in the second place, can thinking: in every act of will there is a commanding thought – and do not imagine that this thought can be separated from the 'willing', as though will would then remain over! Thirdly, will is not only a complex of feeling and thinking, but above all an *affect*: and in fact the affect of command. What is called 'freedom of will' is essentially the affect of superiority over him who must obey: 'I am free, "he" must obey' – this consciousness adheres to every will, as does that tense attention, that straight look which fixes itself exclusively on *one* thing, that unconditional evaluation 'this and nothing else is necessary now', that inner certainty that one will be obeyed, and whatever else pertains to the state of him who gives commands. A man who *wills* – commands something in himself which obeys or which he believes obeys. But now observe the strangest thing of all about the will – about this so complex thing for which people have only *one* word: inasmuch as in the given circumstances we at the same time command *and* obey, and as the side which obeys know the sensations of constraint, compulsion, pressure, resistance, motion which usually begin immediately after the act of will; inasmuch as, on the other hand, we are in the habit of disregarding and deceiving ourselves over this duality by means of the synthetic concept 'I'; so a whole chain of erroneous conclusions and consequently of false evaluations of the will itself has become attached to the will as such – so that he who wills believes wholeheartedly that willing *suffices* for action. Because in the great majority of cases willing takes place only where the effect of the command, that is to say obedience, that is to say the action, was to be *expected*, the *appearance* has translated itself into the sensation, as if there were here a *necessity of effect*. Enough: he who wills believes with a tolerable degree of certainty that will and action are somehow one – he attributes the success, the carrying out of the willing, to the will itself, and thereby enjoys an increase of that sensation of power which all success brings with it. 'Freedom of will' – is the expression for that complex condition of pleasure of the person who wills, who commands and at the same time identifies himself with the executor of the command – who as such also enjoys the triumph over resistances involved but who thinks it was his will itself which overcame these resistances. He who wills adds in this way the sensations of pleasure of the successful executive agents, the serviceable 'under-wills' or under-souls – for our body is only a social structure composed of many souls – to his sensations of pleasure as commander. *L'effet, c'est moi*: what happens here is what happens in every well-constructed and happy commonwealth: the ruling class identifies itself with the successes of the commonwealth. In all willing it is absolutely a question of commanding and obeying, on the basis, as I have said already, of a social structure composed of many 'souls': on which account a philosopher should claim the right to include willing as such within the field of morality: that is, of morality understood as the theory of the relations of dominance under which the phenomenon 'life' arises. –

20

That individual philosophical concepts are not something arbitrary, something growing up autonomously, but on the contrary grow up connected and related to one another; that, however suddenly and arbitrarily they appear to emerge in the history of thought, they none the less belong just as much to a system as do the members of the fauna of a continent: that fact is in the end also shown in the fact that the most diverse philosophers unfailingly fill out again and again a certain basic scheme of *possible* philosophies. Under an invisible spell they always trace once more the identical orbit: however independent of one another they may feel, with their will to criticism or systematism, something in them leads them, something drives them in a definite order one after another: it is precisely that innate systematism and relationship of concepts. Their thinking is in fact not so much a discovering as a recognizing, a remembering, a return and home-coming to a far-off, primordial total household of the soul out of which those concepts once emerged – philosophizing is to that extent a species of atavism of the first rank. The singular family resemblance between all Indian, Greek and German philosophizing is easy enough to explain. Where there exists a language affinity it is quite impossible, thanks to the common philosophy of grammar – I mean thanks to unconscious domination and directing by similar grammatical functions – to avoid everything being prepared in advance for a similar evolution and succession of philosophical systems: just as the road seems to be barred to certain other possibilities of world interpretation. Philosophers within the domain of the Ural-Altaic languages (in which the concept of the subject is least developed) will in all probability look 'into the world' differently and be found on different paths from the Indo-Germans and Moslems: the spell of definite grammatical functions is in the last resort the spell of *physiological* value judgements and racial conditions. – So much by way of retort to Locke's superficiality with regard to the origin of ideas.

21

The *causa sui* is the best self-contradiction hitherto imagined, a kind of logical rape and unnaturalness: but mankind's extravagant pride has managed to get itself deeply and frightfully entangled with precisely this piece of nonsense. For the desire for 'freedom of will' in that metaphysical superlative sense which is unfortunately still dominant in the minds of the half-educated, the desire to bear the whole and sole responsibility for one's actions and to absolve God, world, ancestors, chance, society from responsibility for them, is nothing less than the desire to be precisely that *causa sui* and, with more than Münchhausen temerity, to pull oneself into existence out of the swamp of nothingness by one's own hair. Assuming it is possible in this way to get beyond the peasant simplicity of this celebrated concept 'free will' and banish it from one's mind, I would then ask whoever does that to carry his 'enlightenment' a step further and also banish from his mind the contrary of that unnatural concept 'free will': I mean 'unfree will', which amounts to an abuse of cause and effect. One ought not to make 'cause' and 'effect' *into material things*, as natural scientists do (and those who, like them, naturalize in their thinking –), in accordance with the prevailing mechanistic stupidity which has the cause press and push until it 'produces an effect'; one ought to employ 'cause' and 'effect' only as pure *concepts*, that is to say as conventional fictions for the purpose of designation, mutual understanding, *not* explanation. In the 'in itself' there is nothing of 'causal connection', of 'necessity', of 'psychological unfreedom'; there 'the effect' *does not* 'follow the cause', there no 'law' rules. It is *we* alone who have fabricated causes, succession, reciprocity, relativity, compulsion, number, law, freedom, motive, purpose; and when we falsely introduce this world of symbols into things and mingle it with them as though this symbol-world were an 'in itself', we once more behave as we have always behaved, namely *mythologically*. 'Unfree will' is mythology: in real life it is only a question of *strong* and *weak* wills. – It is almost always a symptom of what is lacking in himself when a thinker detects in every 'causal connection' and 'psychological necessity' something of compulsion, exigency, constraint, pressure, unfreedom: such feelings are traitors, the person who has them gives himself away. And, if I have observed correctly, 'unfreedom of will' is in general conceived as a problem from two completely antithetical standpoints but always in a profoundly *personal* manner: one will at no price give up his 'responsibility', his belief in *himself*, the personal right to *his* deserts (the vain races belong here –), the other, on the contrary, will not be responsible for anything, to blame for anything, and out of an inner self-contempt wants to be able to *shift off* his responsibility for himself somewhere else. This latter, when he writes books, tends today to espouse the cause of the criminal; his most pleasing disguise is a kind of socialist sympathy. And the fatalism of the weak-willed is indeed beautified to an astonishing degree when it can present itself as '*la religion de la souffrance humaine*': that is *its* 'good taste'.

22

You must pardon me as an old philologist who cannot refrain from the maliciousness of putting his finger on bad arts of interpretation: but 'nature's conformity to law' of which you physicists speak so proudly, as though – it exists only thanks to your interpretation and bad 'philology' – it is not a fact, not a 'text', but rather only a naïve humanitarian adjustment and distortion of meaning with which you go more than half-way to meet the democratic instincts of the modern soul! 'Everywhere equality before the law – nature is in this matter no different from us and no better off than we': a nice piece of mental reservation in which vulgar hostility towards everything privileged and autocratic, as well as a second and more subtle atheism, lie once more disguised. '*Ni dieu, ni maître*' – that is your motto too: and therefore 'long live the law of nature!' – isn't that so? But, as aforesaid, that is interpretation, not text; and someone could come along who, with an opposite intention and art of interpretation, knew how to read out of the same nature and with regard to the same phenomena the tyrannically ruthless and inexorable enforcement of power-demands – an interpreter who could bring before your eyes the universality and unconditionality of all 'will to power' in such a way that almost any word and even the word 'tyranny' would finally seem unsuitable or as a weakening and moderating metaphor – as too human – and who none the less ended by asserting of this world the same as you assert of it, namely that it has a 'necessary' and 'calculable' course, but *not* because laws prevail in it but because laws are absolutely *lacking*, and every power draws its ultimate consequences every moment. Granted this too is only interpretation – and you will be eager enough to raise this objection? – well, so much the better. –

23

All psychology has hitherto remained anchored to moral prejudices and timidities: it has not ventured into the depths. To conceive it as morphology and the *development-theory of the will to power*, as I conceive it – has never yet so much as entered the mind of anyone else: in so far as it is permissible to see in what has hitherto been written a symptom of what has hitherto been kept silent. The power of moral prejudices has penetrated deep into the most spiritual world, which is apparently the coldest and most free of presuppositions – and, as goes without saying, has there acted in a harmful, inhibiting, blinding, distorting fashion. A genuine physio-psychology has to struggle with unconscious resistances in the heart of the investigator, it has 'the heart' against it: even a theory of the mutual dependence of the 'good' and the 'wicked' impulses causes, as a more refined immorality, revulsion to a conscience still strong and hearty – and even more a theory of the derivation of all good impulses from wicked ones. Supposing, however, that someone goes so far as to regard the emotions of hatred, envy, covetousness, and lust for domination as life-conditioning emotions, as something which must fundamentally and essentially be present in the total economy of life, consequently must be heightened further if life is to be heightened further – he suffers from such a judgement as from seasickness. And yet even this hypothesis is far from being the strangest and most painful in this tremendous, still almost unexplored realm of dangerous knowledge – and there are in fact a hundred good reasons why everyone should keep away from it who – *can*! On the other hand: if your ship *has* been driven into these seas, very well! Now clench your teeth! Keep your eyes open! Keep a firm hand on the helm! – We sail straight over morality and *past* it, we flatten, we crush perhaps what is left of our own morality by venturing to voyage thither – but what do *we* matter! Never yet has a *deeper* world of insight revealed itself to daring travellers and adventurers: and the psychologist who in this fashion 'brings a sacrifice' – it is *not* the *sacrifizio dell'intelletto*, on the contrary! – will at least be entitled to demand in return that psychology shall again be recognized as the queen of the sciences, to serve and prepare for which the other sciences exist. For psychology is now once again the road to the fundamental problems.

Part Two: The Free Spirit

24

O sancta simplicitas! What strange simplification and falsification mankind lives in! One can never cease to marvel once one has acquired eyes for this marvel! How we have made everything around us bright and free and easy and simple! How we have known how to bestow on our senses a passport to everything superficial, on our thoughts a divine desire for wanton gambolling and false conclusions! – how we have from the very beginning understood how to retain our ignorance so as to enjoy an almost inconceivable freedom, frivolity, impetuosity, bravery, cheerfulness of life, so as to enjoy life! And only on this now firm and granite basis of ignorance has knowledge hitherto been able to rise up, the will to knowledge on the basis of a far more powerful will, the will to non-knowledge, to the uncertain, to the untrue! Not as its antithesis but – as its refinement! For even if, here as elsewhere, *language* cannot get over its coarseness and continues to speak of antitheses where there are only degrees and many subtleties of gradation; even if likewise the incarnate tartuffery of morals which is now part of our invincible 'flesh and blood' twists the words in the mouths even of us men of knowledge: here and there we grasp that fact and laugh at how it is precisely the best knowledge that wants most to hold us in this *simplified*, altogether artificial, fabricated, falsified world, how it is willy-nilly in love with error because, as a living being, it is – in love with life!

25

After so cheerful an exordium a serious word would like to be heard: it addresses itself to the most serious. Take care, philosophers and friends of knowledge, and beware of martyrdom! Of suffering 'for the sake of truth'! Even of defending yourselves! It spoils all the innocence and fine neutrality of your conscience, it makes you obstinate against rebuffs and red rags, it makes you stupid, brutal and bullish if in the struggle with danger, slander, suspicion, casting out and even grosser consequences of hostility you finally even have to act as defenders of truth on earth – as if 'truth' were so innocuous and inept a person she stood in need of defending! And precisely by you, you knights of most sorrowful countenance, you idlers and cobweb-spinners of the spirit! After all, you know well enough that it cannot matter in the least whether precisely *you* are in the right, just as no philosopher hitherto has been in the right, and that a more praiseworthy veracity may lie in every little question-mark placed after your favourite words and favourite theories (and occasionally after yourselves) than in all your solemn gesticulations and smart answers before courts and accusers! Better to step aside! Flee away and conceal yourselves! And have your masks and subtlety, so that you may be misunderstood! Or feared a little! And do not forget the garden, the garden with golden trellis-work. And have about you people who are like a garden – or like music on the waters in the evening, when the day is already becoming a memory; – choose the *good* solitude, the free, wanton, easy solitude which gives you too a right to remain in some sense good! How poisonous, how cunning, how bad every protracted war makes one when it cannot be waged with open force! How *personal* a protracted fear makes one, a protracted keeping watch for enemies, for possible enemies! These outcasts of society, long persecuted and sorely hunted – also the enforced recluses, the Spinozas and Giordano Brunos – in the end always become refined vengeance-seekers and brewers of poison, even if they do so under the most spiritual masquerade and perhaps without being themselves aware of it (just dig up the foundation of Spinoza's ethics and theology!) – not to speak of the stupidity of moral indignation, which is in the philosopher an unfailing sign that he has lost his philosophical sense of humour. The martyrdom of the philosopher, his 'sacrifice for truth', brings to light what there has been in him of agitator and actor; and if one has hitherto regarded him only with artistic curiosity, in the case of many a philosopher it is easy to understand the dangerous desire to see him for once in his degeneration (degenerated into 'martyr', into stage- and platform-ranter). But if one does harbour such a desire, one has to be clear *what* it is one will get to see – merely a satyr play, merely a farcical after-piece, merely a continuing proof that the long tragedy *has come to an end*: supposing that every philosophy was in its inception a long tragedy. –

26

Every superior human being will instinctively aspire after a secret citadel where he is *set free* from the crowd, the many, the majority, where, as its exception, he may forget the rule 'man' – except in the one case in which, as a man of knowledge in the great and exceptional sense, he will be impelled by an even stronger instinct to make straight for this rule. He who, when trafficking with men, does not occasionally glisten with all the shades of distress, green and grey with disgust, satiety, sympathy, gloom and loneliness, is certainly not a man of an elevated taste; but if he does not voluntarily assume this burden and displeasure, if he continually avoids it and, as aforesaid, remains hidden quietly and proudly away in his citadel, then one thing is sure: he is not made, not predestined for knowledge. For if he were, he would one day have to say to himself: 'The devil can take my good taste! the rule is more interesting than the exception – than I, the exception!' – and would go *down*, would above all 'go in'. The study of the *average* human being, protracted, serious, and with much dissembling, self-overcoming, intimacy, bad company – all company is bad company except the company of one's equals – : this constitutes a necessary part of the life story of every philosopher, perhaps the most unpleasant and malodorous part and the part most full of disappointments. If he is lucky, however, as a favourite child of knowledge ought to be, he will encounter means of facilitating and cutting short his task – I mean so-called cynics, that is to say people who recognize the animal, the commonness, the 'rule' in themselves and yet still possess a degree of spirituality and appetite which constrains them to speak of themselves and their kind *before witnesses* – sometimes they even wallow in books as in their own dung. Cynicism is the only form in which common souls come close to honesty; and the higher man must prick up his ears at every cynicism, whether coarse or refined, and congratulate himself whenever a buffoon without shame or a scientific satyr speaks out in his presence. There are even cases in which fascination mingles with the disgust: namely where, by a caprice of nature, such an indiscreet goat and monkey is touched with genius, as in the case of the Abbé Galiani, the profoundest, most sharp-sighted and perhaps also dirtiest man of his century – he was far more profound than Voltaire and consequently also a good deal more silent. It is more often the case that, as already indicated, a scientific head is set on a monkey's body, a refined exceptional understanding on a common soul – no rare occurrence, for instance, among physicians and moral physiologists. And whenever anyone speaks, without bitterness, rather innocuously, of man as a belly with two needs and a head with one; wherever anyone sees, seeks and *wants* to see only hunger, sexual desire, and vanity, as though these were the actual and sole motives of human actions; in brief, whenever anyone speaks 'badly' of man – but does not speak *ill* of him – the lover of knowledge should listen carefully and with diligence, and he should in general lend an ear whenever anyone speaks without indignation. For the indignant man, and whoever is continually tearing and rending himself with his teeth (or, instead of himself, the world, or God, or society) may indeed morally speaking stand higher than the laughing and self-satisfied satyr, but in every other sense he is the more commonplace, less interesting, less instructive case. And no one *lies* so much as the indignant man. –

27

It is hard to be understood: especially when one thinks and lives *gangasrotogati* among men who think and live otherwise,

namely *kurmagati* or at best 'as the frog goes', *mandeikagati* – I
am certainly doing everything I can to be hard to understand
myself! – and one ought to be heartily grateful even for the
will to some subtlety in interpretation. As regards one's 'good
friends', however, who are always too indolent and think that
because they are one's friends they have a right to indolence:
one does well to allow them from the first some room and
latitude for misunderstanding – thus one can laugh at their
expense; – or get rid of them altogether, these good friends –
and still laugh!

28

That which translates worst from one language into another is
the tempo of its style, which has its origin in the character of
the race, or, expressed more physiologically, in the average
tempo of its 'metabolism'. There are honestly meant transla-
tions which, as involuntary vulgarizations of the original, are
almost falsifications simply because it was not possible to
translate also its brave and happy tempo, which leaps over
and puts behind it all that is perilous in things and words.
The German is virtually incapable of *presto* in his language:
thus, it may be fairly concluded, also of many of the most
daring and delightful nuances of free, free-spirited thought.
Just as the *buffo* and the satyr is strange to him, in his body
and in his conscience, so Aristophanes and Petronius are
untranslatable for him. Everything staid, sluggish, ponder-
ously solemn, all long-winded and boring species of style have
been developed in profuse multiplicity among the Germans –
pardon me for the fact that even Goethe's prose is, in its
blend of elegance and stiffness, no exception: it is a reflection
of the 'good old days', to which it belongs, and an expression
of the German taste of a time when there still was a 'German
taste': it was rococo *in moribus et artibus*. Lessing constitutes an
exception, thanks to his histrionic nature, which was versed in
and understood much: he, who was not for nothing the
translator of Bayle and liked to flee to the neighbourhood of
Diderot and Voltaire and even more to that of the Roman

writers of comedy – in tempo too Lessing loved free-spiritedness, escape from Germany. But how could the German language, even in the prose of a Lessing, imitate the tempo of Machiavelli, who in his *Principe* lets us breathe the subtle dry air of Florence and cannot help presenting the most serious affairs in a boisterous *allegrissimo*: not perhaps without a malicious artist's sense of the contrast he is risking – thoughts protracted, difficult, hard, dangerous and the tempo of the gallop and the most wanton good humour. Who, finally, would venture a German translation of Petronius, who was, to a greater degree than any great musician has hitherto been, a master of *presto* in invention, ideas, words – what do all the swamps of the sick wicked world, even of the 'antique world', matter when one has, like him, the feet of a wind, the blast and breath, the liberating scorn of a wind that makes everything healthy by making everything *run*! And as for Aristophanes, that transfiguring, complementary spirit for whose sake one *excuses* all Greece for having existed, assuming one has grasped in all its profundity *what* there is to be excused and transfigured here – I know of nothing that has led me to reflect more on *Plato*'s concealment and sphinx nature than that happily preserved *petit fait* that under the pillow of his death-bed there was discovered no 'Bible', nothing Egyptian, Pythagorean, Platonic – but Aristophanes. How could even a Plato have endured life - a Greek life which he had denied – without an Aristophanes! –

29

Few are made for independence - it is a privilege of the strong. And he who attempts it, having the completest right to it but without being *compelled* to, thereby proves that he is probably not only strong but also daring to the point of recklessness. He ventures into a labyrinth, he multiplies by a thousand the dangers which life as such already brings with it, not the smallest of which is that no one can behold how and where he goes astray, is cut off from others, and is torn to pieces limb from limb by some cave-minotaur of conscience.

If such a one is destroyed, it takes place so far from the understanding of men that they neither feel it nor sympathize – and he can no longer go back! He can no longer go back even to the pity of men! –

30

Our supreme insights must – and should! – sound like follies, in certain cases like crimes, when they come impermissibly to the ears of those who are not predisposed and predestined for them. The exoteric and the esoteric as philosophers formerly distinguished them, among the Indians as among the Greeks, Persians and Moslems, in short wherever one believed in an order of rank and *not* in equality and equal rights – differ one from another not so much in that the exoteric stands outside and sees, evaluates, measures, judges from the outside, not from the inside: what is more essential is that this class sees things from below – but the esoteric sees them *from above*! There are heights of the soul seen from which even tragedy ceases to be tragic; and, taking all the woe of the world together, who could venture to assert that the sight of it would *have* to seduce and compel us to pity and thus to a doubling of that woe? . . . What serves the higher type of man as food or refreshment must to a very different and inferior type be almost poison. The virtues of the common man would perhaps indicate vice and weakness in a philosopher; it may be possible that if a lofty type of man degenerated and perished, he would only thus acquire qualities on whose account it would prove necessary in the lower world into which he had sunk henceforth to venerate him as a saint. There are books which possess an opposite value for soul and health depending on whether the lower soul, the lower vitality, or the higher and more powerful avails itself of them: in the former case they are dangerous, disintegrative books, which produces dissolution, in the latter they are herald calls challenging the most courageous to *their* courage. Books for everybody are always malodorous books: the smell of petty people clings to them. Where the people eats and drinks, even where it worships, there is usually a stink. One should not go into churches if one wants to breathe *pure* air. –

31

In our youthful years we respect and despise without that art of nuance which constitutes the best thing we gain from life, and, as is only fair, we have to pay dearly for having assailed men and things with Yes and No in such a fashion. Everything is so regulated that the worst of all tastes, the taste for the unconditional, is cruelly misused and made a fool of until a man learns to introduce a little art into his feelings and even to venture trying the artificial: as genuine artists of life do. The anger and reverence characteristic of youth seem to allow themselves no peace until they have falsified men and things in such a way that they can vent themselves on them – youth as such is something that falsifies and deceives. Later, when the youthful soul, tormented by disappointments, finally turns suspiciously on itself, still hot and savage even in its suspicion and pangs of conscience: how angry it is with itself now, how it impatiently rends itself, how it takes revenge for its long self-delusion, as if it had blinded itself deliberately! During this transition one punishes oneself by distrusting one's feelings; one tortures one's enthusiasm with doubts, indeed one feels that even a good conscience is a danger, as though a good conscience were a screening of oneself and a sign that one's subtler honesty had grown weary; and above all one takes sides, takes sides on principle, *against* 'youth'. – A decade later: and one grasps that all this too – was still youth!

32

Throughout the longest part of human history – it is called prehistoric times – the value or non-value of an action was derived from its consequences: the action itself came as little into consideration as did its origin, but, in much the same way as today in China a distinction or disgrace reflects back from the child onto its parents, so it was the retroactive force of success or failure which led men to think well or ill of an action. Let us call this period the *pre-moral* period of mankind: the imperative 'know thyself!' was then still unknown. Over the past ten thousand years, on the other hand, one has in a few large tracts of the earth come step by step to the point at which it is no longer the consequences but the origin of the action which determines its value: a great event, taken as a whole, a considerable refinement of vision and standard, the unconscious after-effect of the sovereignty of aristocratic values and of belief in 'origins', the sign of a period which may be called the *moral* in the narrower sense: the first attempt at self-knowledge has been made. Instead of the consequences, the origin: what an inversion of perspectives! And certainly one achieved only after protracted struggles and vacillations! To be sure, a fateful new superstition, a peculiar narrowness of interpretation therewith became dominant: men interpreted the origin of an action in the most definite sense as origin in an *intention*; men became *unanimous* in the belief that the value of an action resided in the value of the intention behind it. The intention as the whole origin and prehistory of an action: it is under the sway of this prejudice that one has morally praised, blamed, judged and philosophized on earth almost to the present day. – But ought we not today to have arrived at the necessity of once again determining upon an inversion and shift of values, thanks to another self-examination and deepening on the part of man – ought we not to stand on the threshold of a period which should be called, negatively at first, the *extra-moral*: today, when among us immoralists at least the suspicion has arisen that the decisive value of an action resides in precisely that which is *not intentional* in it, and that all that in it which is intentional, all of it that can be seen, known, 'conscious', still belongs to its surface and skin – which, like every skin, betrays something but *conceals* still more? In brief, we believe that the intention is only a sign and symptom that needs interpreting, and a sign, moreover, that signifies too many things and which thus taken by itself signifies practically nothing – that morality in the sense in which it has been understood hitherto, that is to say the morality of intentions, has been a prejudice, a precipitancy, perhaps something provisional and precursory, perhaps something of the order of astronomy and alchemy, but in any event something that must be overcome. The overcoming of morality, in a certain sense even the self-overcoming of morality: let this be the name for that protracted secret labour which has been reserved for the subtlest, most honest and also most malicious consciences as living touchstones of the soul. -

33

There is nothing for it: the feelings of devotion, self-sacrifice for one's neighbour, the entire morality of self-renunciation must be taken mercilessly to task and brought to court: likewise the aesthetics of 'disinterested contemplation' through which the emasculation of art today tries, seductively enough, to give itself a good conscience. There is much too much sugar and sorcery in those feelings of 'for others', of '*not* for me', for one not to have to become doubly distrustful here and to ask: 'are they not perhaps – *seductions*?' That they *give pleasure* – to him who has them and to him who enjoys their fruits, also to the mere spectator – does not yet furnish an argument in their *favour*, but urges us rather to caution. So let us be cautious!

34

Whatever standpoint of philosophy we may adopt today: from every point of view the *erroneousness* of the world in which we believe we live is the surest and firmest thing we can get our eyes on – we find endless grounds for it which would like to lure us to suppose a deceptive principle in the 'nature of things'. But he who makes our thinking itself, that is to say 'the mind', responsible for the falsity of the world – an honourable way out taken by every conscious or unconscious *advocatus dei* – : he who takes this world, together with space, time, form, motion, to be the result of a false *conclusion*:

such a one would have good cause, to say the least, to learn finally to mistrust thinking itself: would it not have played on us the biggest hoax ever? and what guarantee would there be that it would not go on doing what it has always done? In all seriousness: the innocence of thinkers has something touching and inspiring of reverence in it which permits them even today to go up to consciousness and ask it to give them *honest* answers: whether it is 'real', for example, and why it really keeps the external world so resolutely at a distance, and other questions of the sort. The belief in 'immediate certainties' is a piece of *moral* naïvety which does honour to us philosophers: but – we ought not to be '*merely* moral' men! Apart from the moral aspect, that belief is a piece of stupidity which does us little honour! In civil life an ever-ready mistrustfulness may count as a sign of 'bad character' and thus be an imprudent thing to have: here among us, beyond the civil world and its Yes and No – what is there to stop us from being imprudent and saying: the philosopher, as the creature which has hitherto always been most fooled on earth, has by now a *right* to 'bad character' – he has today the *duty* to be distrustful, to squint wickedly up out of every abyss of suspicion. – You must forgive me this humorous expression and grimace: for I have long since learned to think differently, to judge differently on the subject of deceiving and being deceived, and I keep in readiness at least a couple of jabs in the ribs for the blind rage with which philosophers resist being deceived. Why *not*? It is no more than a moral prejudice that truth is worth more than appearance; it is even the worst-proved assumption that exists. Let us concede at least this much: there would be no life at all if not on the basis of perspective evaluations and appearances; and if, with the virtuous enthusiasm and awkwardness exhibited by some philosophers, one wanted to abolish the 'apparent world' altogether, well, assuming *you* could do that – at any rate nothing would remain of your 'truth' either! Indeed, what compels us to assume there exists any essential antithesis between 'true' and 'false'? Is it not enough to suppose grades of apparentness and as it were lighter and darker shades and tones of appearance – different *valeurs*, to speak in the language of painters? Why could the world *which is of any concern to us* – not be a fiction? And he who then objects: 'but to the fiction there belongs an author?' – could he not be met with the round retort: *why*? Does this 'belongs' perhaps not also belong to the fiction? Are we not permitted to be a little ironical now about the subject as we are about the predicate and object? Ought the philosopher not to rise above the belief in grammar? All due respect to governesses: but is it not time that philosophy renounced the beliefs of governesses?

35

Oh Voltaire! Oh humanity! Oh imbecility! There is some point to 'truth', to the *search* for truth; and if a human being goes about it too humanely – *'il ne cherche le vrai que pour faire le bien'* – I wager he finds nothing!

36

Granted that nothing is 'given' as real except our world of desires and passions, that we can rise or sink to no other 'reality' than the reality of our drives – for thinking is only the relationship of these drives to one another - : is it not permitted to make the experiment and ask the question whether this which is given does not *suffice* for an understanding even of the so-called mechanical (or 'material') world? I do not mean as a deception, an 'appearance', an 'idea' (in the Berkeleyan and Schopenhaueran sense), but as possessing the same degree of reality as our emotions themselves – as a more primitive form of the world of emotions in which everything still lies locked in mighty unity and then branches out and develops in the organic process (also, as is only fair, is made weaker and more sensitive), as a kind of instinctual life in which all organic functions, together with self-regulation, assimilation, nourishment, excretion, metabolism, are still synthetically bound together – as an *antecedent form* of life? – In the end, it is not merely permitted to make this experiment: it is commanded by the conscience of *method*. Not to assume

several kinds of causality so long as the experiment of getting
along with one has not been taken to its ultimate limits (– to
the point of nonsense, if I may say so): that is a morality of
method which one may not repudiate nowadays – it follows
'from its definition', as a mathematician would say. In the
end, the question is whether we really recognize will as
efficient, whether we believe in the causality of will: if we do
so – and fundamentally belief in *this* is precisely our belief in
causality itself – then we *have* to make the experiment of
positing causality of will hypothetically as the only one. 'Will'
can of course operate only on 'will' – and not on 'matter' (not
on 'nerves', for example –): enough, one must venture the
hypothesis that wherever 'effects' are recognized, will is operat-
ing upon will – and that all mechanical occurrences, in so far
as a force is active in them, are force of will, effects of will. –
Granted finally that one succeeded in explaining our entire
instinctual life as the development and ramification of *one*
basic form of will – as will to power, as is *my* theory – ;
granted that one could trace all organic functions back to this
will to power and could also find in it the solution to the
problem of procreation and nourishment – they are *one* problem – one would have acquired the right to define *all* efficient
force unequivocally as: *will to power*. The world seen from
within, the world described and defined according to its
'intelligible character' – it would be 'will to power' and
nothing else. –

37

'What? Does that, to speak vulgarly, not mean: God is refuted
but the devil is not – ?' On the contrary! On the contrary, my
friends! And who the devil compels you to speak vulgarly! –

38

As happened lately, in all the clarity of modern times, with
the French Revolution, that gruesome and, closely considered,
superfluous farce, into which, however, noble and enthusiastic

spectators all over Europe interpeted from a distance their own indignations and raptures so long and so passionately that *the text disappeared beneath the interpretation*: so a noble posterity could once again misunderstand the entire past and only thus perhaps make the sight of it endurable. – Or rather: has this not already happened? have we ourselves not been this 'noble posterity'? And, in so far as we comprehend this, is it not at this moment – done with?

39

No one is likely to consider a doctrine true merely because it makes happy or makes virtuous: excepting perhaps the dear 'idealists', who rapturize over the good, the true and the beautiful and let all kinds of colourful, clumsy and good-natured desiderata swim about together in their pond. Happiness and virtue are no arguments. But even thoughtful spirits like to forget that making unhappy and making evil are just as little counter-arguments. Something might be true although at the same time harmful and dangerous in the highest degree; indeed, it could pertain to the fundamental nature of existence that a complete knowledge of it would destroy one – so that the strength of a spirit could be measured by how much 'truth' it could take, more clearly, to what degree it *needed* it attenuated, veiled, sweetened, blunted, and falsified. But there can be no doubt that for the discovery of certain *parts* of truth the wicked and unhappy are in a more favourable position and are more likely to succeed; not to speak of the wicked who are happy – a species about whom the moralists are silent. Perhaps severity and cunning provide more favourable conditions for the formation of the strong, independent spirit and philosopher than does that gentle, sweet, yielding good-naturedness and art of taking things lightly which is prized in a scholar and rightly prized. Supposing in advance that the concept 'philosopher' is not limited to the philosopher who writes books – or, worse, writes books of *his* philosophy! – A final trait in the image of the free-spirited philosopher is provided by Stendhal, and in view of what German taste is I do not want to fail to emphasize it – for it goes *against* German taste. '*Pour être bon philosophe*', said this last great psychologist, '*il faut être sec, clair, sans illusion. Un banquier, qui a fait fortune, a une partie du caractère requis pour faire des découvertes en philosophie, c'est-à-dire pour voir clair dans ce qui est.*'

40

Everything profound loves the mask; the profoundest things of all hate even image and parable. Should not nothing less than the *opposite* be the proper disguise under which the shame of a god goes abroad? A questionable question: it would be strange if some mystic or other had not already ventured to meditate some such thing. There are occurrences of so delicate a description that one does well to bury them and make them unrecognizable with a piece of coarseness; there are acts of love and extravagant magnanimity after which nothing is more advisable than to take a stick and give the eyewitness a thrashing and so confuse his memory. Some know how to confuse and mistreat their own memory, so as to take revenge at least on this sole confidant – shame is inventive. It is not the worst things of which one is most ashamed: there is not only deceit behind a mask – there is so much goodness in cunning. I could believe that a man who had something fragile and valuable to conceal might roll through life thick and round as an old, green, thick-hooped wine barrel: the refinement of his shame would have it so. A man whose shame has depth enounters his destinies and delicate decisions too on paths which very few ever reach and of whose existence his intimates and neighbours may not know: his mortal danger is concealed from their eyes, as is the fact that he has regained his sureness of life. Such a hidden man, who instinctively uses speech for silence and conceal-ment and is inexhaustible in evading communication, *wants* a mask of him to roam the heads and hearts of his friends in his stead, and he makes sure that it does so; and supposing he does not want it, he will one day come to see that a mask is there in spite of that – and that that is a good thing. Every profound spirit needs a mask: more, around every profound spirit a mask is continually growing, thanks to the constantly false, that is to say *shallow* interpretation of every word he speaks, every step he takes, every sign of life he gives. –

41

One must test oneself to see whether one is destined for independence and command; and one must do so at the proper time. One should not avoid one's tests, although they are perhaps the most dangerous game one could play and are in the end tests which are taken before ourselves and before no other judge. Not to cleave to another person, though he be the one you love most – every person is a prison, also a nook and corner. Not to cleave to a fatherland, though it be the most suffering and in need of help – it is already easier to sever your heart from a victorious fatherland. Not to cleave to a feeling of pity, though it be for higher men into whose rare torment and helplessness chance allowed us to look. Not to cleave to a science, though it lures one with the most precious discoveries seemingly reserved precisely for *us*. Not to cleave to one's own detachment, to that voluptuous remoteness and strangeness of the bird which flies higher and higher so as to see more and more beneath it – the danger which threatens the flier. Not to cleave to our own virtues and become as a whole the victim of some part of us, of our 'hospitality' for example, which is the danger of dangers for rich and noble souls who expend themselves prodigally, almost indifferently, and take the virtue of liberality to the point where it becomes a vice. One must know how *to conserve oneself*: the sternest test of independence.

42

A new species of philosopher is appearing: I venture to baptize these philosophers with a name not without danger in it. As I divine them, as they let themselves be divined – for it pertains to their nature to *want* to remain a riddle in some respects – these philosophers of the future might rightly, but perhaps also wrongly, be described as *attempters*. This name itself is in the end only an attempt and, if you will, a temptation.

43

Are they new friends of 'truth', these coming philosophers? In all probability: for all philosophers have hitherto loved their truths. But certainly they will not be dogmatists. It must offend their pride, and also their taste, if their truth is supposed to be a truth for everyman, which has hitherto been the secret desire and hidden sense of all dogmatic endeavours. 'My judgement is *my* judgement: another cannot easily acquire a right to it' – such a philosopher of the future may perhaps say. One has to get rid of the bad taste of wanting to be in agreement with many. 'Good' is no longer good when your neighbour takes it into his mouth. And how could there exist a 'common good'! The expression is a self-contradiction: what can be common has ever but little value. In the end it must be as it is and has always been: great things are for the great, abysses for the profound, shudders and delicacies for the refined, and, in sum, all rare things for the rare. –

44

After all this do I still need to say that they too will be free, *very* free spirits, these philosophers of the future – just as surely as they will not be merely free spirits, but something more, higher, greater and thoroughly different that does not want to be misunderstood or taken for what it is not. But in saying this I feel I have a *duty*, almost as much towards them as towards us, their heralds and precursors, us free spirits! – to blow away from all of us an ancient and stupid prejudice and misunderstanding which has all too long obscured the concept 'free spirit' like a fog. In all the countries of Europe and likewise in America there exists at present something that misuses this name, a very narrow, enclosed, chained up species of spirits who desire practically the opposite of that which informs our aims and instincts – not to mention the fact that in regard to those *new* philosophers appearing they must certainly be closed windows and bolted doors. They belong, in short and regrettably, among the *levellers*, these falsely named 'free spirits' – eloquent and tirelessly scribbling slaves of the democratic taste and its 'modern ideas', men without solitude one and all, without their own solitude, good clumsy fellows who, while they cannot be denied courage and moral respectability, are unfree and ludicrously superficial, above all in their fundamental inclination to see in the forms of existing society the cause of practically *all* human failure and misery: which is to stand the truth happily on its head! What with all their might they would like to strive after is the universal green pasture happiness of the herd, with security, safety, comfort and an easier life for all; their two most oft-recited doctrines and ditties are 'equality of rights' and 'sympathy for all that suffers' – and suffering itself they take for something that has to be *abolished*. We, who are the opposite of this, and have opened our eyes and our conscience to the question where and how the plant 'man' has hitherto grown up most vigorously, we think that this has always happened under the opposite conditions, that the perilousness of his situation had first to become tremendous, his powers of invention and dissimulation (his 'spirit' –) had, under protracted pressure and constraint, to evolve into subtlety and daring, his will to life had to be intensified into unconditional will to power – we think that severity, force, slavery, peril in the street and in the heart, concealment, stoicism, the art of experiment and devilry of every kind, that everything evil, dreadful, tyrannical, beast of prey and serpent in man serves to enhance the species 'man' just as much as does its opposite – we do not say enough when we say even that much, and at any rate we are, in what we say and do not say on this point, at the *other* end from all modern ideology and herd desiderata: at its antipodes perhaps? Is it any wonder we 'free spirits' are not precisely the most communicative of spirits? that we do not want to betray in every respect *from what* a spirit can free itself and *to what* it is then perhaps driven? And as for the dangerous formula 'beyond good and evil' with which we at any rate guard against being taken for what we are not: we *are* something different from '*libres-penseurs*', '*liberi pensatori*', '*Freidenker*', or whatever else all these worthy advocates of 'modern ideas' like to call themselves. At home in many countries of the spirit, or at least having been guests there; having again and again eluded the agreeable musty nooks and corners into which predilection and prejudice, youth, origin, the accidents of people and books, or even weariness from wandering seemed to have consigned us; full of malice towards the lures of dependence which reside in honours, or money, or offices, or raptures of the senses; grateful even to distress and changeful illness because it has always liberated us from some rule and its 'prejudice', grateful to the god, devil, sheep and worm in us, curious to the point of vice, investigators to the point of cruelty, with rash fingers for the ungraspable, with teeth and stomach for the most indigestible, ready for every task that demands acuteness and sharp senses, ready for every venture thanks to a superfluity of 'free will', with fore- and back-souls into whose ultimate intentions no one can easily see, with fore- and backgrounds to whose end no foot may go, hidden under mantles of light, conquerors even though we look like heirs and prodigals, collectors and arrangers from morn till night, misers of our riches and our full-crammed cupboards, thrifty in learning and forgetting, inventive in schemata, sometimes proud of tables of categories, sometimes pedants, sometimes night owls of labour even in broad daylight; yes, even scarecrows when we need to be – and today we need to be: in so far, that is, as we are born, sworn, jealous friends of *solitude*, of our own deepest, most midnight, most midday solitude – such a type of man are we, we free spirits! and perhaps *you* too are something of the same type, you coming men? you *new* philosophers? –

Part Three: The Religious Nature

45

The human soul and its frontiers, the compass of human inner experience in general attained hitherto, the heights, depths and distances of this experience, the entire history of the soul *hitherto* and its still unexhausted possibilities: this is the pre-destined hunting-ground for a born psychologist and lover of the 'big-game hunt'. But how often must he say despairingly to himself: 'one man! alas, but one man! and this great forest and jungle!' And thus he wishes he had a few hundred beaters and subtle well-instructed tracker dogs whom he could send into the history of the human soul and there round up *his* game. In vain: he discovers again and again, thoroughly and bitterly, how hard it is to find beaters and dogs for all the things which arouse his curiosity. The drawback in sending scholars out into new and dangerous hunting-grounds where courage, prudence, subtlety in every sense are needed is that they cease to be of any use precisely where the '*big* hunt', but also the big danger, begins – precisely there do they lose their keenness of eye and keenness of nose. To divine and establish, for example, what sort of history the problem of *knowledge and conscience* has had in the soul of *homines religiosi* one would oneself perhaps have to be as profound, as wounded, as monstrous as Pascal's intellectual conscience was – and then there would still be needed that broad heaven of bright, malicious spirituality capable of looking down on this turmoil of dangerous and painful experiences, surveying and ordering them and forcing them into formulas. – But who could do me this service! And who could have the time to wait for such servants! – they appear too rarely, they are at all times so very improbable! In the end one has to do everything *oneself* if one is to know a few things oneself: that is to say, one has *much* to do! – But a curiosity like mine is after all the most pleasurable of vices – I beg your pardon! I meant to say: the love of truth has its reward in Heaven, and already upon earth. –

46

The faith such as primitive Christianity demanded and not infrequently obtained in the midst of a sceptical and southerly free-spirited world with a centuries-long struggle between philosophical schools behind it and in it, plus the education in tolerance provided by the *Imperium Romanum* – this faith is *not* that gruff, true-hearted liegeman's faith with which a Luther, say, or a Cromwell, or some other northern barbarian of the spirit cleaved to his God and his Christianity; it is rather that faith of Pascal which resembles in a terrible fashion a protracted suicide of reason – of a tough, long-lived, wormlike reason which is not to be killed instantaneously with a single blow. The Christian faith is from the beginning sacrifice: sacrifice of all freedom, all pride, all self-confidence of the spirit, at the same time enslavement and self-mockery, self-mutilation. There is cruelty and religious Phoenicianism in this faith exacted of an over-ripe, manifold and much-indulged conscience: its presupposition is that the subjection of the spirit is indescribably *painful*, that the entire past and habitude of such a spirit resists the *absurdissimum* which 'faith' appears to it to be. Modern men, with their obtuseness to all Christian nomenclature, no longer sense the gruesome superlative which lay for an antique taste in the paradoxical formula 'god on the cross'. Never and nowhere has there hitherto been a comparable boldness in inversion, anything so fearsome, questioning and questionable, as this formula: it promised a revaluation of all antique values. – It is the orient, the *innermost* orient, it is the oriental slave who in this fashion took vengeance on Rome and its noble and frivolous tolerance, on Roman 'catholicism' of faith – and it has never been faith but always freedom from faith, that half-stoical and smiling unconcern with the seriousness of faith, that has enraged slaves in their masters and against their masters. 'Enlightenment' enrages: for the slave wants the unconditional, he understands in the domain of morality too only the tyrannical, he loves as he hates, without nuance, into the depths of him, to the point of pain, to the point of sickness – the great *hidden* suffering he feels is enraged at the noble taste which seems to *deny* suffering. Scepticism towards suffering, at bottom no more than a pose of aristocratic morality, was likewise not the least contributory cause of the last great slave revolt which began with the French Revolution.

47

Wherever the religious neurosis has hitherto appeared on earth we find it tied to three dangerous dietary prescriptions: solitude, fasting and sexual abstinence – but without our being able to decide with certainty which is cause here and which effect, or *whether* any relation of cause and effect is involved here at all. The justification of the latter doubt is that one of the most frequent symptoms of the condition, in the case of savage and tame peoples, is the most sudden and most extravagant voluptuousness which is then, just as suddenly, reversed into a convulsion of penitence and a denial of world and will: both perhaps interpretable as masked epilepsy? But nowhere is it more necessary to renounce interpretations: around no other type has there grown up such an abundance of nonsense and superstition, none seems to have hitherto interested men, even philosophers, more – the time has come to cool down a little on this matter, to learn caution: better, to look away, *to go away*. – Still in the background of the most recent philosophy, the Schopenhaueran, there stands, almost as the problem in itself, this gruesome question-mark of the religious crisis and awakening. How is denial of the will *possible*? How is the saint possible? – this really seems to have been the question over which Schopenhauer became a philosopher and set to work. And thus it showed a genuinely Schopenhaueran outcome that his most convinced adherent (perhaps also his last adherent, so far as Germany is concerned –), namely Richard Wagner, brought his own life's work to an end at precisely this point and at last introduced that dreadful and eternal type onto the stage as Kundry, *type vécu*, just as it is; and at the very time when the psychiatrists of almost all the nations of Europe had an opportunity of studying it at close quarters wherever the religious neurosis – or, as I call it, 'the religious nature' – staged its latest epidemic parade and outbreak as the 'Salvation Army'. – But if one asks what it has really been in this whole phenomenon of the saint that has interested men of all types and ages, even philosophers, so immoderately, then the answer is, beyond doubt, the appearance of the miraculous adhering to it, namely the direct *succession of opposites*, of morally antithetical states of soul: here it seemed a palpable fact that a 'bad man' all at once became a 'saint', a good man. Pschology has hitherto come to grief at this point: has it not been principally because it has acknowledged the dominion of morality, because it itself *believed* in antithetical moral values and saw, read, *interpreted* these antitheses into the text *and* the facts? – What? The 'miracle' only an error of interpretation? A lack of philology? –

48

It seems that their Catholicism is much more an intrinsic part of the Latin races than the whole of Christianity in general is of us northerners; and that unbelief consequently signifies something altogether different in Catholic countries from what it does in Protestant – namely a kind of revolt against the spirit of the race, while with us it is rather a return to the spirit (or lack of spirit –) of the race. We northerners are undoubtedly descended from barbarian races also in respect of our talent for religion: we have *little* talent for it. We may except the Celts, who therefore supplied the best soil for the reception of the Christian infection in the north – the Christian ideal came to blossom, so far as the pale northern sun permitted it, in France. How uncongenially pious are to our taste even these latest French sceptics when they have in them any Celtic blood! How Catholic, how un-German does Auguste Comte's sociology smell to us with its Roman logic of the instincts! How Jesuitical that clever and charming cicerone of

Port-Royal, Sainte-Beuve, despite all his hostility towards the Jesuits! And even more so Ernest Renan: how inaccessible to us northerners is the language of a Renan, in whom every other minute some nothingness of religious tension topples a soul which is in a refined sense voluptuous and relaxed! Repeat these beautiful words of his – and what malice and high spirits are at once aroused in reply in our probably less beautiful and sterner, that is to say German, souls: – '*Disons donc hardiment que la religion est un produit de l'homme normal, que l'homme est le plus dans le vrai quand il est le plus religieux et le plus assuré d'une destinée infinie . . . C'est quand il est bon qu'il veut que la vertu corresponde à une ordre éternelle, c'est quand il contemple les choses d'une manière désintéressée qu'il trouve la mort révoltante et absurde. Comment ne pas supposer que c'est dans ces moments-là, que l'homme voit le mieux? . . .*' These words are so totally *antipodal* to my ears and habits that when I discovered them my immediate anger wrote beside them '*la niaiserie religieuse par excellence!*' – until my subsequent anger actually began to like them, these words with their upside-down-truth! It is so pleasant, so distinguishing, to possess one's own antipodes!

49

What astonishes one about the religiosity of the ancient Greeks is the tremendous amount of gratitude that emanates from it – the kind of man who stands *thus* before nature and before life is a very noble one! – Later, when the rabble came to predominate in Greece, *fear* also overran religion; and Christianity was preparing itself. –

50

The passion for God: there is the peasant, true-hearted and importunate kind, like Luther's – the whole of Protestantism lacks southern *delicatezza*. There is an oriental ecstatic kind, like that of a slave who has been undeservedly pardoned and elevated, as for example in the case of Augustine, who lacks in an offensive manner all nobility of bearing and desire.

There is the womanly tender and longing kind which presses bashfully and ignorantly for a *unio mystica et physica*: as in the case of Madame de Guyon. In many cases it appears strangely enough as a disguise for the puberty of a girl or a youth; now and then even as the hysteria of an old maid, also as her final ambition – the church has more than once canonized the woman in question.

51

Hitherto the mightiest men have still bowed down reverently before the saint as the enigma of self-constraint and voluntary final renunciation: why did they bow? They sensed in him – as it were behind the question-mark presented by his fragile and miserable appearance – the superior force that sought to prove itself through such a constraint, the strength of will in which they recognized and knew how to honour their own strength and joy in ruling: they honoured something in themselves when they honoured the saint. In addition to this, the sight of the saint aroused a suspicion in them: such an enormity of denial, of anti-nature, will not have been desired for nothing, they said to themselves. Is there perhaps a reason for it, a very great danger about which the ascetic, thanks to his secret visitors and informants, might possess closer knowledge? Enough, the mighty of the world learned in face of him a new fear, they sensed a new power, a strange enemy as yet unsubdued – it was the 'will to power' which constrained them to halt before the saint. They had to question him –.

52

In the Jewish 'Old Testament', the book of divine justice, there are men, things and speeches of so grand a style that Greek and Indian literature have nothing to set beside it. One stands in reverence and trembling before these remnants of what man once was and has sorrowful thoughts about old Asia and its little jutting-out promontory Europe, which would like to signify as against Asia the 'progress of man'. To be sure: he who is only a measly tame domestic animal and knows only the needs of a domestic animal (like our cultured people of today, the Christians of 'cultured' Christianity included –) has no reason to wonder, let alone to sorrow, among those ruins – the taste for the Old Testament is a touchstone in regard to 'great' and 'small' – : perhaps he will find the New Testament, the book of mercy, more after his own heart (there is in it a great deal of the genuine delicate, musty odour of devotee and petty soul). To have glued this New Testament, a species of rococo taste in every respect, on to the Old Testament to form a *single* book, as 'bible', as 'the book of books': that is perhaps the greatest piece of temerity and 'sin against the spirit' that literary Europe has on its conscience.

53

Why atheism today? – 'The father' in God is thoroughly refuted; likewise 'the judge', 'the rewarder'. Likewise his 'free will': he does not hear – and if he heard he would still not know how to help. The worst thing is: he seems incapable of making himself clearly understood: is he himself vague about what he means? – These are what, in the course of many conversations, asking and listening, I found to be the causes of the decline of European theism; it seems to me that the religious instinct is indeed in vigorous growth – but that it rejects the theistic answer with profound mistrust.

54

What, at bottom, is the whole of modern philosophy doing? Since Descartes – and indeed rather in spite of him than on the basis of his precedent – all philosophers have been making an *attentat* on the ancient soul concept under the cloak of a critique of the subject-and-predicate concept – that is to say, an *attentat* on the fundamental presupposition of Christian doctrine. Modern philosophy, as an epistemological scepticism, is, covertly or openly, *anti-Christian*: although, to speak to more refined ears, by no means anti-religious. For in the past one believed in 'the soul' as one believed in grammar and the grammatical subject: one said 'I' is the condition, 'think' is the predicate and conditioned – thinking is an activity to which a subject *must* be thought of as cause. Then one tried with admirable artfulness and tenacity to fathom whether one could not get out of this net – whether the reverse was not perhaps true: 'think' the condition, 'I' conditioned; 'I' thus being only a synthesis *produced* by thinking. *Kant* wanted fundamentally to prove that, starting from the subject, the subject could not be proved – nor could the object: the possibility of an *apparent existence* of the subject, that is to say of 'the soul', may not always have been remote from him, that idea which, as the philosophy of the Vedanta, has exerted immense influence on earth before.

55

There is a great ladder of religious cruelty with many rungs; but three of them are the most important. At one time one sacrificed human beings to one's god, perhaps precisely those human beings one loved best – the sacrifice of the first-born present in all prehistoric religions belongs here, as does the sacrifice of the Emperor Tiberius in the Mithras grotto on the isle of Capri, that most horrible of all Roman anachronisms. Then, in the moral epoch of mankind, one sacrificed to one's god the strongest instincts one possessed, one's 'nature'; the joy of *this* festival glitters in the cruel glance of the ascetic, the inspired 'anti-naturist'. Finally: what was left to be sacrificed? Did one not finally have to sacrifice everything comforting, holy, healing, all hope, all faith in a concealed harmony, in a future bliss and justice? Did one not have to sacrifice God himself and out of cruelty against oneself worship stone, stupidity, gravity, fate, nothingness? To sacrifice God for nothingness – this paradoxical mystery of the ultimate act of cruelty was reserved for the generation which is even now arising: we all know something of it already.

56

He who, prompted by some enigmatic desire, has, like me, long endeavoured to think pessimism through to the bottom and to redeem it from the half-Christian, half-German simplicity and narrowness with which it finally presented itself to this century, namely in the form of the Schopenhaueran philosophy; he who has really gazed with an Asiatic and more than Asiatic eye down into the most world-denying of all possible modes of thought – beyond good and evil and no longer, like Buddha and Schopenhauer, under the spell and illusion of morality – perhaps by that very act, and without really intending to, may have had his eyes opened to the opposite ideal: to the ideal of the most exuberant, most living and most world-affirming man, who has not only learned to get on and treat with all that was and is but who wants to have it again *as it was and is* to all eternity, insatiably calling out *da capo* not only to himself but to the whole piece and play, and not only to a play but fundamentally to him who needs precisely this play – and who makes it necessary: because he needs himself again and again – and makes himself necessary – What? And would this not be – *circulus vitiosus deus*?

57

With the strength of his spiritual sight and insight the distance, and as it were the space, around man continually expands: his world grows deeper, ever new stars, ever new images and enigmas come into view. Perhaps everything on which the spirit's eye has exercised its profundity and acuteness has been really but an opportunity for its exercise, a game, something for children and the childish. Perhaps the most solemn concepts which have occasioned the most strife and suffering, the concepts 'God' and 'sin', will one day seem to us of no more importance than a child's toy and a child's troubles seem to an old man – and perhaps 'old man' will then have need of another toy and other troubles – still enough of a child, an eternal child!

58

Has it been observed to what extent a genuine religious life
(both for its favourite labour of microscopic self-examination
and that gentle composure which calls itself 'prayer' and
which is a constant readiness for the 'coming of God' –)
requires external leisure or semi-leisure, I mean leisure with a
good conscience, inherited, by blood, which is not altogether
unfamiliar with the aristocratic idea that work *degrades* – that
is to say, makes soul and body common? And that consequently modern, noisy, time-consuming, proud and stupidly
proud industriousness educates and prepares precisely for
'unbelief' more than anything else does? Among those in
Germany for example who nowadays live without religion, I
find people whose 'free-thinking' is of differing kinds and
origins but above all a majority of those in whom industriousness from generation to generation has extinguished the
religious instincts: so that they no longer have any idea what
religions are supposed to be for and as it were merely register
their existence in the world with a kind of dumb amazement.
They feel they are already fully occupied, these worthy people,
whether with their businesses or with their pleasures, not to
speak of the 'fatherland' and the newspapers and 'family
duties': it seems that they have no time at all left for religion,
especially as it is not clear to them whether it involves another
business or another pleasure – for they tell themselves it is not
possible that one goes to church simply to make oneself
miserable. They are not opposed to religious usages; if partici-
pation in such usages is demanded in certain cases, by the
state for instance, they do what is demanded of them as one
does so many things – with patient and modest seriousness
and without much curiosity and discomfort – it is only that
they live too much aside and outside even to feel the need for
any for or against in such things. The great majority of
German middle-class Protestants can today be numbered
among these indifferent people, especially in the great industrious centres of trade and commerce; likewise the great majority
of industrious scholars and the entire university equipage

(excepting the theologians, whose possibility and presence there provides the psychologist with ever more and ever subtler enigmas to solve). Pious or even merely church-going people seldom realize *how much* good will, one might even say willfulness, it requires nowadays for a German scholar to take the problem of religion seriously; his whole trade (and, as said above, the tradesmanlike industriousness to which his modern conscience obliges him) disposes him to a superior, almost good-natured merriment in regard to religion, sometimes mixed with a mild contempt directed at the 'uncleanliness' of spirit which he presupposes wherever one still belongs to the church. It is only with the aid of history (thus *not* from his personal experience) that the scholar succeeds in summoning up a reverent seriousness and a certain shy respect towards religion; but if he intensifies his feelings towards it even to the point of feeling grateful to it, he has still in his own person not got so much as a single step closer to that which still exists as church or piety: perhaps the reverse. The practical indifference to religious things in which he was born and raised is as a rule sublimated in him into a caution and cleanliness which avoids contact with religious people and things; and it can be precisely the depth of his tolerance and humanity that bids him evade the subtle distress which tolerance itself brings with it. – Every age has its own divine kind of naïvety for the invention of which other ages may envy it – and how much naïvety, venerable, childlike and boundlessly stupid naïvety there is in the scholar's belief in his superiority, in the good conscience of his tolerance, in the simple unsuspecting certainty with which his instinct treats the religious man as an inferior and lower type which he himself has grown beyond and *above* – he, the little presumptuous dwarf and man of the mob, the brisk and busy head- and handyman of 'ideas', of 'modern ideas'!

59

He who has seen deeply into the world knows what wisdom there is in the fact that men are superficial It is their instinct for preservation which teaches them to be fickle, light and false. Here and there, among philosophers as well as artists, one finds a passionate and exaggerated worship of 'pure forms': let no one doubt that he who *needs* the cult of surfaces to that extent has at some time or other made a calamitous attempt to get *beneath* them. Perhaps there might even exist an order of rank in regard to these burnt children, these born artists who can find pleasure in life only in the intention of falsifying its image (as it were in a long-drawn-out revenge on life –): one could determine the degree to which life has been spoiled for them by the extent to which they want to see its image falsified, attenuated and made otherworldly and divine – one could include the *homines religiosi* among the artists as their *highest* rank. It is the profound suspicious fear of an incurable pessimism which compels whole millennia to cling with their teeth to a religious interpretation of existence: the fear born of that instinct which senses that one might get hold of the truth *too soon*, before mankind was sufficiently strong, sufficiently hard, sufficient of an artist ... Piety, the 'life in God', would, viewed in this light, appear as the subtlest and ultimate product of the *fear* of truth, as the artist's worship of an intoxication before the most consistent of all falsifications, as the will to inversion of truth, to untruth at any price. Perhaps there has up till now been no finer way of making man himself more beautiful than piety: through piety man can become to so great a degree of art, surface, play of colours, goodness, that one no longer suffers at the sight of him. –

60

To love men *for the sake of God* – that has been the noblest and most remote feeling attained to among men up till now. That love of man without some sanctifying ulterior objective is one piece of stupidity and animality *more*, that the inclination to this love of man has first to receive its measure, its refinement, its grain of salt and drop of amber from a higher inclination – whatever man it was who first felt and 'experienced' this, however much his tongue may have faltered as it sought to express such a delicate thought, let him be holy and venerated to us for all time as the man who has soared the highest and gone the most beautifully astray!

61

The philosopher as *we* understand him, we free spirits — as the man of the most comprehensive responsibility who has the conscience for the collective evolution of mankind: this philosopher will make use of the religions for his work of education and breeding, just as he will make use of existing political and economic conditions. The influence on selection and breeding, that is to say the destructive as well as the creative and formative influence which can be exercised with the aid of the religions, is manifold and various depending on the kind of men placed under their spell and protection. For the strong and independent prepared and predestined for command, in whom the art and reason of a ruling race is incarnated, religion is one more means of overcoming resistance so as to be able to rule: as a bond that unites together ruler and ruled and betrays and hands over to the former the consciences of the latter, all that is hidden and most intimate in them which would like to exclude itself from obedience; and if some natures of such noble descent incline through lofty spirituality to a more withdrawn and meditative life and reserve to themselves only the most refined kind of rule (over select disciples or brothers), then religion can even be used as a means of obtaining peace from the noise and effort of *cruder* modes of government, and cleanliness from the *necessary* dirt of all politics. Thus did the Brahmins, for example, arrange things: with the aid of a religious organization they gave themselves the power of nominating their kings for the people, while keeping and feeling themselves aside and outside as men of higher and more than kingly tasks. In the meantime, religion also gives a section of the ruled guidance and opportunity for preparing itself for future rule and command; that is to say, those slowly rising orders and classes in which through fortunate marriage customs the strength and joy of the will, the will to self-mastery is always increasing – religion presents them with sufficient instigations and temptations to take the road to higher spirituality, to test the feelings of great self-overcoming, of silence and solitude – asceticism and puritanism are virtually indispensable means of education and ennobling if a race wants to become master over its origins in the rabble, and work its way up towards future rule. To ordinary men, finally, the great majority, who exist for service and general utility and who *may* exist only for that purpose, religion gives an invaluable contentment with their nature and station, manifold peace of heart, an ennobling of obedience, one piece of joy and sorrow more to share with their fellows, and some transfiguration of the whole everydayness, the whole lowliness, the whole half-bestial poverty of their souls. Religion and the religious significance of life sheds sunshine over these perpetual drudges and makes their own sight tolerable to them, it has the effect which an Epicurean philosophy usually has on sufferers of a higher rank, refreshing, refining, as it were *making the most use of* suffering, ultimately even sanctifying and justifying. Perhaps nothing in Christianity and Buddhism is so venerable as their art of teaching even the lowliest to set themselves through piety in an apparently higher order of things and thus to preserve their contentment with the real order, within which they live hard enough lives – and necessarily have to!

62

In the end, to be sure, to present the debit side of the account to these religions and to bring into the light of day their uncanny perilousness – it costs dear and terribly when religions hold sway, *not* as means of education and breeding in the hands of the philosopher, but in their own right and as *sovereign*, when they themselves want to be final ends and not means beside other means. Among men, as among every other species, there is a surplus of failures, of the sick, the degenerate, the fragile, of those who are bound to suffer; the successful cases are, among men too, always the exception, and, considering that man is the animal *whose nature has not yet been fixed*, the rare exception. But worse still: the higher the type of man a man represents, the greater the improbability he will *turn out well*: chance, the law of absurdity in the total economy of mankind, shows itself in its most dreadful shape in its destructive effect on higher men, whose conditions of life are subtle, manifold and difficult to compute. Now what is the attitude of the above-named two chief religions towards this *surplus* of unsuccessful cases? They seek to preserve, to retain in life, whatever can in any way be preserved, indeed they side with it as a matter of principle as religions *for sufferers*, they maintain that all those who suffer from life as from an illness are in the right, and would like every other feeling of life to be counted false and become impossible. However highly one may rate this kindly preservative solicitude, inasmuch as, together with all the other types of man, it has been and is applied to the highest type, which has hitherto almost always been the type that has suffered most: in the total accounting the hitherto *sovereign* religions are among the main reasons the type 'man' has been kept on a lower level – they have preserved too much of that *which ought to perish*. We have inestimable benefits to thank them for; and who is sufficiently rich in gratitude not to be impoverished in face of all that the 'spiritual men' of Christianity, for example, have hitherto done for Europe! And yet, when they gave comfort to the suffering, courage to the oppressed and despairing, a staff and stay to the irresolute, and lured those who were inwardly shattered and had become savage away from society into monasteries and houses of correction for the soul: what did they have to do in addition so as thus, with a good conscience, as a matter of principle, to work at the preservation of everything sick and suffering, which means in fact and truth at the *corruption of the European race*? Stand all evaluations *on their head* – *that* is what they had to do! And smash the strong, contaminate great hopes, cast suspicion on joy in beauty, break down everything autocratic, manly, conquering, tyrannical, all the instincts proper to the highest and most successful of the type 'man', into uncertainty, remorse of conscience, self-destruction, indeed reverse the whole love of the earthly and of dominion over the earth into hatred of the earth and the earthly – *that* is the task the church set itself and had to set itself, until in its evaluation 'unworldliness', 'unsensuality', and 'higher man' were finally fused together into *one* feeling. Supposing one were able to view the strangely painful and at the same time coarse and subtle comedy of European Christianity with the mocking and unconcerned eye of an Epicurean god, I believe there would be no end to one's laughter and amazement: for does it not seem that *one* will has dominated Europe for eighteen centuries, the will to make of man a *sublime abortion*? But he who, with an opposite desire, no longer Epicurean but with some divine hammer in his hand, approached this almost deliberate degeneration and stunting of man such as constitutes the European Christian (Pascal for instance), would he not have to cry out in rage, in pity, in horror: 'O you fools, you presumptuous, pitying fools, what have you done! Was this a work for your hands! How you have bungled and botched my beautiful stone! What a thing for *you* to take upon yourselves!' – What I am saying is: Christianity has been the most fatal kind of self-presumption ever. Men not high or hard enough for the artistic refashioning of *mankind*; men not strong or farsighted enough for the sublime self-constraint needed to *allow* the foreground law of thousandfold failure and perishing to prevail; men not noble enough to see the abysmal disparity in order of rank and abysm of rank between men and man – it is *such* men who, with their 'equal before God', have hitherto ruled over the destiny of Europe, until at last a shrunken, almost ludicrous species, a herd animal, something full of good will, sickly and mediocre has been bred, the European of today . . .

63

He who is a teacher from the very heart takes all things seriously only with reference to his students – even himself.

64

'Knowledge for its own sake' – this is the last snare set by morality: one therewith gets completely entangled with it once more.

65

The charm of knowledge would be small if so much shame did not have to be overcome on the road to it.

65a

One is most dishonest towards one's God: he is not *permitted* to sin!

66

The inclination to disparage himself, to let himself be robbed, lied to and exploited, could be the self-effacement of a god among men.

67

Love of *one* is a piece of barbarism: for it is practised at the expense of all others. Love of God likewise.

68

'I have done that,' says my memory. 'I cannot have done that' – says my pride, and remains adamant. At last – memory yields.

69

One has been a bad spectator of life if one has not also seen the hand that in a considerate fashion – kills.

70

If one has character one also has one's typical experience which recurs again and again.

71

The sage as astronomer. – As long as you still feel the stars as being something 'over you' you still lack the eye of the man of knowledge.

72

It is not the strength but the duration of exalted sensations which makes exalted men.

73

He who attains his ideal by that very fact transcends it.

73a

Many a peacock hides his peacock tail from all eyes – and calls it his pride.

74

A man with genius is unendurable if he does not also possess at least two other things: gratitude and cleanliness.

75

The degree and kind of a man's sexuality reaches up into the topmost summit of his spirit.

76

Under conditions of peace the warlike man attacks himself.

77

With one's principles one seeks to tyrannize over one's habits or to justify or honour or scold or conceal them – two people with the same principles probably seek something fundamentally different with them.

78

He who despises himself still nonetheless respects himself as one who despises.

79

A soul which knows it is loved but does not itself love betrays its dregs – its lowest part comes up.

80

A thing explained is a thing we have no further concern with. -- What did that god mean who counselled: 'know thyself!'? Does that perhaps mean: 'Have no further concern with thyself! become objective!' – And Socrates? – And the 'man of science'? –

81

It is dreadful to die of thirst in the sea. Do you have to salt your truth so much that it can no longer even – quench thirst?

82

'Pity for all' – would be harshness and tyranny for *you*, my neighbour!

83

Instinct – When the house burns down one forgets even one's dinner. – Yes: but one retrieves it from the ashes.

84

Woman learns how to hate to the extent that she unlearns how – to charm.

85

The same emotions in man and woman are, however, different in tempo: therefore man and woman never cease to mis-understand one another.

86

Behind all their personal vanity women themselves always have their impersonal contempt – for 'woman'. –

87

Bound heart, free spirit – If one binds one's heart firmly and imprisons it one can allow one's spirit many liberties: I have said that before. But no one believes it if he does not already know it . . .

88

One begins to mistrust very clever people when they become embarrassed.

89

Terrible experiences make one wonder whether he who experiences them is not something terrible.

90

Heavy, melancholy people grow lighter through precisely that which makes others heavy, through hatred and love, and for a while they rise to their surface.

91

So cold, so icy one burns one's fingers on him! Every hand that grasps him starts back! - And for just that reason many think he is glowing hot.

92

Who has not - for the sake of his reputation - sacrificed himself? -

93

There is no hatred for men in geniality, but for just that reason all too much contempt for men.

94

Mature manhood: that means to have rediscovered the seriousness one had as a child at play.

95

To be ashamed of one's immorality: that is a step on the ladder at the end of which one is also ashamed of one's morality.

96

One ought to depart from life as Odysseus departed from Nausicaa – blessing rather than in love with it.

97

What? A great man? I always see only the actor of his own ideal.

98

If one trains one's conscience it will kiss us as it bites.

99

The disappointed man speaks. – 'I listened for an echo and I heard only praise –.'

100

Before ourselves we all pose as being simpler than we are: thus do we take a rest from our fellow men.

101

Today a man of knowledge might easily feel as if he were God become animal.

102

To discover he is loved in return ought really to disenchant the lover with the beloved. 'What? *She* is so modest as to love even you? Or so stupid? Or – or –.'

103

The danger in happiness. – 'Now everything is turning out well for me, now I love every destiny – who would like to be my destiny?'

104

It is not their love for men but the impotence of their love for men which hinders the Christians of today from – burning us.

105

The free spirit, the 'pious man of knowledge' – finds *pia fraus* even more offensive to his taste (to *his* kind of 'piety') than *impia fraus*. Hence the profound lack of understanding of the church typical of the 'free spirit' – *his* kind of unfreedom.

106

By means of music the passions enjoy themselves.

107

To close your ears to even the best counter-argument once the decision has been taken: sign of a strong character. Thus an occasional will to stupidity.

108

There are no moral phenomena at all, only a moral interpretation of phenomena . . .

109

The criminal is often enough not equal to his deed: he disparages and slanders it.

110

A criminal's lawyers are seldom artists enough to turn the beautiful terribleness of the deed to the advantage of him who did it.

111

Our vanity is hardest to wound precisely when our pride has just been wounded.

112

He who feels predestined to regard and not believe finds all believers too noisy and importunate: he rebuffs them.

113

'You want to make him interested in you? Then pretend to be embarrassed in his presence –'

114

The tremendous expectation in regard to sexual love and the shame involved in this expectation distorts all a woman's perspectives from the start.

115

Where neither love nor hate is in the game a woman is a mediocre player.

116

The great epochs of our life are the occasions when we gain the courage to rebaptize our evil qualities as our best qualities.

117

The will to overcome an emotion is ultimately only the will of another emotion or of several others.

118

There is an innocence in admiration: he has it to whom it has not yet occurred that he too could one day be admired.

119

Disgust with dirt can be so great that it prevents us from cleaning ourselves – from 'justifying' ourselves.

120

Sensuality often makes love grow too quickly, so that the root remains weak and is easy to pull out.

121

It was a piece of subtle refinement that God learned Greek when he wanted to become a writer – and that he did not learn it better.

122

To enjoy praise is with some people only politeness of the heart – and precisely the opposite of vanity of the spirit.

123

Even concubinage has been corrupted: – by marriage.

124

He who rejoices even at the stake triumphs not over pain but at the fact that he feels no pain where he had expected to feel it. A parable.

125

When we have to change our opinion about someone we hold the inconvenience he has therewith caused us greatly to his discredit.

126

A people is a detour of nature to get to six or seven great men. – Yes: and then to get round them.

127

Science offends the modesty of all genuine women. They feel as if one were trying to look under their skin – or worse! under their clothes and finery.

128

The more abstract the truth you want to teach the more you must seduce the senses to it.

129

The devil has the widest perspectives for God, and that is why he keeps so far away from him – the devil being the oldest friend of knowledge.

130

What a person *is* begins to betray itself when his talent declines – when he ceases to show what he can *do*. Talent is also finery; finery is also a hiding place.

131

The sexes deceive themselves about one another: the reason being that fundamentally they love and honour only them-

selves (or their own ideal, to express it more pleasantly –).
Thus man wants woman to be peaceful – but woman is
essentially unpeaceful, like the cat, however well she may have
trained herself to present an appearance of peace.

132

One is punished most for one's virtues.

133

He who does not know how to find the road to *his* ideal lives
more frivolously and impudently than the man without an
ideal.

134

All credibility, all good conscience, all evidence of truth
comes only from the senses.

135

Pharisaism is not degeneration in a good man: a good part of
it is rather the condition of all being good.

136

One seeks a midwife for his thoughts, another someone to
whom he can be a midwife: thus originates a good conversation.

137

When one has dealings with scholars and artists it is easy to
miscalculate in opposite directions: behind a remarkable
scholar one not infrequently finds a mediocre man, and behind
a mediocre artist often – a very remarkable man.

138

What we do in dreams we also do when we are awake: we invent and fabricate the person with whom we associate – and immediately forget we have done so.

139

In revenge and in love woman is more barbarous than man.

140

Counsel as conundrum – 'If the bonds are not to burst – you must try to cut them first.'

141

The belly is the reason man does not so easily take himself for a god.

142

The chastest expression I have ever heard: *'Dans le véritable amour c'est l'âme, qui enveloppe le corps.'*

143

Our vanity would have just that which we do best count as that which is hardest for us. The origin of many a morality.

144

When a woman has scholarly inclinations there is usually something wrong with her sexuality. Unfruitfulness itself disposes one to a certain masculinity of taste; for man is, if I may be allowed to say so, 'the unfruitful animal'.

145

Comparing man and woman in general one may say: woman would not have the genius for finery if she did not have the instinct for the *secondary* role.

146

He who fights with monsters should look to it that he himself does not become a monster. And when you gaze long into an abyss the abyss also gazes into you.

147

From old Florentine novels, moreover – from life: '*buona femmina e mala femmina vuol bastone*'. Sacchetti, Nov. 86.

148

To seduce one's neighbour to a good opinion and afterwards faithfully to believe in this good opinion of one's neighbour: who can do this trick as well as women?

149

That which an age feels to be evil is usually an untimely after-echo of that which was formerly felt to be good – the atavism of an older ideal.

150

Around the hero everything becomes a tragedy, around the demi-god a satyr-play; and around God everything becomes – what? Perhaps a 'world'? –

151

It is not enough to possess a talent: one must also possess your permission to possess it – eh, my friends?

152

'Where the tree of knowledge stands is always Paradise': thus speak the oldest and youngest serpents.

153

That which is done out of love always takes place beyond good and evil.

154

Objection, evasion, happy distrust, pleasure in mockery are signs of health: everything unconditional belongs in pathology.

155

The sense of the tragic increases and diminishes with sensuality.

156

Madness is something rare in individuals – but in groups, parties, peoples, ages it is the rule.

157

The thought of suicide is a powerful solace: by means of it one gets through many a bad night.

158

To our strongest drive, the tyrant in us, not only our reason but also our conscience submits.

159

One *has* to requite good and ill: but why to precisely the person who did us good or ill?

160

One no longer loves one's knowledge enough when one has communicated it.

161

Poets behave impudently towards their experiences: they exploit them.

162

'Our neighbour is not our neighbour but our neighbour's neighbour' – thus thinks every people.

163

Love brings to light the exalted and concealed qualities of a lover – what is rare and exceptional in him: to that extent it can easily deceive as to what is normal in him.

164

Jesus said to his Jews: 'The law was made for servants – love God as I love him, as his son! What have we sons of God to do with morality!' –

165

Concerning every party – A shepherd always has need of a bell-wether – or he must himself occasionally be one.

166

You may lie with your mouth, but with the mouth you make as you do so you none the less tell the truth.

167

With hard men intimacy is a thing of shame – and something precious.

168

Christianity gave Eros poison to drink – he did not die of it, to be sure, but degenerated into vice.

169

To talk about oneself a great deal can also be a means of concealing oneself.

170

In praise there is more importunity than in blame.

171

Pity in a man of knowledge seems almost ludicrous, like sensitive hands on a cyclops.

172

From love of man one sometimes embraces anyone (because one cannot embrace everyone): but one must never let this anyone know it . . .

173

One does not hate so long as one continues to rate low, but only when one has come to rate equal or higher.

174

You utilitarians, you too love everything *useful* only as a *vehicle* of your inclinations – you too really find the noise of its wheels intolerable?

175

Ultimately one loves one's desires and not that which is desired.

176

The vanity of others offends our taste only when it offends our vanity.

177

Perhaps no one has ever been sufficiently truthful about what 'truthfulness' is.

178

Clever people are not credited with their follies: what a deprivation of human rights!

179

The consequences of our actions take us by the scruff of the neck, altogether indifferent to the fact that we have 'improved' in the meantime.

180

There is an innocence in lying which is the sign of good faith in a cause.

181

It is inhuman to bless where one is cursed.

182

The familiarity of the superior embitters, because it may not be returned.

183

'Not that you lied to me but that I no longer believe you – that is what has distressed me –.'

184

There is a wild spirit of good-naturedness which looks like malice.

185

'I do not like it.' – Why? – 'I am not up to it.' – Has anyone ever answered like that?

Moral sensibility is as subtle, late, manifold, sensitive and refined in Europe today as the 'science of morals' pertaining to it is still young, inept, clumsy and coarse-fingered – an interesting contrast which sometimes even becomes visible and incarnate in the person of a moralist. Even the expression 'science of morals' is, considering what is designated by it, far too proud, and contrary to *good* taste: which is always accustomed to choose the more modest expressions. One should, in all strictness, admit *what* will be needful here for a long time to come, *what* alone is provisionally justified here: assembly of material, conceptual comprehension and arrangement of a vast domain of delicate value-feelings and value-distinctions which live, grow, beget and perish – and perhaps attempts to display the more frequent and recurring forms of these living crystallizations – as preparation of a *typology* of morals. To be sure: one has not been so modest hitherto. Philosophers one and all have, with a strait-laced seriousness that provokes laughter, demanded something much higher, more pretentious, more solemn of themselves as soon as they have concerned themselves with morality as a science: they wanted to furnish the *rational ground* of morality – and every philosopher hitherto has believed he has furnished this rational ground; morality itself, however, was taken as 'given'. How far from their clumsy pride was that apparently insignificant task left in dust and mildew, the task of description, although the most delicate hands and senses could hardly be delicate enough for it! It was precisely because moral philosophers knew the facts of morality only somewhat vaguely in an arbitrary extract or as a chance abridgement, as morality of their environment, their class, their church, the spirit of their times, their climate and zone of the earth, for instance – it was precisely because they were ill informed and not even very inquisitive about other peoples, ages and former times, that they did not so much as catch sight of the real problems of morality – for these come into view only if we compare *many* moralities. Strange though it may sound, in all 'science of morals' hitherto the problem of morality itself has been *lacking*: the suspicion was lacking that there was anything problematic here. What philosophers called 'the rational ground of morality' and sought to furnish was, viewed in the proper light, only a scholarly form of *faith* in the prevailing morality, a new way of *expressing* it, and thus itself a fact within a certain morality, indeed even in the last resort a kind of denial that this morality *ought* to be conceived of as a problem – and in any event the opposite of a testing, analysis, doubting and vivisection of this faith. Hear, for example, with what almost venerable innocence Schopenhauer still presented his task, and draw your own conclusions as to how scientific a 'science' is whose greatest masters still talk like children and old women: – 'The principle', he says (*Fundamental Problems of Ethics*),

> the fundamental proposition on whose content all philosophers of ethics are *actually* at one: *neminem laede, immo omnes, quantum potes, juva* – is *actually* the proposition of which all the teachers of morals endeavour to furnish the rational ground ... the *actual* foundation of ethics which has been sought for centuries like the philosopher's stone.

– The difficulty of furnishing the rational ground for the above-quoted proposition may indeed be great – as is well known, Schopenhauer too failed to do it – ; and he who has ever been certain how insipidly false and sentimental this proposition is in a world whose essence is will to power – may like to recall that Schopenhauer, although a pessimist, *actually* – played the flute ... Every day, after dinner: read his biographers on this subject. And by the way: a pessimist, a world-denier and God-denier, who *comes to a halt* before morality – who affirms morality and plays the flute, affirms *laede neminem* morality: what? is that actually – a pessimist?

187

Quite apart from the value of such assertions as 'there exists in us a categorical imperative' one can still ask: what does such an assertion say of the man who asserts it? There are moralities which are intended to justify their authors before others; other moralities are intended to calm him and make him content with himself; with others he wants to crucify and humiliate himself; with others he wants to wreak vengeance, with others hide himself, with others transfigure himself and set himself on high; this morality serves to make its author forget, that to make him or something about him forgotten; many moralists would like to exercise power and their creative moods on mankind; others, Kant perhaps among them, give to understand with their morality: 'what is worthy of respect in me is that I know how to obey — and things *ought* to be no different with you!' — in short, moralities too are only a *sign-language of the emotions*.

188

Every morality is, as opposed to *laisser aller*, a piece of tyranny against 'nature', likewise against 'reason': but that can be no objection to it unless one is in possession of some other morality which decrees that any kind of tyranny and unreason is impermissible. The essential and invaluable element in every morality is that it is a protracted constraint: to understand Stoicism or Port-Royal or Puritanism one should recall the constraint under which every language has hitherto attained strength and freedom — the metrical constraint, the tyranny of rhyme and rhythm. How much trouble the poets and orators of every nation have given themselves! — not excluding a few present-day prose writers in whose ear there dwells an inexor-able conscience — 'for the sake of foolishness', as the utilitarian fools say, thinking they are clever — 'from subjection to arbitrary laws', as the anarchists say, feeling themselves 'free', even free-spirited. But the strange fact is that all there is or has been on earth of freedom, subtlety, boldness, dance and masterly certainty, whether in thinking itself, or in ruling, or in speaking and persuasion, in the arts as in morals, has evolved only by virtue of the 'tyranny of such arbitrary laws'; and, in all seriousness, there is no small probability that precisely this is 'nature' and 'natural' – and *not* that *laisser aller*! Every artist knows how far from the feeling of letting himself go his 'natural' condition is, the free ordering, placing, disposing, forming in the moment of 'inspiration' – and how strictly and subtly he then obeys thousandfold laws which precisely on account of their severity and definiteness mock all formulation in concepts (even the firmest concept is by comparison something fluctuating, manifold, ambiguous –). The essential thing 'in heaven and upon earth' seems, to say it again, to be a protracted *obedience* in *one* direction: from out of that there always emerges and has always emerged in the long run something for the sake of which it is worthwhile to live on earth, for example virtue, art, music, dance, reason, spirituality – something transfiguring, refined, mad and divine. Protracted unfreedom of spirit, mistrustful constraint in the communicability of ideas, the discipline thinkers imposed on themselves to think within an ecclesiastical or courtly rule or under Aristotelian presuppositions, the protracted spiritual will to interpret all events according to a Christian scheme and to rediscover and justify the Christian God in every chance occurrence – all these violent, arbitrary, severe, gruesome and antirational things have shown themselves to be the means by which the European spirit was disciplined in its strength, ruthless curiosity and subtle flexibility: though admittedly an irreplaceable quantity of force and spirit had at the same time to be suppressed, stifled and spoiled (for here as everywhere 'nature' shows itself as it is, in all its prodigal and *indifferent* magnificence, which is noble though it outrage our feelings). That for thousands of years European thinkers thought only so as to prove something – today, on the contrary, we suspect any thinker who 'wants to prove something' – that they always knew in advance that which was *supposed* to result from the most rigorous cogitation, as used to be the case with Asiatic astrology and is still the case with the innocuous Christian-moral interpretation of the most intimate personal experiences 'to the glory of God' and 'for the salvation of the soul' – this tyranny, this arbitrariness, this rigorous and grandiose stupidity has *educated* the spirit; it seems that slavery, in the cruder and in the more refined sense, is the indispensable means also for spiritual discipline and breeding. Regard any morality from this point of view: it is 'nature' in it which teaches hatred of *laisser aller*, of too great freedom, and which implants the need for limited horizons and immediate tasks – which teaches the *narrowing of perspective*, and thus in a certain sense stupidity, as a condition of life and growth. 'Thou shalt obey someone and for a long time: *otherwise* thou shalt perish and lose all respect for thyself' – this seems to me to be nature's imperative, which is, to be sure, neither 'categorical' as old Kant demanded it should be (hence the 'otherwise' –), nor addressed to the individual (what do individuals matter to nature!), but to peoples, races, ages, classes, and above all to the entire animal 'man', to *mankind*.

189

The industrious races find leisure very hard to endure: it was a masterpiece of *English* instinct to make Sunday so extremely holy and boring that the English unconsciously long again for their week- and working-days – as a kind of cleverly devised and cleverly intercalated *fast*, such as is also to be seen very frequently in the ancient world (although, as one might expect in the case of southern peoples, not precisely in regard to work –). There have to be fasts of many kinds; and wherever powerful drives and habits prevail legislators have to see to it that there are intercalary days on which such a drive is put in chains and learns to hunger again. Seen from a higher viewpoint, entire generations and ages, if they are infected with some moral fanaticism or other, appear to be such intercalated periods of constraint and fasting, during which a drive learns to stoop and submit, but also to *purify* and *intensify* itself; certain philosophical sects (for example the Stoa in the midst of the Hellenistic culture, with its air grown rank and over-charged with aphrodisiac vapours) likewise permit of a similar interpretation. – This also provides a hint towards the elucidation of that paradox why it was precisely during Europe's Christian period and only under the impress of Christian value judgements that the sexual drive sublimated itself into love (*amour-passion*).

190

There is something in Plato's morality which does not really belong to Plato but is only to be met with in his philosophy, one might say in spite of Plato: namely Socratism, for which he was really too noble. 'No one wants to do injury to himself, therefore all badness is involuntary. For the bad man does injury to himself: this he would not do if he knew that badness is bad. Thus the bad man is bad only in consequence of an error; if one cures him of his error, one necessarily makes him – good.' – This way of reasoning smells of the *mob*, which sees in bad behaviour only its disagreeable consequences and actually judges 'it is *stupid* to act badly'; while it takes 'good' without further ado to be identical with 'useful and pleasant'. In the case of every utilitarian morality one may conjecture in advance a similar origin and follow one's nose: one will seldom go astray. – Plato did all he could to interpret something refined and noble into his teacher's proposition, above all himself – he, the most intrepid of interpreters, who picked up the whole of Socrates only in the manner of a popular tune from the streets, so as to subject it to infinite and impossible variations: that is, to make it into all his own masks and multiplicities. One might ask in jest, and in Homeric jest at that: what is the Platonic Socrates if not *prosthe Platōn opithen te Platōn messē te chimaira*?

191

The old theological problem of 'faith' and 'knowledge' – or, more clearly, of instinct and reason – that is to say, the

question whether in regard to the evaluation of things instinct
deserves to have more authority than rationality, which wants
to evaluate and act according to reasons, according to a
'why?', that is to say according to utility and fitness for a
purpose – this is still that old moral problem which first
appeared in the person of Socrates and was already dividing
the minds of men long before Christianity. Socrates himself,
to be sure, had, with the taste appropriate to his talent – that
of a superior dialectician – initially taken the side of reason;
and what indeed did he do all his life long but laugh at the
clumsy incapacity of his noble Athenians, who were men of
instinct, like all noble men, and were never able to supply
adequate information about the reasons for their actions?
Ultimately, however, in silence and secrecy, he laughed at
himself too: he found in himself, before his more refined
conscience and self-interrogation, the same difficulty and incapacity. But why, he exhorted himself, should one therefore
abandon the instincts! One must help both them *and* reason to
receive their due – one must follow the instincts, but persuade
reason to aid them with good arguments. This was the actual
falsity of that great ironist, who had so many secrets; he
induced his conscience to acquiesce in a sort of self-outwitting:
fundamentally he had seen through the irrational aspect of
moral judgement. – Plato, more innocent in such things and
without the craftiness of the plebeian, wanted at the expenditure of all his strength – the greatest strength any philosopher
has hitherto had to expend! – to prove to himself that reason
and instinct move of themselves towards *one* goal, towards the
good, towards 'God'; and since Plato all theologians and
philosophers have followed the same path – that is to say, in
moral matters instinct, or as the Christians call it 'faith', or as
I call it 'the herd', has hitherto triumphed. One might have to
exclude Descartes, the father of rationalism (and consequently
the grandfather of the Revolution), who recognized only the
authority of reason: but reason is only an instrument, and
Descartes was superficial.

192

He who has followed the history of an individual science will find in its evolution a clue to the comprehension of the oldest and most common processes of all 'knowledge and understanding': in both cases it is the premature hypotheses, the fictions, the good stupid will to 'believe', the lack of mistrust and patience which are evolved first – it is only late, and then imperfectly, that our senses learn to be subtle, faithful, cautious organs of understanding. It is more comfortable for our eye to react to a particular object by producing again an image it has often produced before than by retaining what is new and different in an impression: the latter requires more strength, more 'morality'. To hear something new is hard and painful for the ear; we hear the music of foreigners badly. When we hear a foreign language we involuntarily attempt to form the sounds we hear into words which have a more familiar and homely ring: thus the Germans, for example, once heard *arcubalista* and adapted it into *Armbrust*. The novel finds our senses, too, hostile and reluctant; and even in the case of the 'simplest' processes of the senses, the emotions, such as fear, love, hatred, and the passive emotions of laziness, *dominate*. – As little as a reader today reads all the individual words (not to speak of the syllables) of a page – he rather takes about five words in twenty haphazardly and 'conjectures' their probable meaning – just as little do we see a tree exactly and entire with regard to its leaves, branches, colour, shape; it is so much easier for us to put together an approximation of a tree. Even when we are involved in the most uncommon experiences we still do the same thing: we fabricate the greater part of the experience and can hardly be compelled *not* to contemplate some event as its 'inventor'. All this means: we are from the very heart and from the very first – *accustomed to lying*. Or, to express it more virtuously and hypocritically, in short more pleasantly: one is much more of an artist than one realizes. – In a lively conversation I often see before me the face of the person with whom I am speaking so clearly and subtly determined by the thought he is expressing or which I believe has been called up in him that this degree of clarity far surpasses the *power* of my eyesight – so that the play of the muscles and the expression of the eyes *must* have been invented by me. Probably the person was making a quite different face or none whatever.

193

Quidquid luce fuit, tenebris agit: but also the other way round. That which we experience in dreams, if we experience it often, is in the end just as much a part of the total economy of our soul as is anything we 'really' experience: we are by virtue of it richer or poorer, feel one need more or one need fewer, and finally are led along a little in broad daylight and even in the most cheerful moments of our waking spirit by the habits of our dreams. Suppose someone has often flown in his dreams and finally as soon as he starts dreaming becomes conscious of a power and art of flying as if it were a privilege he possessed, likewise as his personal and enviable form of happiness: such a man as believes he can realize any arc and angle with the slightest impulse, as knows the feeling of a certain divine frivolity, a 'going up' without tension or constraint, a 'going down' without condescension or abasement – without *gravity*! – how should the man who knew such dream-experiences and dream-habits not find at last that the word 'happiness' had a different colour and definition in his waking hours too! How should he not have a *different* kind of – desire for happiness? 'Soaring rapture' as the poets describe it must seem to him, in comparison with this 'flying', too earthy, muscular, violent, too 'grave'.

194

The diversity of men is revealed not only in the diversity of their tables of what they find good, that is to say in the fact that they regard diverse goods worth striving for and also differ as to what is more or less valuable, as to the order of rank of the goods they all recognize – it is revealed even more in what they regard as actually *having* and *possessing* what they find good. In regard to a woman, for example, the more modest man counts the simple disposal of her body and sexual gratification as a sufficient and satisfactory sign of having, of possession; another, with a more jealous and demanding thirst for possession, sees the 'question-mark', the merely apparent quality of such a having and requires subtler tests, above all in order to know whether the woman not only gives herself to him but also gives up for his sake what she has or would like to have – : only *thus* does she count to him as 'possessed'. A third, however, is not done with jealousy and desire for having even then; he asks himself whether, when the woman gives up everything for him, she does not perhaps do so for a phantom of him: he demands that she know him to the very heart before she is able to love him at all, he dares to let himself be unravelled – . He feels that his beloved is fully in his possession only when she no longer deceives herself about him but loves him as much for his devilry and hidden insatiability as she does for his goodness, patience and spirituality. One would like to possess a people: and all the higher arts of a Cagliostro and Catiline seem to him right for that end. Another, with a more refined thirst for possession, says to himself: 'one may not deceive where one wants to possess' – he is irritated and dissatisfied at the idea that it is a mask of him which rules the hearts of the people: 'so I must *let* myself be known and, first of all, know myself!' Among helpful and charitable people one almost always finds that clumsy deceitfulness which first adjusts and adapts him who is to be helped: as if, for example, he 'deserved' help, desired precisely *their* help, and would prove profoundly grateful, faithful and submissive to them in return for all the help he had received – with these imaginings they dispose of those in need as if they were possessions, and are charitable and helpful at all only from a desire for possessions. They are jealous if one frustrates or anticipates them when they want to help. Parents involuntarily make of their child something similar to themselves – they call it 'education' – and at the bottom of her heart no mother doubts that in her child she has borne a piece of property, no father disputes his right to subject it to *his* concepts and values. Indeed, in former times (among the ancient Germans, for instance) it seemed proper for fathers to possess power of life or death over the newborn and to use it as they thought fit. And as formerly the father, so still today the teacher, the class, the priest, the prince unhesitatingly see in every new human being an opportunity for a new possession. From which it follows . . .

195

The Jews – a people 'born for slavery' as Tacitus and the whole ancient world says, 'the chosen people' as they themselves say and believe – the Jews achieved that miracle of inversion of values thanks to which life on earth has for a couple of millennia acquired a new and dangerous fascination – their prophets fused 'rich', 'godless', 'evil', 'violent', 'sensual' into one and were the first to coin the word 'world' as a term of infamy. It is in this inversion of values (with which is involved the employment of the word for 'poor' as a synonym of 'holy' and 'friend') that the significance of the Jewish people resides: with *them* there begins the *slave revolt in morals*.

196

It is to be *inferred* that there exist countless dark bodies close to the sun – such as we shall never see. This is, between ourselves, a parable; and a moral psychologist reads the whole starry script only as a parable and sign-language by means of which many things can be kept secret.

197

One altogether misunderstands the beast of prey and man of prey (Cesare Borgia for example), one misunderstands 'nature', so long as one looks for something 'sick' at the bottom of these healthiest of all tropical monsters and growths, or even for an inborn 'hell' in them–: as virtually all moralists have done hitherto. It seems, does it not, that there exists in moralists a hatred for the jungle and the tropics? And that the 'tropical man' has to be discredited at any cost, whether as the sickness and degeneration of man or as his own hell and self-torment? But why? For the benefit of 'temperate zones'? The benefit of temperate men? Of the 'moral'? Of the mediocre? – This for the chapter 'Morality as Timidity'.

198

All these moralities which address themselves to the individual person, for the promotion of his 'happiness' as they say – what are they but prescriptions for behaviour in relation to the degree of *perilousness* in which the individual person lives with himself; recipes to counter his passions, his good and bad inclinations in so far as they have will to power in them and would like to play the tyrant; great and little artifices and acts of prudence to which there clings the nook-and-cranny odour of ancient household remedies and old-woman wisdom; one and all baroque and unreasonable in form – because they address themselves to 'all', because they generalize where generalization is impermissible – speaking unconditionally one and all, taking themselves for unconditional, flavoured with more than *one* grain of salt, indeed tolerable only, and occasionally even tempting, when they learn to smell over-spiced and dangerous, to smell above all of 'the other world': all this is, from an intellectual point of view, of little value and far from constituting 'science', not to speak of 'wisdom', but rather, to say it again and to say it thrice, prudence, prudence, prudence, mingled with stupidity, stupidity, stupidity – whether it be that indifference and statuesque coldness towards the passionate folly of the emotions which the Stoics advised and applied; or that no-more-laughing and no-more-weeping of Spinoza, that destruction of the emotions through analysis and vivisection which he advocated so naïvely; or that depression of the emotions to a harmless mean at which they may be satisfied, the Aristotelianism of morals; even morality as enjoyment of the emotions in a deliberate thinning down and spiritualization through the symbolism of art, as music for instance, or as love of God or love of man for the sake of God – for in religion the passions again acquire civic rights, assuming that . . .; finally, even that easygoing and roguish surrender to the emotions such as Hafiz and Goethe taught, that bold letting fall of the reins, that spiritual-physical *licentia morum* in the exceptional case of wise old owls and drunkards for whom there is 'no longer much risk in it'. This too for the chapter 'Morality as Timidity'.

199

Inasmuch as ever since there have been human beings there have also been human herds (family groups, communities, tribes, nations, states, churches), and always very many who obey compared with the very small number of those who command – considering, that is to say, that hitherto nothing has been practised and cultivated among men better or longer than obedience, it is fair to suppose that as a rule a need for it is by now innate as a kind of *formal conscience* which commands: 'thou shalt unconditionally do this, unconditionally not do that', in short 'thou shalt'. This need seeks to be satisfied and to fill out its form with a content; in doing so it grasps about wildly, according to the degree of its strength, impatience and tension, with little discrimination, as a crude appetite, and accepts whatever any commander – parent, teacher, law, class prejudice, public opinion – shouts in its ears. The strange narrowness of human evolution, its hesitations, its delays, its frequent retrogressions and rotations, are due to the fact that the herd instinct of obedience has been inherited best and at the expense of the art of commanding. If we think of this instinct taken to its ultimate extravagance there would be no commanders or independent men at all; or, if they existed, they would suffer from a bad conscience and in order to be able to command would have to practise a deceit upon themselves: the deceit, that is, that they too were only obeying. This state of things actually exists in Europe today: I call it the moral hypocrisy of the commanders. They know no way of defending themselves against their bad conscience other than to pose as executors of more ancient or higher commands (commands of ancestors, of the constitution, of justice, of the law or even of God), or even to borrow herd maxims from the herd's way of thinking and appear as 'the first servant of the people' for example, or as 'instruments of the common good'. On the other hand, the herd-man in Europe today makes himself out to be the only permissible kind of man and glorifies the qualities through which he is tame, peaceable and useful to the herd as the real human virtues: namely public spirit, benevolence, consideration, industriousness, moderation, modesty, forbearance, pity. In those cases, however, in which leaders and bell-wethers are thought to be indispensable, there is attempt after attempt to substitute for them an adding-together of clever herd-men: this, for example, is the origin of all parliamentary constitutions. All this notwithstanding, what a blessing, what a release from a burden becoming intolerable, the appearance of an unconditional commander is for this herd-animal European, the effect produced by the appearance of Napoleon is the latest great witness – the history of the effect of Napoleon is almost the history of the higher happiness this entire century has attained in its most valuable men and moments.

200

The man of an era of dissolution which mixes the races together and who therefore contains within him the inheritance of a diversified descent, that is to say contrary and often not merely contrary drives and values which struggle with one another and rarely leave one another in peace – such a man of late cultures and broken lights will, on average, be a rather weak man: his fundamental desire is that the war which he *is* should come to an end; happiness appears to him, in accord with a sedative (for example Epicurean or Christian) medicine and mode of thought, pre-eminently as the happiness of repose, of tranquillity, of satiety, of unity at last attained, as a 'Sabbath of Sabbaths', to quote the holy rhetorician Augustine,

who was himself such a man. — If, however, the contra-
riety and war in such a nature should act as one *more*
stimulus and enticement to life — and if, on the other hand, in
addition to powerful and irreconcilable drives, there has also
been inherited and cultivated a proper mastery and subtlety in
conducting a war against oneself, that is to say self-control,
self-outwitting: then there arise those marvellously in- comprehensible and unfathomable men, those enigmatic men predestined for victory and the seduction of others, the fairest
examples of which are Alcibiades and Caesar (— to whom I
should like to add that *first* European agreeable to my taste,
the Hohenstaufen Friedrich II), and among artists perhaps
Leonardo da Vinci. They appear in precisely the same ages as
those in which that rather weak type with his desire for rest
comes to the fore: the two types belong together and originate
in the same causes.

201

So long as the utility which dominates moral value-judgements
is solely that which is useful to the herd, so long as the object
is solely the preservation of the community and the immoral
is sought precisely and exclusively in that which seems to
imperil the existence of the community: so long as that is the
case there can be no 'morality of love of one's neighbour'.
Supposing that even there a constant little exercise of consideration, pity, fairness, mildness, mutual aid was practised, supposing that even at that stage of society all those drives are active
which are later honourably designated 'virtues' and are finally
practically equated with the concept 'morality': in that era
they do not yet by any means belong to the domain of moral
valuations — they are still *extra-moral*. An act of pity, for
example, was during the finest age of Rome considered neither
good nor bad, neither moral nor immoral; and even if it was
commended, this commendation was entirely compatible with
a kind of involuntary disdain, as soon, that is, as it was set
beside any action which served the welfare of the whole, of
the *res publica*. Ultimately 'love of one's neighbour' is always

something secondary, in part conventional and arbitrarily illusory, when compared with *fear of one's neighbour*. Once the structure of society seems to have been in general fixed and made safe from external dangers, it is this fear of one's neighbour which again creates new perspectives of moral valuation. There are certain strong and dangerous drives, such as enterprisingness, foolhardiness, revengefulness, craft, rapacity, ambition, which hitherto had not only to be honoured from the point of view of their social utility – under different names, naturally, from those chosen here – but also mightily developed and cultivated (because they were constantly needed to protect the community as a whole against the enemies of the community as a whole); these drives are now felt to be doubly dangerous – now that the diversionary outlets for them are lacking – and are gradually branded as immoral and given over to calumny. The antithetical drives and inclinations now come into moral honour; step by step the herd instinct draws its conclusions. How much or how little that is dangerous to the community, dangerous to equality, resides in an opinion, in a condition or emotion, in a will, in a talent, that is now the moral perspective: here again fear is the mother of morality. When the highest and strongest drives, breaking passionately out, carry the individual far above and beyond the average and lowlands of the herd conscience, the self-confidence of the community goes to pieces, its faith in itself, its spine as it were, is broken: consequently it is precisely these drives which are most branded and calumniated. Lofty spiritual independence, the will to stand alone, great intelligence even, are felt to be dangerous; everything that raises the individual above the herd and makes his neighbour quail is henceforth called *evil*; the fair, modest, obedient, self-effacing disposition, the *mean and average* in desires, acquires moral names and honours. Eventually, under very peaceful conditions, there is less and less occasion or need to educate one's feelings in severity and sternness; and now every kind of severity, even severity in justice, begins to trouble the conscience; a stern and lofty nobility and self-responsibility is received almost as an offence and awakens mistrust, 'the lamb', even more 'the sheep', is held in higher and higher respect. There comes a point of morbid mellowing and over-tenderness in the history of society at which it takes the side even of him who harms it, the *criminal*, and does so honestly and wholeheartedly. Punishment: that seems to it somehow unfair – certainly the idea of 'being punished' and 'having to punish' is unpleasant to it, makes it afraid. 'Is it not enough to render him *harmless*? why punish him as well? To administer punishment is itself dreadful!' – with this question herd morality, the morality of timidity, draws its ultimate conclusion. Supposing all danger, the cause of fear, could be abolished, this morality would therewith also be abolished: it would no longer be necessary, it would no longer *regard itself* as necessary! – He who examines the conscience of the present-day European will have to extract from a thousand moral recesses and hiding-places always the same imperative, the imperative of herd timidity: 'we wish that there will one day *no longer be anything to fear*!' One day – everywhere in Europe the will and way to *that* day is now called 'progress'.

202

Let us straight away say once more what we have already said a hundred times: for ears today offer such truths – *our* truths – no ready welcome. We know well enough how offensive it sounds when someone says plainly and without metaphor that man is an animal; but it will be reckoned almost a *crime* in us that precisely in regard to men of 'modern ideas' we constantly employ the terms 'herd', 'herd instinct', and the like. But what of that! we can do no other: for it is precisely here that our new insight lies. We have found that in all principal moral judgements Europe has become unanimous, including the lands where Europe's influence predominates: one manifestly *knows* in Europe what Socrates thought he did not know, and what that celebrated old serpent once promised to teach – one 'knows' today what is good and evil. Now it is bound to make a harsh sound and one not easy for ears to hear when we insist again and again: that which here believes it knows, that which here glorifies itself with its praising and blaming and calls itself good, is the instinct of the herd-animal man: the instinct which has broken through and come to predominate and prevail over the other instincts and is coming to do so more and more in proportion to the increasing physiological approximation and assimilation of which it is the symptom. *Morality is in Europe today herd-animal morality* – that is to say, as we understand the thing, only *one* kind of human morality beside which, before which, after which many other, above all *higher*, moralities are possible or ought to be possible. But against such a 'possibility', against such an 'ought', this morality defends itself with all its might: it says, obstinately and stubbornly, 'I am morality itself, and nothing is morality besides me!' – indeed, with the aid of a religion which has gratified and flattered the sublimest herd-animal desires, it has got to the point where we discover even in political and social institutions an increasingly evident expression of this morality: the *democratic* movement inherits the Christian. But that the tempo of this movement is much too slow and somnolent for the more impatient, for the sick and suffering of the said instinct, is attested by the ever more frantic baying, the ever more undisguised fang-baring of the anarchist dogs which now rove the streets of European culture: apparently the reverse of the placidly industrious democrats and revolutionary ideologists, and even more so of the stupid philosophasters and brotherhood fanatics who call themselves socialists and want a 'free society', they are in fact at one with them all in their total and instinctive hostility towards every form of society other than that of the *autonomous* herd (to the point of repudiating even the concepts 'master' and 'servant' – *ni dieu ni maître* says a socialist formula –); at one in their tenacious opposition to every special claim, every special right and privilege (that is to say, in the last resort to *every* right: for when everyone is equal no one will need any 'rights' –); at one in their mistrust of punitive justice (as if it were an assault on the weaker, an injustice against the necessary consequence of all previous society –); but equally at one in the religion of pity, in sympathy with whatever feels, lives, suffers (down as far as the animals, up as far as 'God' – the extravagance of 'pity for God' belongs in a democratic era –); at one, one and all, in the cry and impatience of pity, in mortal hatred for suffering in general, in their almost feminine incapacity to remain spectators of suffering, to *let* suffer; at one in their involuntary gloom and sensitivity, under whose spell Europe seems threatened with a new Buddhism; at one in their faith in the morality of *mutual* pity, as if it were morality in itself and the pinnacle, the *attained* pinnacle of man, the sole hope of the future, the consolation of the present and the great redemption from all the guilt of the past – at one, one and all, in their faith in the community as the *saviour*, that is to say in the herd, in 'themselves' . . .

203

We, who have a different faith – we, to whom the democratic movement is not merely a form assumed by political organization in decay but also a form assumed by man in decay, that is to say in diminishment, in process of becoming mediocre and losing his value: whither must *we* direct our hopes? – Towards *new philosophers*, we have no other choice; towards spirits strong and original enough to make a start on antithetical evaluations and to revalue and reverse 'eternal values'; towards heralds and forerunners, towards men of the future who in the present knot together the constraint which compels the will of millennia on to *new* paths. To teach man the future of man as his *will*, as dependent on a human will, and to prepare for great enterprises and collective experiments in discipline and breeding so as to make an end of that gruesome dominion of chance and nonsense that has hitherto been called 'history' – the nonsense of the 'greatest number' is only its latest form – : for that a new kind of philosopher and commander will some time be needed, in face of whom whatever has existed on earth of hidden, dreadful and benevolent spirits may well look pale and dwarfed. It is the image of such leaders which hovers before *our* eyes – may I say that aloud, you free spirits?

The circumstances one would have in part to create, in part to employ, to bring them into existence; the conjectural paths and tests by virtue of which a soul could grow to such height and power it would feel *compelled* to these tasks; a revaluation of values under whose novel pressure and hammer a conscience would be steeled, a heart transformed to brass, so that it might endure the weight of such a responsibility; on the other hand, the need for such leaders, the terrible danger they might not appear or might fail or might degenerate – these are *our* proper cares and concerns, do you know that, you free spirits? These are the heavy, remote thoughts and thunder clouds that pass across *our* life's sky. There are few more grievous pains than once to have beheld, divined, sensed, how an extraordinary man missed his way and degenerated: but he who has the rare eye for the collective danger that 'man' himself *may degenerate*, he who, like us, has recognized the tremendous fortuitousness which has hitherto played its game with the future of man – a game in which no hand, not even a 'finger of God' took any part! – he who has divined the fatality that lies concealed in the idiotic guilelessness and blind confidence of 'modern ideas', even more in the whole of Christian-European morality: he suffers from a feeling of anxiety with which no other can be compared – for he comprehends in a *single* glance all that which, given a favourable accumulation and intensification of forces and tasks, could be *cultivated out of man*, he knows with all the knowledge of his conscience how the greatest possibilities in man are still unexhausted and how often before the type man has been faced with strange decisions and new paths – he knows even better from his most painful memories against what wretched things an evolving being of the highest rank has hitherto usually been shattered and has broken off, sunk and has itself become wretched. The *collective degeneration of man* down to that which the socialist dolts and blockheads today see as their 'man of the future' – as their ideal! – this degeneration and diminution of man to the perfect herd animal (or, as they say, to the man of the 'free society'), this animalization of man to the pygmy animal of equal rights and equal pretensions is *possible*, there is no doubt about that! He who has once thought this possibility through to the end knows one more kind of disgust than other men do – and perhaps also a new *task*! . . .

Part Six: We Scholars

204

At the risk that moralizing will here too prove to be what it has always been – namely an undismayed *montrer ses plaies*, as Balzac says – I should like to venture to combat a harmful and improper displacement of the order of rank between science and philosophy which is today, quite unnoticed and as if with a perfect good conscience, threatening to become established. In my view it is only from one's *experience* – experience always means bad experience, does it not? – that one can acquire the right to speak on such a higher question of rank: otherwise one will talk like a blind man about colours or like women and artists *against* science ('oh this wicked science', their modesty and instinct sighs, 'it always exposes the *facts*!'–). The Declaration of Independence of the man of science, his emancipation from philosophy, is one of the more subtle after-effects of the democratic form and formlessness of life: the self-glorification and presumption of the scholar now stands everywhere in full bloom and in its finest springtime – which does not mean to say that in this case self-praise smells sweetly. 'Away with all masters!' – that is what the plebeian instinct desires here too; and now that science has most successfully resisted theology, whose 'hand-maid' it was for too long, it is now, with great high spirits and a plentiful lack of understanding, taking it upon itself to lay down laws for philosophy and for once to play the 'master' – what am I saying? to play the *philosopher* itself. My memory – the memory of a man of science, if I may say so! – is full of arrogant naïveties I have heard about philosophy and philosophers from young scientists and old physicians (not to speak of the most cultured and conceited of all scholars, the philologists and schoolmen, who are both by profession –). Now it was the specialist and jobbing workman who instinct-ively opposed synthetic undertakings and capacities in general;

now the industrious labourer who had got a scent of the *otium* and noble luxury in the philosopher's physical economy and felt wronged and diminished by it. Now it was that colour blindness of the utility man who sees in philosophy nothing but a series of *refuted* systems and a wasteful expenditure which 'benefits' nobody. Now a fear of disguised mysticism and a rectification of the frontiers of knowledge leaped out; now a disrespect for an individual philosopher which had involuntarily generalized itself into a disrespect for philosophy. Finally, what I found most frequently among young scholars was that behind the arrogant disdain for philosophy there lay the evil after-effect of a philosopher himself, from whom they had, to be sure, withdrawn their allegiance, without, however, having got free from the spell of his disparaging evaluation of other philosophers – the result being a feeling of ill humour towards philosophy in general. (This is the sort of after-effect which, it seems to me, Schopenhauer, for example, has had on Germany in recent years – with his unintelligent rage against Hegel he succeeded in disconnecting the entire last generation of Germans from German culture, which culture was, all things considered, a high point and divinatory refinement of the *historical sense*: but Schopenhauer himself was in precisely this respect poor, unreceptive and un-German to the point of genius.) In general and broadly speaking, it may have been above all the human, all too human element, in short the poverty of the most recent philosophy itself, which has been most thoroughly prejudicial to respect for philosophy and has opened the gates to the instinct of the plebeian. For one must admit how completely the whole species of a Heraclitus, a Plato, an Empedocles, and whatever else these royal and splendid hermits of the spirit were called, is lacking in our modern world; and to what degree, in face of such representatives of philosophy as are, thanks to fashion, at present as completely on top as they are completely abysmal (in Germany, for example, the two lions of Berlin, the anarchist Eugen Dühring and the amalgamist Eduard von Hartmann) – a worthy man of science is *justified* in feeling he is of a better species and descent. It is, in particular, the sight of those hotchpotch-philosophers who call themselves 'philosophers of reality' or 'positivists' which is capable of implanting a perilous mistrust in the soul of an ambitious young scholar: these gentlemen are at best scholars and specialists themselves, that fact is palpable! – they are one and all defeated men *brought back* under the sway of science, who at some time or other demanded *more* of themselves without having the right to this 'more' and the responsibility that goes with it – and who now honourably, wrathfully, revengefully represent by word and deed the *unbelief* in the lordly task and lordliness of philosophy. Finally: how could things be otherwise! Science is flourishing today and its good conscience shines in its face, while that to which the whole of modern philosophy has gradually sunk, this remnant of philosophy, arouses distrust and displeasure when it does not arouse mockery and pity. Philosophy reduced to 'theory of knowledge', actually no more than a timid epochism and abstinence doctrine: a philosophy that does not even get over the threshold and painfully *denies* itself the right of entry – that is philosophy at its last gasp, an end, an agony, something that arouses pity. How could such a philosophy – *rule*!

205

The perils in the way of the evolution of the philosopher are in truth so manifold today one may well doubt whether this fruit can still ripen at all. The compass and tower-building of the sciences has grown enormous, and therewith the probability has also grown enormous that the philosopher will become weary while still no more than a learner, or that he will let himself be stopped somewhere and 'specialize': so that he will never reach his proper height, the height from which he can survey, look around and *look down*. Or that he will reach this height too late, when his best time is past and his best strength spent; or damaged, coarsened, degenerate, so that his view, his total value judgement, no longer means much. Perhaps it is the very refinement of his intellectual conscience which makes him linger on the way and arrive late; he fears he may be seduced into dilettantism, into becoming an insect with a thousand feet and a thousand antennae, he knows too well that one who has lost respect for himself can no longer command, can no longer *lead* as a man of knowledge either, unless he wants to become a great actor, a philosophical Cagliostro and pied piper of the spirit, in short a mis-leader. This is ultimately a question of taste even if it were not a question of conscience. In addition to this, so as to redouble his difficulties, there is the fact that the philosopher demands of himself a judgement, a Yes or No, not in regard to the sciences but in regard to life and the value of life – that he is reluctant to believe he has a right, to say nothing of a duty, to come to such a judgement, and has to find his way to this right and this faith only through the widest – perhaps most disturbing and shattering – experiences, and often hesitating, doubting, and being struck dumb. Indeed, the mob has long confounded and confused the philosopher with someone else, whether with the man of science or with the religiously exalted, dead to the senses, 'dead to the world' fanatic and drunkard of God; and today if one hears anyone commended for living 'wisely' or 'like a philosopher', it means hardly more than 'prudently and apart'. Wisdom: that seems to the rabble to be a kind of flight, an artifice and means for getting oneself out of a dangerous game; but the genuine philosopher – as he seems to *us*, my friends? – lives 'un-philosophically' and 'unwisely', above all *imprudently*, and bears the burden and duty of a hundred attempts and temptations of life – he risks *himself* constantly, he plays *the* dangerous game . . .

206

In comparison with a genius, that is to say with a being which either *begets* or *bears*, both words taken in their most comprehensive sense – the scholar, the average man of science, always has something of the old maid about him: for, like her, he has no acquaintanceship with the two most valuable functions of mankind. To both of them, indeed, to the scholar and to the old maid, one concedes respectability, by way of compensation as it were – one emphasizes the respectability in these cases – and experiences the same feeling of annoyance at having been constrained to this concession. Let us look more closely: what is the man of science? An ignoble species of man for a start, with the virtues of an ignoble, that is to say subservient, unauthoritative and un-self-sufficient species of man: he possesses industriousness, patient acknowledgement of his proper place in the rank and file, uniformity and moderation in abilities and requirements, he possesses the instinct for his own kind and for that which his own kind have need of, for example that little bit of independence and green pasture without which there is no quiet work, that claim to honour and recognition (which first and foremost presupposes recognizability –), that sunshine of a good name, that constant affirmation of his value and his utility with which his inner *distrust*, the dregs at the heart of all dependent men and herd animals, have again and again to be overcome. The scholar also possesses, as is only to be expected, the diseases and ill breeding of an ignoble species: he is full of petty envy and has very keen eyes for what is base in those natures to whose heights he is unable to rise. He is trusting, but only like one who sometimes lets himself go but never lets himself *flow out*; and it is precisely in the presence of men who do flow out that he becomes the more frosty and reserved – his eye is then like a reluctant smooth lake whose surface is disturbed by no ripple of delight or sympathy. The worst and most dangerous thing of which a scholar is capable comes from the instinct of mediocrity which characterizes his species: from that Jesuitism of mediocrity which instinctively works for the destruction of the uncommon man and tries to break or – better still! – relax every bent bow. For relaxing – with consideration, with indulgent hand, naturally, *relaxing* with importunate pity: that is the true art of Jesuitism, which has always understood how to introduce itself as the religion of pity. –

207

However gratefully one may go to welcome an *objective* spirit – and who has not been sick to death of everything subjective and its accursed ipsissimosity! – in the end one has to learn to be cautious with one's gratitude too and put a stop to the exaggerated way in which the depersonalization of the spirit is today celebrated as redemption and transfiguration, as if it were the end in itself: as is usually the case within the pessimist school, which also has good reason to accord the highest honours to 'disinterested knowledge'. The objective man who no longer scolds or curses as the pessimist does, the *ideal* scholar in whom the scientific instinct, after thousandfold total and partial failure, for once comes to full bloom, is certainly one of the most precious instruments there are: but he belongs in the hand of one who is mightier. He is only an instrument, let us say a *mirror* – he is not an 'end in himself'. And the objective man is in fact a mirror: accustomed to submitting to whatever wants to be known, lacking any other pleasure than that provided by knowledge, by 'mirroring' – he waits until something comes along and then gently spreads himself out, so that not even the lightest footsteps and the fluttering of ghostly beings shall be lost on his surface and skin. Whatever still remains to him of his 'own person' seems to him accidental, often capricious, more often disturbing: so completely has he become a passage and reflection of forms and events not his own. He finds it an effort to think about 'himself', and not infrequently he thinks about himself mistakenly; he can easily confuse himself with another, he fails to understand his own needs and is in this respect alone unsubtle and negligent. Perhaps he is troubled by his health or by the pettiness and stuffiness of his wife and friends, or by a lack of companions and company – yes, he forces himself to reflect on his troubles: but in vain! Already his thoughts are roaming, off to a *more general* case, and tomorrow he will know as little how to help himself as he did yesterday. He no longer knows how to take himself seriously, nor does he have the time for it: he is cheerful, *not* because he has no troubles but because he has no fingers and facility for dealing with *his troubles*. His habitual going out to welcome everything and every experience, the sunny and ingenuous hospitality with which he accepts all he encounters, his inconsiderate benevolence, his perilous unconcernedness over Yes and No: alas, how often he has to suffer for these his virtues! – and as a human being in general he can all too easily become the *caput mortuum* of these virtues. If love and hatred are demanded of him, I mean love and hatred as God, woman and animal understand them –: he will do what he can and give what he can. But one ought not to be surprised if it is not very much – if he proves spurious, brittle, questionable and soft. His love and his hatred are artificial and more of a *tour de force*, a piece of vanity and exaggeration. For he is genuine only when he can be objective: only in his cheerful totalism can he remain 'nature' and 'natural'. His mirroring soul, for ever polishing itself, no longer knows how to affirm or how to deny; he does not command, neither does he destroy. '*Je ne méprise presque rien*' – he says with Leibniz: one should not overlook or underestimate the *presque*! Nor is he an exemplar; he neither leads nor follows; he sets himself altogether too far off to have any reason to take sides between good and evil. When he was for so long confused with the *philosopher*, with the Caesarian cultivator and *Gewaltmensch* of culture, he was done much too great honour and what is essential in him was overlooked – he is an instrument, something of a slave, if certainly the sublimest kind of slave, but in himself he is nothing – *presque rien*! The objective man is an instrument, a precious, easily damaged and tarnished measuring instrument and reflecting apparatus which ought to be respected and taken good care of; but he is not an end, a termination and ascent, a complementary man in whom the *rest* of existence is justified, a conclusion – and even less a beginning, a begetting and first cause, something solid, powerful and based firmly on itself that wants to be master: but rather only a delicate, empty, elegant, flexible mould which has first to wait for some content so as 'to form' itself by it – as a rule a man without content, a 'selfless' man. Consequently nothing for women either, *in parenthesis*. –

208

When a philosopher today gives us to understand that he is not a sceptic – I hope the foregoing account of the objective

spirit has brought this out? – all the world is offended to hear
it; thereafter he is regarded with a certain dread, there is so
much one would like to ask him ... indeed, among timid
listeners, of whom there are nowadays a very great number,
he is henceforth considered dangerous. It is as if, in his
rejection of scepticism, they seemed to hear some evil, menacing
sound from afar, as if some new explosive were being tested
somewhere, a dynamite of the spirit, perhaps a newly discovered Russian nihiline, a pessimism *bonae voluntatis* which
does not merely say No, will No, but – dreadful thought! *does*
No. Against this kind of 'good will' – a will to the actual
active denial of life – there is today confessedly no better
sedative and soporific than scepticism, the gentle, gracious,
lulling poppy scepticism; and even *Hamlet* is prescribed by the
doctors of our time against the 'spirit' and its noises under the
ground. 'Are our ears not already filled with nasty sounds?'
says the sceptic as a friend of sleep and almost as a kind of
security police: 'this subterranean No is terrible! Be quiet, you
pessimistic moles!' For the sceptic, that delicate creature, is all
too easily frightened; his conscience is schooled to wince at
every No, indeed even at a hard decisive Yes, and to sense
something like a sting. Yes! and No! – that is to him contrary
to morality; on the other hand, he likes his virtue to enjoy a
noble continence, perhaps by saying after Montaigne 'What
do I know?' Or after Socrates: 'I know that I know nothing.'
Or: 'Here I do not trust myself, here no door stands open to
me.' Or: 'If it did stand open, why go straight in?' Or: 'What
is the point of hasty hypotheses? To make no hypothesis at all
could well be a part of good taste. Do you absolutely have to
go straightening out what is crooked? Absolutely have to stop
up every hole with oakum? Is there not plenty of time? Does
time not have time? Oh you rogues, are you unable to *wait*?
Uncertainty too has its charms, the sphinx too is a Circe, Circe
too was a philosopher.' – Thus does a sceptic console himself;
and it is true he stands in need of some consolation. For
scepticism is the most spiritual expression of a certain complex
physiological condition called in ordinary language nervous
debility and sickliness; it arises whenever races or classes long

separated from one another are decisively and suddenly crossed. In the new generation, which has as it were inherited varying standards and values in its blood, all is unrest, disorder, doubt, experiment; the most vital forces have a retarding effect, the virtues themselves will not let one another grow and become strong, equilibrium, centre of balance, upright certainty are lacking in body and soul. But that which becomes most profoundly sick and degenerates in such hybrids is the *will*: they no longer have any conception of independence of decision, of the valiant feeling of pleasure in willing – even in their dreams they doubt the 'freedom of the will'. Our Europe of today, the scene of a senselessly sudden attempt at radical class – and *consequently* race – mixture, is as a result sceptical from top to bottom, now with that agile scepticism which springs impatiently and greedily from branch to branch, now gloomily like a cloud overcharged with question-marks – and often sick to death of its will! Paralysis of will: where does one not find this cripple sitting today! And frequently so dressed up! How seductively dressed up! There is the loveliest false finery available for this disease; and that most of that which appears in the shop windows today as 'objectivity', 'scientificality', '*l'art pour l'art*', 'pure will-less knowledge' is merely scepticism and will-paralysis dressed up – for this diagnosis of the European sickness I am willing to go bail. – Sickness of will is distributed over Europe unequally: it appears most virulently and abundantly where culture has been longest, indigenous it declines according to the extent to which 'the barbarian' still – or again – asserts his rights under the loose-fitting garment of Western culture. In present-day France, consequently, as one can as easily deduce as actually see, the will is sickest; and France, which has always possessed a masterly adroitness in transforming even the most fateful crises of its spirit into something charming and seductive, today really demonstrates its cultural ascendency over Europe as the school and showcase for all the fascinations of scepticism. The strength to will, and to will one thing for a long time, is somewhat stronger already in Germany, and stronger again in the north of Germany than in the centre of

Germany; considerably stronger in England, Spain and Corsica, there in association with dullness, here with hardness of head – not to speak of Italy, which is too young to know what it wants and first has to prove whether it is capable of willing – but strongest of all and most astonishing in that huge empire-in-between, where Europe as it were flows back into Asia, in Russia. There the strength to will has for long been stored up and kept in reserve, there the will is waiting menacingly – uncertain whether it is a will to deny or a will to affirm – in readiness to discharge itself, to borrow one of the physicists' favourite words. It may need not only wars in India and Asian involvements to relieve Europe of the greatest danger facing it, but also internal eruptions, the explosion of the empire into small fragments, and above all the introduction of the parliamentary imbecility, including the obligation upon everyone to read his newspaper at breakfast. I do not say this because I desire it: the reverse would be more after my heart – I mean such an increase in the Russian threat that Europe would have to resolve to become equally threatening, namely *to acquire a single will* by means of a new caste dominating all Europe, a protracted terrible will of its own which could set its objectives thousands of years ahead – so that the long-drawn-out comedy of its petty states and the divided will of its dynasties and democracies should finally come to an end. The time for petty politics is past: the very next century will bring with it the struggle for mastery over the whole earth – the *compulsion* to grand politics.

209

To what extent the new warlike age upon which we Europeans have obviously entered may perhaps also be favourable to the evolution of a new and stronger species of scepticism: on that question I should like for the moment to speak only in a parable which amateurs of German history will easily understand. That unscrupulous enthusiast for tall handsome grenadiers who, as king of Prussia, brought into existence a military and sceptical genius – and therewith at bottom that new type of German which has just triumphantly emerged – the questionable mad father of Frederick the Great, himself had on *one* point the grasp and lucky clutch of genius: he knew what was then lacking in Germany and which deficiency was a hundred times more alarming and pressing than any deficiency in culture or social polish – his antipathy for the youthful Frederick was the product of a deep instinctual fear. *Men were lacking*; and he suspected, with the bitterest vexation, that his own son was not enough of a man. In that he was deceived: but who would not have been deceived in his place? He saw his son lapse into the atheism, the *esprit*, the pleasure-seeking frivolity of ingenious Frenchmen – he saw in the background the great blood-sucker, the spider scepticism, he suspected the incurable wretchedness of a heart which is no longer hard enough for evil or for good, of a broken will which no longer commands, *can* no longer command. But in the meantime there grew up in his son that more dangerous and harder new species of scepticism – who knows *to what extent* favoured by precisely the father's hatred and the icy melancholy of a will sent into solitude? – the scepticism of audacious manliness, which is related most closely to genius for war and conquest and which first entered Germany in the person of the great Frederick. This scepticism despises and yet grasps to itself; it undermines and takes into possession; it does not believe but retains itself; it gives perilous liberty to the spirit but it keeps firm hold on the heart; it is the *German* form of scepticism which, as a continuation of Frederick-ism intensified into the most spiritual domain, for a long time brought Europe under the dominion of the German spirit and its critical and historical mistrust. Thanks to the indomitably strong and tough masculinity of the great German philologists and critical historians (who, seen aright, were also one and all artists in destruction and disintegration), there became established, gradually and in spite of all the romanticism in music and philosophy, a *new* conception of the German spirit in which the trait of manly scepticism decisively predominated: whether as intrepidity of eye, as bravery and sternness of dissecting hand, or as tenacious will for perilous voyages of discovery, for

North Pole expeditions of the spirit beneath desolate and dangerous skies. There may be good reason for warm-blooded and superficial humanitarians to cross themselves before precisely this spirit: *cet esprit fataliste, ironique, mephistophelique* Michelet calls it, not without a shudder. But if one wishes to appreciate what a mark of distinction is this fear of the 'man' in the German spirit through which Europe was awoken from its 'dogmatic slumber', one might like to recall the earlier conception which it had to overcome – and how it is not very long since a masculinized woman could, with unbridled presumption, venture to commend the Germans to Europe's sympathy as gentle, good-hearted, weak-willed and poetic dolts. One should at last have a sufficiently profound comprehension of Napoleon's astonishment when he caught sight of Goethe: it betrays what had for centuries been thought was meant by the 'German spirit'. '*Voilà un homme!*' – which is to say: 'but that is a *man*! And I had expected only a German!' –

210

Supposing, then, that in the image of the philosophers of the future some trait provokes the question whether they will not have to be sceptics in the sense last suggested, this would still designate only something about them – and *not* them themselves. They might with equal justification let themselves be called critics; and they will certainly be experimenters. Through the name with which I have ventured to baptize them I have already expressly emphasized experiment and the delight in experiment: was this because, as critics body and soul, they like to employ experiment in a new, perhaps wider, perhaps more dangerous sense? Will they, in their passion for knowledge, have to go further with audacious and painful experiments than the tender and pampered taste of a democratic century can approve of? – There can be no doubt that these coming men will want to dispense least with those serious and not indubious qualities which distinguish the critic from the sceptic: I mean certainty in standards of value,

conscious employment of a unity of method, instructed courage, independence and ability to justify oneself; indeed, they
confess to taking a *pleasure* in negating and dissecting and to a
certain self-possessed cruelty which knows how to wield the
knife with certainty and deftness even when the heart bleeds.
They will be *harder* (and perhaps not always only against
themselves) than humane men might wish, they will not
consort with 'truth' so as to be 'pleased' by it or 'elevated'
and 'inspired' – they will rather be little disposed to believe
that *truth* of all things should be attended by such pleasures.
They will smile, these stern spirits, if someone should say in
their presence: 'This thought elevates me: how should it not
be true?' Or: 'This work delights me: how should it not be
beautiful?' Or: 'This artist enlarges me: how should he not be
great?' – perhaps they will have not only a smile but a feeling
of genuine disgust for all such fawning enthusiasm, idealism,
feminism, hermaphroditism, and he who could penetrate into
the secret chambers of their hearts would hardly discover
there the intention of reconciling 'Christian feelings' with
'classical taste' and perhaps even with 'modern parlia-
mentarianism' (as such a conciliatory spirit is said to exist
even among philosophers in our very uncertain and consequently conciliatory century). Critical discipline and every
habit conducive to cleanliness and severity in things of the
spirit will be demanded by these philosophers not only of
themselves: they could even display them as their kind of
decoration – none the less they still do not want to be called
critics on that account. It seems to them no small insult to
philosophy when it is decreed, as is so happily done today:
'Philosophy itself is criticism and critical science – and nothing
whatever besides!' This evaluation of philosophy may enjoy
the applause of every positivist in France and Germany (–
and it might possibly have flattered the heart and taste of
Kant: one should recall the titles of his principal works): our
new philosophers will still say: critics are the philosophers'
instruments and for that reason very far from being philosophers themselves! Even the great Chinaman of Königsberg
was only a great critic. –

211

I insist that philosophical labourers and men of science in general should once and for all cease to be confused with philosophers – that on precisely this point 'to each his own' should be strictly applied, and not much too much given to the former, much too little to the latter. It may be required for the education of a philosopher that he himself has also once stood on all those steps on which his servants, the scientific labourers of philosophy, remain standing – *have* to remain standing; he himself must perhaps have been critic and sceptic and dogmatist and historian and, in addition, poet and collector and traveller and reader of riddles and moralist and seer and 'free spirit' and practically everything, so as to traverse the whole range of human values and value-feelings and be *able* to gaze from the heights into every distance, from the depths into every height, from the nook-and-corner into every broad expanse with manifold eyes and a manifold conscience. But all these are only preconditions of his task: this task itself demands something different – it demands that he *create values*. Those philosophical labourers after the noble exemplar of Kant and Hegel have to take some great fact of evaluation – that is to say, former *assessments* of value, creations of value which have become dominant and are for a while called 'truths' – and identify them and reduce them to formulas, whether in the realm of *logic* or of *politics* (morals) or of *art*. It is the duty of these scholars to take everything that has hitherto happened and been valued, and make it clear, distinct, intelligible and manageable, to abbreviate everything long, even 'time' itself, and to *subdue* the entire past: a tremendous and wonderful task in the service of which every subtle pride, every tenacious will can certainly find satisfaction. *Actual philosophers, however, are commanders and law-givers:* they say 'thus it *shall* be!', it is they who determine the Wherefore and Whither of mankind, and they possess for this task the preliminary work of all the philosophical labourers, of all those who have subdued the past – they reach for the future with creative hand, and everything that is or has been becomes for them a means, an instrument, a hammer. Their 'knowing' is *creating*, their creating is a law-giving, their will to truth is *–will to power*. – Are there such philosophers today? Have there been such philosophers? *Must* there not be such philosophers? . . .

212

It seems to me more and more that the philosopher, being *necessarily* a man of tomorrow and the day after tomorrow, has always found himself and *had* to find himself in contradiction to his today: his enemy has always been the ideal of today. Hitherto these extraordinary promoters of mankind who have been called philosophers and have seldom felt themselves to be friends of knowledge but, rather, disagreeable fools and dangerous question-marks – have found their task, their hard, unwanted, unavoidable task, but finally the greatness of their task, in being the bad conscience of their age. By laying the knife vivisectionally to the bosom of the very *virtues of the age* they betrayed what was their own secret: to know a *new* greatness of man, a new untrodden path to his enlargement. Each time they revealed how much hypocrisy, indolence, letting oneself go and letting oneself fall, how much falsehood was concealed under the most honoured type of their contemporary morality, how much virtue was *outlived*; each time they said: 'We have to go thither, out yonder, where *you* today are least at home.' In face of a world of 'modern ideas' which would like to banish everyone into a corner and 'speciality', a philosopher, assuming there could be philosophers today, would be compelled to see the greatness of man, the concept 'greatness', precisely in his spaciousness and multiplicity, in his wholeness in diversity: he would even determine value and rank according to how much and how many things one could endure and take upon oneself, how *far* one could extend one's responsibility. Today the taste of the age and the virtue of the age weakens and attenuates the will, nothing is so completely timely as weakness of will: consequently, in the philosopher's ideal precisely strength of will, the hardness and capacity for protracted decisions, must constitute part of the concept 'greatness'; with just as much justification as the opposite doctrine and the ideal of a shy, renunciatory, humble, selfless humanity was appropriate to an opposite age, to one such as, like the sixteenth century, suffered from its accumulation of will and the stormiest waters and flood-tides of selfishness. In the age of Socrates, among men of nothing but wearied instincts, among conservative ancient Athenians who let themselves go – 'towards happiness', as they said, towards pleasure, as they behaved – and who at the same time had in their mouth the old pretentious words to which their lives had long ceased to give them any right, *irony* was perhaps required for greatness of soul, that Socratic malicious certitude of the old physician and plebeian who cut remorselessly into his own flesh as he did into the flesh and heart of the 'noble', with a look which said distinctly enough: 'do not dissemble before me! Here – we are equal!' Today, conversely, when the herd animal alone obtains and bestows honours in Europe, when 'equality of rights' could all too easily change into equality in wrongdoing: I mean into a general war on everything rare, strange, privileged, the higher man, the higher soul, the higher duty, the higher responsibility, creative fullness of power and mastery – today, being noble, wanting to be by oneself, the ability to be different, independence and the need for self-responsibility pertains to the concept 'greatness'; and the philosopher will betray something of his ideal when he asserts: 'He shall be the greatest who can be the most solitary, the most concealed, the most divergent, the man beyond good and evil, the master of his virtues, the superabundant of will; this shall be called greatness: the ability to be as manifold as whole, as vast as full.' And, to ask it again: is greatness – *possible* today?

213

What a philosopher is, is hard to learn, because it cannot be taught: one has to 'know' it from experience – or one ought to be sufficiently proud *not* to know it. But that nowadays all the world talks of things of which it *cannot* have experience is most and worst evident in respect of philosophers and the philosophical states of mind – very few know them or are permitted to know them, and all popular conceptions of them are false. Thus, for example, that genuinely philosophical combination of a bold exuberant spirituality which runs *presto* and a dialectical severity and necessity which never takes a false step is to most thinkers and scholars unknown from experience and consequently, if someone should speak of it in their presence, incredible. They imagine every necessity as a state of distress, as a painful compelled conformity and constraint; and thought itself they regard as something slow, hesitant, almost as toil and often as 'worthy of the *sweat* of the noble' – and not at all as something easy, divine, and a closest relation of high spirits and the dance! 'Thinking' and 'taking something seriously', giving it 'weighty consideration' – to them these things go together: that is the only way they have 'experienced' it. Artists may here have a more subtle scent: they know only too well that it is precisely when they cease to act 'voluntarily' and do everything of necessity that their feeling of freedom, subtlety, fullness of power, creative placing, disposing, shaping reaches its height – in short, that necessity and 'freedom of will' are then one in them. In the last resort there exists an order of rank of states of soul with which the order of rank of problems accords; and the supreme problems repel without mercy everyone who ventures near them without being, through the elevation and power of his spirituality, predestined to their solution. Of what avail is it if nimble commonplace minds or worthy clumsy mechanicals and empiricists crowd up to them, as they so often do today, and with their plebeian ambition approach as it were this 'court of courts'! But coarse feet may never tread such carpets: that has been seen to in the primal law of things; the doors remain shut against such importunates, though they may batter and shatter their heads against them! For every elevated world one has to be born or, expressed more clearly, *bred* for it: one has a right to philosophy – taking the word in the grand sense – only by virtue of one's origin; one's ancestors, one's 'blood' are the decisive thing here too. Many generations must have worked to prepare for the philosopher; each of his virtues must have been individually acquired, tended, inherited, incorporated, and not only the bold, easy, delicate course and cadence of his thoughts but above all the readiness for great responsibilities, the lofty glance that rules and looks down, the feeling of being segregated from the mob and its duties and virtues, the genial protection and defence of that which is misunderstood and calumniated, be it god or devil, the pleasure in and exercise of grand justice, the art of commanding, the breadth of will, the slow eye which seldom admires, seldom looks upward, seldom loves . . .

Part Seven: Our Virtues

214

Our virtues? – it is probable that we too still have our virtues,
although naturally they will not be those square and simple
virtues on whose account we hold our grandfathers in high
esteem but also hold them off a little. We Europeans of the
day after tomorrow, we first-born of the twentieth century –
with all our dangerous curiosity, our multiplicity and art of
disguise, our mellow and as it were sugared cruelty in spirit
and senses – *if* we are to have virtues we shall presumably
have only such virtues as have learned to get along with our
most secret and heartfelt inclinations, with our most fervent
needs: very well, let us look for them within our labyrinths! –
where, as is well known, such a variety of things lose themselves, such a variety of things get lost for ever. And is there
anything nicer than to *look for* one's own virtues? Does this
not almost mean: to *believe in* one's own virtue? But this
'believing in one's virtue' – is this not at bottom the same
thing as that which one formerly called one's 'good
conscience', that venerable long conceptual pigtail which our
grandfathers used to attach to the back of their heads and
often enough to the back of their minds as well? It seems that,
however little we may think ourselves old-fashioned and
grandfatherly-respectable in other respects, in one thing we are
none the less worthy grandsons of these grandfathers, we last
Europeans with a good conscience: we too still wear their
pigtail. – Alas! if only you knew how soon, how very soon,
things will be – different! . . .

215

As in the realm of the stars it is sometimes two suns which
determine the course of a planet, as in certain cases suns of
differing colour shine on a single planet now with a red light,

147

now with a green light, and sometimes striking it at the same time and flooding it with many colours: so we modern men are, thanks to the complicated mechanism of our 'starry firmament', determined by *differing* moralities; our actions shine alternately in differing colours, they are seldom un-equivocal – and there are cases enough in which we perform *many-coloured* actions.

216

Love of one's enemies? I think that has been well learned: it happens thousandfold today, on a large and small scale; indeed, occasionally something higher and more sublime happens – we learn to *despise* when we love, and precisely when we love best – but all this unconsciously, without noise, without ostentation, with that modesty and concealment of goodness which forbids the mouth solemn words and the formulas of virtue. Morality as a posture – goes against our taste today. This too is progress: just as it was progress when religion as a posture finally went against the taste of our fathers, including hostility and Voltarian bitterness towards religion (and whatever else formerly belonged to the gesture-language of free-thinkers). It is the music in our conscience, the dance in our spirit, with which puritan litanies, moral preaching and philistinism will not chime.

217

Beware of those who set great store on being credited with moral tact and subtlety in moral discrimination! If once they blunder *in our presence* (not to speak of *in respect of us*) they never forgive us – they unavoidably take to slandering and derogat-ing us, even if they still remain our 'friends'. – Blessed are the forgetful: for they shall 'have done' with their stupidities too.

218

The psychologists of France – and where else today are there psychologists? – have still not yet exhausted the bitter and

manifold pleasure they take in the *bêtise bourgeoise*, just as if . . .
enough, they thereby betray something. Flaubert, for example,
the worthy citizen of Rouen, in the end no longer saw, heard
or tasted anything else – it was his mode of self-torment and
more refined cruelty. I now suggest, by way of a change – for
this is getting boring – a new object of enjoyment: the
unconscious cunning of the attitude adopted by all good, fat,
worthy spirits of mediocrity towards more exalted spirits and
their tasks, that subtle, barbed, Jesuitical cunning which is a
thousand times subtler than the taste and understanding of
this middle class in its best moments – subtler even than the
understanding of its victims – : another demonstration that,
of all forms of intelligence discovered hitherto, 'instinct' is the
most intelligent. In brief: study, psychologists, the philosophy
of the 'rule' in its struggle with the 'exception': there you
have a spectacle fit for the gods and for divine maliciousness!
Or, still more clearly: carry out vivisection on the 'good man',
on the *'homo bonae voluntatis'* . . . on *yourselves*!

219

Moral judgement and condemnation is the favourite form of
revenge of the spiritually limited on those who are less so,
likewise a form of compensation for their having been neg-
lected by nature, finally an occasion for acquiring spirit and
becoming refined – malice spiritualizes. Deep in their hearts
they are glad there exists a standard according to which those
overloaded with the goods and privileges of the spirit are
their equals – they struggle for the 'equality of all before God'
and it is virtually for that purpose that they *need* the belief in
God. It is among them that the most vigorous opponents of
atheism are to be found. Anyone who told them 'a lofty
spirituality is incompatible with any kind of worthiness and
respectability of the merely moral man' would enrage them –
I shall take care not to do so. I should, rather, like to flatter
them with my proposition that a lofty spirituality itself exists
only as the final product of moral qualities; that it is a
synthesis of all those states attributed to the 'merely moral'

man after they have been acquired one by one through protracted discipline and practice, perhaps in the course of whole chains of generations; that lofty spirituality is the spiritualization of justice and of that benevolent severity which knows itself empowered to maintain *order of rank* in the world among things themselves – and not only among men

220

Now that the 'disinterested' are praised so widely one has, perhaps not without some danger, to become conscious of *what* it is the people are really interested in, and what in general the things are about which the common man is profoundly and deeply concerned: including the educated, even the scholars and, unless all appearance deceives, perhaps the philosophers as well. The fact then emerges that the great majority of those things which interest and stimulate every higher nature and more refined and fastidious taste appear altogether 'uninteresting' to the average man – if he none the less notices a devotion to these things, he calls it '*désintéressé*' and wonders how it is possible to act 'disinterestedly'. There have been philosophers who have known how to lend this popular wonderment a seductive and mystical-otherwordly expression (– perhaps because they did not know the higher nature from experience?) – instead of stating the naked and obvious truth that the 'disinterested' act is a *very* interesting and interested act, provided that . . . 'And love?' – what! Even an act performed out of love is supposed to be 'un-egoistic'? But you blockheads – ! 'And commendation of him who sacrifices?' – But he who has really made sacrifices knows that he wanted and received something in return – perhaps something of himself in exchange for something of himself – that he gave away here in order to have more there, perhaps in general to be more or to feel himself 'more'. But this is a domain of questions and answers in which a more fastidious taste prefers not to linger: truth has so much to stifle her yawns here when answers are demanded of her. She is, after all, a woman: one ought not to violate her.

221

It can happen, said a pettyfogging moral pedant, that I honour and respect an unselfish man: but not because he is unselfish but because he seems to me to have the right to be useful to another man at his own expense. Enough: the question is always who *he* is and who the *other* is. In one made and destined for command, for example, self-abnegation and modest retirement would be not a virtue but the waste of a virtue: so it seems to me. Every unegoistic morality which takes itself as unconditional and addresses itself to everybody is not merely a sin against taste: it is an instigation to sins of omission, one seduction *more* under the mask of philanthropy – and a seduction and injury for precisely the higher, rarer, privileged. Moralities must first of all be forced to bow before *order of rank*, their presumption must be brought home to them – until they at last come to understand that it is *immoral* to say: 'What is good for one is good for another.' – Thus my moralistic pedant and *bonhomme*: does he deserve to be laughed at for thus exhorting moralities to morality? But one should not be too much in the right if one wants to have the laughers on *one's own* side; a grain of wrong is even an element of good taste.

222

Where pity and fellow-suffering is preached today – and, heard aright, no other religion is any longer preached now – the psychologist should prick up his ears: through all the vanity, all the noise characteristic of these preachers (as it is of all preachers) he will hear a hoarse, groaning, genuine note of self-contempt. It is part of that darkening and uglification of Europe which has now been going on for a hundred years (the earliest symptoms of which were first recorded in a thoughtful letter of Galiani's to Madame d'Epinay): *if it is not the cause of it!* The man of 'modern ideas', that proud ape, is immoderately dissatisfied with himself: that is certain. He suffers: and his vanity would have him only 'suffer with his fellows' . . .

223

The hybrid European – a tolerably ugly plebeian, all in all – definitely requires a costume: he needs history as his storeroom for costumes. He realizes, to be sure, that none of them fits him properly – he changes and changes. Consider the nineteenth century with regard to these rapid predilections and changes in the style-masquerade; notice too the moments of despair because 'nothing suits' us –. It is in vain we parade ourselves as romantic or classical or Christian or Florentine or baroque or 'national', *in moribus et artibus*: the 'cap doesn't fit'! But the 'spirit', especially the 'historical spirit', perceives an advantage even in this despair: again and again another piece of the past and of foreignness is tried out, tried on, taken off, packed away, above all *studied* – we are the first studious age *in puncto* of 'costumes', I mean those of morality, articles of faith, artistic tastes and religions, prepared as no other age has been for the carnival in the grand style, for the most spiritual Shrovetide laughter and wild spirits, for the transcendental heights of the most absolute nonsense and Aristophanic universal mockery. Perhaps it is precisely here that we are discovering the realm of our *invention*, that realm where we too can still be original, perhaps as parodists of world history and God's buffoons – perhaps, even if nothing else of today has a future, precisely our *laughter* may still have a future!

224

The *historical sense* (or the capacity for divining quickly the order of rank of the evaluations according to which a people, a society, a human being has lived, the 'divinatory instinct' for the relationships of these evaluations, for the relation of the authority of values to the authority of effective forces): this historical sense, to which we Europeans lay claim as our speciality, has come to us in the wake of the mad and fascinating *semi-barbarism* into which Europe has been plunged through the democratic mingling of classes and races – only the nineteenth century knows this sense, as its sixth sense.

The past of every form and mode of life, of cultures that formerly lay close beside or on top of one another, streams into us 'modern souls' thanks to this mingling, our instincts now run back in all directions, we ourselves are a kind of chaos − : in the end, as I said before, 'the spirit' perceives its advantage in all this. Through our semi-barbarism in body and desires we have secret access everywhere such as a noble age never had, above all the access to the labyrinth of unfinished cultures and to every semi-barbarism which has ever existed on earth; and, in so far as the most considerable part of human culture hitherto has been semi-barbarism, 'historical sense' means virtually the sense and instinct for everything, the taste and tongue for everything: which at once proves it to be an *ignoble* sense. We enjoy Homer again, for instance: perhaps it is our happiest advance that we know how to appreciate Homer, whom the men of a noble culture (the French of the seventeenth century, for example, such as Saint-Evremond, who reproached him for his *esprit vaste*, and even their dying echo, Voltaire) cannot and could not assimilate so easily − whom they hardly permitted themselves to enjoy. The very definite Yes and No of their palate, their easily aroused disgust, their hesitant reserve with regard to everything strange, their horror of the tastelessness even of a lively curiosity, and in general that unwillingness of a noble and self-sufficient culture to admit to a new desire, a dissatisfaction with one's own culture, an admiration for what is foreign: all this disposes them unfavourably towards even the best things in the world which are not their property and *could* not become their prey − and no sense is so unintelligible to such men as the historical sense and its obsequious plebeian curiosity. It is no different with Shakespeare, that astonishing Spanish-Moorish-Saxon synthesis of tastes over which an ancient Athenian of the circle of Aeschylus would have half-killed himself with laughter or annoyance: but we − we accept precisely this confusion of colours, this medley of the most delicate, the coarsest and the most artificial, with a secret confidence and cordiality, we enjoy him as an artistic refinement reserved precisely for us and allow ourselves to be as little disturbed by the repellent fumes and the proximity of the English rabble in which Shakespeare's art and taste live as we do on the Chiaja of Naples, where we go our way enchanted and willing with all our senses alert, however much the sewers of the plebeian quarters may fill the air. That as men of the 'historical sense' we have our virtues is not to be denied – we are unpretentious, selfless, modest, brave, full of self-restraint, full of devotion, very grateful, very patient, very accommodating – with all that, we are perhaps not very 'tasteful'. Let us finally confess it to ourselves: that which we men of the 'historical sense' find hardest to grasp, to feel, taste, love, that which at bottom finds us prejudiced and almost hostile, is just what is complete and wholly mature in every art and culture, that which constitutes actual nobility in works and in men, their moment of smooth sea and halcyon self-sufficiency, the goldness and coldness displayed by all things which have become perfect. Perhaps our great virtue of the historical sense necessarily stands opposed to *good* taste, or to the very best taste at any rate, and it is precisely the brief little pieces of good luck and transfiguration of human life that here and there come flashing up which we find most difficult and laboursome to evoke in ourselves: those miraculous moments when a great power voluntarily halted before the boundless and immeasurable – when a superfluity of subtle delight in sudden restraint and petrifaction, in standing firm and fixing oneself, was enjoyed on a ground still trembling. *Measure* is alien to us, let us admit it to ourselves; what we itch for is the infinite, the unmeasured. Like a rider on a charging steed we let fall the reins before the infinite, we modern men, like semi-barbarians – and attain *our* state of bliss only when we are most – *in danger*.

225

Whether it be hedonism or pessimism or utilitarianism or eudaemonism: all these modes of thought which assess the value of things according to *pleasure* and *pain*, that is to say according to attendant and secondary phenomena, are fore-

ground modes of thought and naïveties which anyone conscious of *creative* powers and an artist's conscience will look
down on with derision, though not without pity. Pity for *you*!
That, to be sure, is not pity for social 'distress', for 'society'
and its sick and unfortunate, for the vicious and broken from
the start who lie all around us; even less is it pity for the
grumbling, oppressed, rebellious slave classes who aspire after
domination – they call it 'freedom'. *Our* pity is a more
elevated, more farsighted pity – we see how *man* is diminishing
himself, how *you* are diminishing him! – and there are times
when we behold *your* pity with an indescribable anxiety, when
we defend ourselves against this pity – when we find your
seriousness more dangerous than any kind of frivolity. You
want if possible – and there is no madder 'if possible' – *to
abolish suffering*; and we? – it really does seem that *we* would
rather increase it and make it worse than it has ever been!
Wellbeing as you understand it – that is no goal, that seems to
us an *end*! A state which soon renders man ludicrous and
contemptible – which makes it *desirable* that he should perish!
The discipline of suffering, of *great* suffering – do you not
know that it is *this* discipline alone which has created every
elevation of mankind hitherto? That tension of the soul in
misfortune which cultivates its strength, its terror at the sight
of great destruction, its inventiveness and bravery in undergo-
ing, enduring, interpreting, exploiting misfortune, and whatever of depth, mystery, mask, spirit, cunning and greatness
has been bestowed upon it – has it not been bestowed
through suffering, through the discipline of great suffering?
In man, *creature* and *creator* are united: in man there is matter,
fragment, excess, clay, mud, madness, chaos; but in man there
is also creator, sculptor, the hardness of the hammer, the
divine spectator and the seventh day – do you understand this
antithesis? And that *your* pity is for the 'creature in man', for
that which has to be formed, broken, forged, torn, burned,
annealed, refined – that which has to *suffer* and *should* suffer?
And *our* pity – do you not grasp whom our *opposite* pity is for
when it defends itself against your pity as the worst of all
pampering and weakening? – Pity *against* pity, then! – But, to

repeat, there are higher problems than the problems of pleasure and pain and pity; and every philosophy that treats only of them is a piece of naïvety. -

226

We immoralists! – This world which concerns *us*, in which *we* have to love and fear, this almost invisible, inaudible world of subtle commanding, subtle obeying, a world of 'almost' in every respect, sophistical, insidious, sharp, tender: it is well defended, indeed, against clumsy spectators and familiar curiosity! We are entwined in an austere shirt of duty and *cannot* get out of it – and in this we are 'men of duty', we too! Sometimes, it is true, we may dance in our 'chains' and between our 'swords'; often, it is no less true, we gnash our teeth at it and frown impatiently at the unseen hardship of our lot. But do what we will, fools and appearances speak against us and say 'these are men *without* duty' – we always have fools and appearances against us!

227

Honesty - granted that this is our virtue, from which we cannot get free, we free spirits – well, let us labour at it with all love and malice and not weary of 'perfecting' ourselves in *our* virtue, the only one we have: may its brightness one day overspread this ageing culture and its dull, gloomy seriousness like a gilded azure mocking evening glow! And if our honesty should one day none the less grow weary, and sigh, and stretch its limbs, and find us too hard, and like to have things better, easier, gentler, like an agreeable vice: let us remain *hard*, we last of the Stoics! And let us send to the aid of our honesty whatever we have of devilry in us – our disgust at the clumsy and casual, our *'nitimur in vetitum'*, our adventurer's courage, our sharp and fastidious curiosity, our subtlest, most disguised, most spiritual will to power and world-overcoming which wanders avidly through all the realms of the future – let us go to the aid of our 'god' with all our 'devils'! It is probable that we shall be misunderstood and taken for what we are not: but what of that! People will say: 'Their "honesty" – is their devilry and nothing more!' But what of that! And even if they were right! Have all gods hitherto not been such devils grown holy and been rebaptized? And what do we know of ourselves, when all's said and done? And what the spirit which leads us on would like to be *called* (it is a question of names)? And how many spirits we harbour? Our honesty, we free spirits – let us see to it that our honesty does not become our vanity, our pomp and finery, our limitation, our stupidity! Every virtue tends towards stupidity, every stupidity towards virtue; 'stupid to the point of saintliness' they say in Russia – let us see to it that through honesty we do not finally become saints and bores! Is life not a hundred times too short to be – bored in it? One would have to believe in eternal life to . . .

228

May I be forgiven the discovery that all moral philosophy hitherto has been boring and a soporific – and that 'virtue' has in my eyes been harmed by nothing more than it has been by this *boringness* of its advocates; in saying which, however, I should not want to overlook their general utility. It is important that as few people as possible should think about morality – consequently it is *very* important that morality should not one day become interesting! But do not worry! It is still now as it has always been: I see no one in Europe who has (or *propagates*) any idea that thinking about morality could be dangerous, insidious, seductive – that *fatality* could be involved! Consider, for example, the indefatigable, inevitable English utilitarians and with what clumsy and worthy feet they walk, stalk (a Homeric metaphor says it more plainly) along in the footsteps of Bentham, just as he himself had walked in the footsteps of the worthy Helvétius (no, he was not a dangerous man, this Helvétius, *ce senateur Pococurante* as Galiani called him –). No new idea, no subtle expression or turn of an old idea, not even a real history of what had been thought before: an *impossible* literature altogether, unless one knows how to leaven it with a little malice. For into these moralists too (whom one has to read with mental reservations if one *has* to read them at all –) there has crept that old English vice called *cant*, which is *moral tartuffery*, this time concealed in the new form of scientificality; there are also signs of a secret struggle with pangs of conscience, from which a race of former Puritans will naturally suffer. (Is a moralist not the opposite of a Puritan? That is to say, as a thinker who regards morality as something questionable, as worthy of question-marks, in short as a problem? Is moralizing not – immoral?) Ultimately they all want *English* morality to prevail: inasmuch as mankind, or the 'general utility', or 'the happiness of the greatest number', no! the happiness of *England* would best be served; they would like with all their might to prove to themselves that to strive after *English* happiness, I mean after comfort and fashion (and, as the supreme goal, a seat in Parliament), is at the same time the true path of virtue, indeed that all virtue there has ever been on earth has consisted in just such a striving. Not one of all these ponderous herd animals with their uneasy conscience (who undertake to advocate the cause of egoism as the cause of the general welfare –) wants to know or scent that the 'general welfare' is not an ideal, or a goal, or a concept that can be grasped at all, but only an emetic – that what is right for one *cannot* by any means therefore be right for another, that the demand for *one* morality for all is detrimental to precisely the higher men, in short that there exists an *order of rank* between man and man, consequently also between morality and morality. They are a modest and thoroughly mediocre species of man, these English utilitarians, and, as aforesaid, in so far as they are boring one cannot think sufficiently highly of their utility. One ought even to *encourage* them: which is in part the objective of the following rhymes.

> Hail, continual plodders, hail!
> 'Lengthen out the tedious tale',
> Pedant still in head and knee,
> Dull, of humour not a trace,
> Permanently commonplace,
> *Sans génie et sans esprit!*

In late ages which may be proud of their humaneness there remains so much fear, so much *superstitious* fear of the 'savage cruel beast', to have mastered which constitutes the very pride of those more humane ages, that even palpable truths as if by general agreement, remain unspoken for centuries, because they seem as though they might help to bring back to life that savage beast which has been finally laid to rest. Perhaps I am risking something when I let one of these truths escape: let others capture it again and give it sufficient of the 'milk of pious thoughts' for it to lie still and forgotten in its old corner. – One should open one's eyes and take a new look at cruelty; one should at last grow impatient, so that the kind of immodest fat errors which have, for example, been fostered about tragedy by ancient and modern philosophers should no longer go stalking virtuously and confidently about. Almost everything we call 'higher culture' is based on the spiritualization and intensification of *cruelty* – this is my proposition; the 'wild beast' has not been laid to rest at all, it lives, it flourishes, it has merely become – deified. That which constitutes the painful voluptuousness of tragedy is cruelty; that which produces a pleasing effect in so-called tragic pity, indeed fundamentally in everything sublime up to the highest and most refined thrills of metaphysics, derives its sweetness solely from the ingredient of cruelty mixed in with it. What the Roman in the arena, the Christian in the ecstasies of the Cross, the Spaniard watching burnings or bullfights, the Japanese of today crowding in to the tragedy, the Parisian suburban workman who has a nostalgia for bloody revolutions, the Wagnerienne who, with will suspended, 'experiences' *Tristan und Isolde* – what all of these enjoy and look with secret ardour to imbibe is the spicy potion of the great Circe 'cruelty'. Here, to be sure, we must put aside the thick-witted psychology of former times which had to teach of cruelty only that it had its origin in the sight of the sufferings of *others*: there is also an abundant, over-abundant enjoyment of one's own suffering, of making oneself suffer – and wherever man allows himself to be persuaded to self-denial in the *religious* sense, or to self-mutilation, as among Phoenicians and ascetics, or in general to desensualization, decarnalization, contrition, to Puritanical spasms of repentance, to conscience-vivisection and to a Pascalian *sacrifizio dell'intelletto*, he is secretly lured and urged onward by his cruelty, by the dangerous thrills of cruelty directed *against himself*. Consider, finally, how even the man of knowledge, when he compels his spirit to knowledge which is *counter* to the inclination of his spirit and frequently also to the desires of his heart – by saying No, that is, when he would like to affirm, love, worship – disposes as an artist in and transfigurer of cruelty; in all taking things seriously and thoroughly, indeed, there is already a violation, a desire to hurt the fundamental will of the spirit, which ceaselessly strives for appearance and the superficial – in all desire to know there is already a drop of cruelty.

230

Perhaps what I have said here of a 'fundamental will of the spirit' may not be immediately comprehensible: allow me to explain. – That commanding something which the people calls 'spirit' wants to be master within itself and around itself and to feel itself master: out of multiplicity it has the will to simplicity, a will which binds together and tames, which is imperious and domineering. In this its needs and capacities are the same as those which physiologists posit for everything that lives, grows and multiplies. The power of the spirit to appropriate what is foreign to it is revealed in a strong inclination to assimilate the new to the old, to simplify the complex, to overlook or repel what is wholly contradictory: just as it arbitrarily emphasizes, extracts and falsifies to suit itself certain traits and lines in what is foreign to it, in every piece of 'external world'. Its intention in all this is the incorporation of new 'experiences', the arrangement of new things within old divisions – growth, that is to say; more precisely, the *feeling* of growth, the feeling of increased power.

This same will is served by an apparently antithetical drive of
the spirit, a sudden decision for ignorance, for arbitrary
shutting-out, a closing of the windows, an inner denial of this
or that thing, a refusal to let it approach, a kind of defensive
posture against much that can be known, a contentment with
the dark, with the closed horizon, an acceptance and approval
of ignorance: all this being necessary according to the degree
of its power to appropriate, its 'digestive power', to speak in a
metaphor – and indeed 'the spirit' is more like a stomach than
anything else. It is here that there also belongs the occasional
will of the spirit to let itself be deceived, perhaps with a
mischievous notion that such and such is *not* the case, that it is
only being allowed to pass for the case, a joy in uncertainty
and ambiguity, an exultant enjoyment of the capricious narrowness and secrecy of a nook-and-corner, of the all too
close, of the foreground, of the exaggerated, diminished,
displaced, beautified, an enjoyment of the capriciousness of all
these expressions of power. Finally there also belongs here
that not altogether innocent readiness of the spirit to deceive
other spirits and to dissemble before them, that continual
pressing and pushing of a creative, formative, changeable
force: in this the spirit enjoys the multiplicity and cunning of
its masks, it enjoys too the sense of being safe that this brings
– for it is precisely through its protean arts that it is best
concealed and protected! *This* will to appearance, to simplification, to the mask, to the cloak, in short to the superficial – for
every surface is a cloak – is *counteracted* by that sublime
inclination in the man of knowledge which takes a profound,
many-sided and thorough view of things and *will* take such a
view: as a kind of cruelty of the intellectual conscience and
taste which every brave thinker will recognize in himself,
provided he has hardened and sharpened for long enough his
own view of himself, as he should have, and is accustomed to
stern discipline and stern language. He will say 'there is
something cruel in the inclination of my spirit' – let the
amiable and virtuous try to talk him out of that! In fact, it
would be nicer if, instead of with cruelty, we were perhaps
credited with an 'extravagant honesty' – we free, *very* free

spirits – and perhaps *that* will actually one day be our posthumous fame? In the meantime – for it will be a long time before that happens – we ourselves are likely to be least inclined to dress up in moralistic verbal tinsel and valences of this sort: all our labour hitherto has spoiled us for this taste and its buoyant luxuriousness. They are beautiful, glittering, jingling, festive words: honesty, love of truth, love of wisdom, sacrifice for the sake of knowledge, heroism of the truthful – there is something about them that makes one's pride swell. But we hermits and marmots long ago became convinced that this worthy verbal pomp too belongs among the ancient false finery, lumber and gold-dust of unconscious human vanity, and that under such flattering colours and varnish too the terrible basic text *homo natura* must again be discerned. For to translate man back into nature; to master the many vain and fanciful interpretations and secondary meanings which have been hitherto scribbled and daubed over that eternal basic text *homo natura*; to confront man henceforth with man in the way in which, hardened by the discipline of science, man today confronts the *rest* of nature, with dauntless Oedipus eyes and stopped-up Odysseus ears, deaf to the siren songs of old metaphysical bird-catchers who have all too long been piping to him 'you are more! you are higher! you are of a different origin!' – that may be a strange and extravagant task but it is a *task* – who would deny that? Why did we choose it, this extravagant task? Or, to ask the question differently: 'why knowledge at all?' – Everyone will ask us about that. And we, thus pressed, we who have asked ourselves the same question a hundred times, we have found and can find no better answer . . .

231

Learning transforms us, it does that which all nourishment does which does not merely 'preserve' –: as the physiologist knows. But at the bottom of us, 'right down deep', there is, to be sure, something unteachable, a granite stratum of spiritual fate, of predetermined decision and answer to predetermined selected questions. In the case of every cardinal problem there speaks an unchangeable 'this is I'; about man and woman, for example, a thinker cannot relearn but only learn fully – only discover all that is 'firm and settled' within him on this subject. One sometimes comes upon certain solutions to problems which inspire strong belief in *us*; perhaps one thenceforth calls them one's 'convictions'. Later – one sees them only as footsteps to self-knowledge, signposts to the problem which we *are* – more correctly, to the great stupidity which we are, to our spiritual fate, to the *unteachable* 'right down deep'. – Having just paid myself such a deal of pretty compliments I may perhaps be more readily permitted to utter a few truths about 'woman as such': assuming it is now understood from the outset to how great an extent these are only – *my* truths. –

232

Woman wants to be independent: and to that end she is beginning to enlighten men about 'woman as such' – *this* is one of the worst developments in the general *uglification* of Europe. For what must these clumsy attempts on the part of female scientificality and self-exposure not bring to light! Woman has so much reason for shame; in woman there is concealed so much pedanticism, superficiality, schoolmarm-ishness, petty presumption, petty unbridledness and petty immodesty – one needs only to study her behaviour with children! – which has fundamentally been most effectively controlled and repressed hitherto by *fear* of man. Woe when the 'eternal-boring in woman' – she has plenty of that! – is allowed to venture forth! When she begins radically and on principle to forget her arts and best policy: those of charm, play, the banishing of care, the assuaging of grief and taking lightly, together with her subtle aptitude for agreeable desires! Already female voices are raised which, by holy Aristophanes! make one tremble; there are threatening and medically explicit statements of what woman *wants* of man. Is it not in the worst of taste when woman sets about becoming scientific in that fashion? Enlightenment in this field has hitherto been the affair and endowment of men – we remained 'among ourselves' in this; and whatever women write about 'woman', we may in the end reserve a good suspicion as to whether woman really *wants* or *can* want enlightenment about herself . . . Unless a woman is looking for a new *adornment* for herself in this way – self-adornment pertains to the eternal-womanly, does it not? – she is trying to inspire fear of herself – perhaps she is seeking dominion. But she does not *want* truth: what is truth to a woman! From the very first nothing has been more alien, repugnant, inimical to woman than truth – her great art is the lie, her supreme concern is appearance and beauty. Let us confess it, we men: it is precisely *this* art and *this* instinct in woman which we love and honour: we who have a hard time and for our refreshment like to associate with creatures under whose hands, glances and tender follies our seriousness, our gravity and profundity appear to us almost as folly. Finally I pose the question: has any woman ever conceded profundity to a woman's mind or justice to a woman's heart? And is it not true that on the whole 'woman' has hitherto been slighted most by woman herself – and not at all by us? – We men want woman to cease compromising herself through enlightenment: just as it was man's care and consideration for woman which led the Church to decree: *mulier taceat in ecclesia*! It was to the benefit of woman when Napoleon gave the all too eloquent Madame de Staël to understand: *mulier taceat in politicis*! – and I think it is a true friend of women who calls on them today: *mulier taceat de muliere*!

233

It betrays corruption of the instincts – quite apart from the fact that it betrays bad taste – when a woman appeals precisely to Madame Roland or Madame de Staël or Monsieur George Sand as if something *in favour* of 'woman as such' were thereby demonstrated. Among men the above-named are the three *comic* women as such – nothing more! – and precisely the best involuntary *counter-arguments* against emancipation and female autocracy.

234

Stupidity in the kitchen; woman as cook; the dreadful thought-lessness with which the nourishment of the family and the master of the house is provided for! Woman does not understand what food *means*: and she wants to be the cook! If woman were a thinking creature she would, having been the cook for thousands of years, surely have had to discover the major facts of physiology, and likewise gained possession of the art of healing. It is through bad female cooks – through the complete absence of reason in the kitchen, that the evolution of man has been longest retarded and most harmed: even today things are hardly any better. A lecture for high-school girls.

235

There are fortunate turns of the spirit, there are epigrams, a little handful of words, in which an entire culture, a whole society is suddenly crystallized. Among these is Madame de Lambert's remark to her son: '*mon ami, ne vous permettez jamais que de folies, qui vous feront grand plaisir*' – the most motherly and prudent remark, incidentally, that was ever addressed to a son.

236

That which Dante and Goethe believed of woman – the former when he sang '*ella guardava suso, ed io in lei*', the latter when he translated it 'the eternal-womanly draws us *upward*' – : I do not doubt that every nobler woman will resist this belief, for *that* is precisely what she believes of the eternal-manly . . .

237

Seven Proverbs for Women

How the slowest tedium flees when a man comes on his
  knees!

Age and scientific thought give even virtue some support.

Sober garb and total muteness dress a woman with – astute-
  ness.

Who has brought me luck today? God! – and my *couturier*.

Young: a cavern decked about. Old: a dragon sallies out.

Noble name, a leg that's fine, man as well: oh were *he* mine!

Few words, much meaning – slippery ground, many a poor
  she-ass has found!

Men have hitherto treated women like birds which have
strayed down to them from the heights: as something more
delicate, more fragile, more savage, stranger, sweeter, soulful
– but as something which has to be caged up so that it shall not
fly away.

238

To blunder over the fundamental problem of 'man and
woman', to deny here the most abysmal antagonism and the
necessity of an eternally hostile tension, perhaps to dream here
of equal rights, equal education, equal claims and duties: this
is a *typical* sign of shallow-mindedness, and a thinker who has
proved himself to be shallow on this dangerous point –
shallow of instinct! – may be regarded as suspect in general,
more, as betrayed, as found out: he will probably be too
'short' for all the fundamental questions of life, those of life in
the future too, incapable of *any* depth. On the other hand, a
man who has depth, in his spirit as well as in his desires, and
also that depth of benevolence which is capable of hardness
and severity and is easily confused with them, can think of
woman only in an *oriental* way – he must conceive of woman
as a possession, as property with lock and key, as something
predestined for service and attaining her fulfilment in service
– in this matter he must take his stand on the tremendous

intelligence of Asia, on Asia's superiority of instinct, as the Greeks formerly did: they were Asia's best heirs and pupils and, as is well known, from Homer to the age of Pericles, with the *increase* of their culture and the amplitude of their powers, also became step by step *more strict* with women, in short more oriental. *How* necessary, *how* logical, *how* humanly desirable even, this was: let each ponder for himself!

239

The weak sex has in no age been treated by men with such respect as it is in ours – that pertains to the democratic inclination and fundamental taste, as does disrespectfulness to old age –: is it any wonder if this respect is immediately abused? She wants more, she learns to demand, in the end she finds this tribute of respect almost offensive, she would prefer competition for rights, indeed a real stand-up fight: enough, woman loses in modesty. Let us add at once that she also loses in taste. She unlearns *fear* of man: but the woman who 'unlearns fear' sacrifices her most womanly instincts. That woman should venture out when the fear-inspiring in man, let us put it more precisely and say the *man* in man, is no longer desired and developed, is fair enough, also comprehensible enough; what is harder to comprehend is that, through precisely this fact – woman degenerates. This is what is happening today: let us not deceive ourselves! Wherever the spirit of industry has triumphed over the military and aristocratic spirit woman now aspires to the economic and legal independence of a clerk: 'woman as clerk' stands inscribed on the portal of the modern society now taking shape. As she thus seizes new rights, looks to become 'master', and inscribes the 'progress' of woman on her flags and banners, the reverse is happening with dreadful clarity: *woman is retrogressing*. Since the French Revolution the influence of woman in Europe has grown *less* in the same proportion as her rights and claims have grown greater; and the 'emancipation of woman', in so far as it has been demanded and advanced by women themselves (and not only by male shallow-pates), is thus revealed as a noteworthy symptom of the growing enfeeblement and blunting of the most feminine instincts. There is *stupidity* in this movement, an almost masculine stupidity, of which a real woman – who is always a clever woman – would have to be ashamed from the very heart. To lose her sense for the ground on which she is most sure of victory; to neglect to practise the use of her own proper weapons; to let herself go before the man, perhaps even 'to the extent of producing a book', where formerly she kept herself in check and in subtle cunning humility; to seek with virtuous assurance to destroy man's belief that a fundamentally different ideal is *wrapped up* in woman, that there is something eternally, necessarily feminine; emphatically and loquaciously to talk man out of the idea that woman has to be maintained, cared for, protected, indulged like a delicate, strangely wild and often agreeable domestic animal; the clumsy and indignant parade of all of slavery and bondage that woman's position in the order of society has hitherto entailed and still entails (as if slavery were a counter-argument and not rather a condition of every higher culture, of every enhancement of culture) – what does all this mean if not a crumbling of the feminine instinct, a defeminizing? To be sure, there are sufficient idiotic friends and corrupters of woman among the learned asses of the male sex who advise woman to defeminize herself in this fashion and to imitate all the stupidities with which 'man' in Europe, European 'manliness', is sick – who would like to reduce woman to the level of 'general education', if not to that of newspaper reading and playing at politics. Here and there they even want to turn women into free-spirits and *literati*: as if a woman without piety would not be something utterly repellent or ludicrous to a profound and godless man –; almost everywhere her nerves are being shattered by the most morbid and dangerous of all the varieties of music (our latest German music), and she is being rendered more and more hysterical with every day that passes and more and more incapable of her first and last profession, which is to bear strong children. There is a desire to make her in general more 'cultivated' and, as they say, to make the 'weak sex' *strong* through culture: as if history did not teach in the most emphatic manner possible that making human beings 'culti-vated' and making them weaker – that is to say, enfeebling, fragmenting, contaminating, the *force of the will*, have always gone hand in hand, and that the world's most powerful and influential women (most recently the mother of Napoleon) owed their power and ascendancy over men precisely to the force of their will – and not to schoolmasters! That in woman which inspires respect and fundamentally fear is her *nature*, which is more 'natural' than that of the man, her genuine, cunning, beast-of-prey suppleness, the tiger's claws beneath the glove, the naïvety of her egoism, her ineducability and inner savagery, and how incomprehensible, capacious and prowling her desires and virtues are . . . That which, all fear notwithstanding, evokes pity for this dangerous and beautiful cat 'woman' is that she appears to be more afflicted, more vulnerable, more in need of love and more condemned to disappointment than any other animal. Fear and pity: it is with these feelings that man has hitherto stood before woman, always with one foot in tragedy, which lacerates as it delights. – What? And is this now over with? And is woman now being deprived of her *enchantment*? Is woman slowly being made boring? O Europe! Europe! We know the horned beast which always attracted you most, which again and again threatens you with danger! Your ancient fable could once again become 'history' – once again a monstrous stupidity could master you and carry you off! And no god concealed within it, no! merely an 'idea', a 'modern idea'! . . .

Part Eight: Peoples and Fatherlands

240

I have heard, once again for the first time — Richard Wagner's overture to the *Meistersinger*: it is a magnificent, overladen, heavy and late art which has the pride to presuppose for its understanding that two centuries of music are still living — it is to the credit of the Germans that such a pride was not misplaced! What forces and juices, what seasons and zones are not mixed together here! Now it seems archaic, now strange, acid and too young, it is as arbitrary as it is pompous-traditional, it is not infrequently puckish, still more often rough and uncouth — it has fire and spirit and at the same time the loose yellow skin of fruits which ripen too late. It flows broad and full: and suddenly a moment of inexplicable hesitation, as it were a gap between cause and effect, an oppression producing dreams, almost a nightmare — but already the old stream of wellbeing broadens and widens again, the stream of the most manifold wellbeing, of happiness old and new, *very* much including the happiness of the artist in himself, which he has no desire to conceal, his happy, astonished knowledge of the masterliness of the means he is here employing, new, newly acquired, untried artistic means, as his art seems to betray to us. All in all, no beauty, nothing of the south or of subtle southerly brightness of sky, nothing of gracefulness, no dance, hardly any will to logic; a certain clumsiness, even, which is actually emphasized, as if the artist wanted to say: 'it is intentional'; a cumbersome drapery, something capriciously barbarous and solemn, a fluttering of venerable learned lace and conceits; something German in the best and worst sense of the word, something manifold, formless and inexhaustible in the German fashion; a certain German powerfulness and overfullness of soul which is not afraid to hide itself among the refinements of decay — which perhaps feels itself most at ease there; a true, genuine token of the German soul, which is at once young and aged, over-mellow and still too rich in future. This kind of music best expresses what I consider true of the Germans: they are of the day before yesterday and the day after tomorrow – *they have as yet no today.*

241

We 'good Europeans': we too have our hours when we permit ourselves a warm-hearted patriotism, a lapse and regression into old loves and narrownesses – I have just given an example of it – hours of national ebullition, of patriotic palpitations and floods of various outmoded feelings. More ponderous spirits than we may have done with what in our case is confined to a few hours and is then over only after a longer period: one takes half a year, another half a life, according to the speed and power with which he digests it and of his 'metabolism'. Indeed, I can imagine dull, sluggish races which, even in our fast-moving Europe, would need half a century to overcome such atavistic attacks of patriotism and cleaving to one's native soil and to be restored to reason, I mean to 'good Europeanism'. And, while digressing on this possibility, I chanced to become the ear-witness of a conversation between two old 'patriots' – it is clear they were both hard of hearing and thus spoke all the louder. '*He* has and knows as much philosophy as a peasant or a fraternity student', said one of them: 'he is still innocent. But what does that matter nowadays! It is the age of the masses: they fall on their faces before anything massive. And *in politics* likewise. A statesman who builds for them another Tower of Babel, some monstrosity of empire and power, they call "great" – what does it matter if we, more cautious and reserved than they, persist in the old belief that it is the great idea alone which can bestow greatness on a deed or a cause. Suppose a statesman were to put his nation in the position of having henceforth to pursue "grand politics", for which it was ill equipped and badly prepared by nature, so that it had to sacrifice its old and sure virtues for the sake of a new and doubtful mediocrity –suppose a statesman were to condemn his nation to "politicizing" at all, while that nation had hitherto had something better to do and think about and in the depths of its soul still retained a cautious disgust for the restlessness, emptiness and noisy wrangling of those nations which actually do practise politics – suppose such a statesman were to goad the slumbering passions and desires of his nation, turn its former diffidence and desire to stand aside into a stigma and its predilection for foreign things and its secret infiniteness into a fault, devalue its most heartfelt inclinations in its own eyes, reverse its conscience, make its mind narrow and its taste "national" – what! a statesman who did all this, a statesman for whom his nation would have to atone for all future time, assuming it had a future – would such a statesman be *great*?' 'Undoubtedly!' the other patriot replied vehemently: 'otherwise he would not have been *able* to do it! Perhaps you may say it was mad to want to do such a thing? But perhaps everything great has been merely mad to begin with!' – 'Misuse of words!' cried the other: – 'strong! strong! strong and mad! *Not* great!' – The old men had obviously grown heated as they thus shouted their 'truths' in one another's faces; I, however, in my happiness and beyond, considered how soon a stronger will become master of the strong; and also that when one nation becomes spiritually shallower there is a compensation for it: another nation becomes deeper. –

242

Whether that which now distinguishes the European be called 'civilization' or 'humanization' or 'progress'; whether one calls it simply, without implying any praise or blame, the *democratic* movement in Europe: behind all the moral and political foregrounds indicated by such formulas a great *physiological* process is taking place and gathering greater and ever greater impetus – the process of the assimilation of all Europeans, their growing detachment from the conditions under which races dependent on climate and class originate, their increasing independence of any *definite* milieu which, through making the same demands for centuries, would like to inscribe itself on soul and body – that is to say, the slow emergence of an essentially supra-national and nomadic type of man which, physiologically speaking, possesses as its typical distinction a maximum of the art and power of adaptation. This process of the *becoming European*, the tempo of which can be retarded by great relapses but which will perhaps precisely through them gain in vehemence and depth – the still-raging storm and stress of 'national feeling' belongs here, likewise the anarchism now emerging –: this process will probably lead to results which its naïve propagators and panegyrists, the apostles of 'modern ideas', would be least inclined to anticipate. The same novel conditions which will on average create a levelling and mediocritizing of man – a useful, industrious, highly serviceable and able herd-animal man – are adapted in the highest degree to giving rise to exceptional men of the most dangerous and enticing quality. For while that power of adaptation which continually tries out changing conditions and begins a new labour with every new generation, almost with every new decade, cannot make possible the *powerfulness* of the type; while the total impression produced by such future Europeans will probably be that of multifarious, garrulous, weak-willed and highly employable workers who *need* a master, a commander, as they need their daily bread; while, therefore, the democratization of Europe will lead to the production of a type prepared for *slavery* in the subtlest sense: in individual and exceptional cases the *strong* man will be found to turn out stronger and richer than has perhaps ever happened before – thanks to the unprejudiced nature of his schooling, thanks to the tremendous multiplicity of practice, art and mask. What I mean to say is that the democratization of Europe is at the same time an involuntary arrangement for the breeding of *tyrants* – in every sense of that word, including the most spiritual.

243

I hear with pleasure that our sun is moving rapidly in the direction of the constellation of *Hercules*: and I hope that men on the earth will in this matter emulate the sun. And we at their head, we good Europeans! –

244

There was a time when it was usual to call the Germans 'profound', and this was meant as a term of distinction: now, when the most successful type of the new Germanism thirsts after quite different honours and perhaps feels that anything profound lacks 'dash', it is almost timely and patriotic to doubt whether that commendation of former days was not founded on self-deception: whether German profundity is not at bottom something different and worse – and something which, thanks be to God, one is on the verge of successfully getting rid of. Let us therefore try to learn anew about German profundity: all that is required is a little vivisection of the German soul. – The German soul is above all manifold, of diverse origins, put together and superimposed rather than actually constructed: the reason for that is its source. A German who would make bold to say 'two souls, alas, within my bosom dwell' would err very widely from the truth, more correctly he would fall short of the truth by a large number of souls. As a people of the most tremendous mixture and mingling of races, perhaps even with a preponderance of the pre-Aryan element, as the 'people of the middle' in every sense, the Germans are more incomprehensible, more comprehensive, more full of contradictions, more unknown, more incalculable, more surprising, even more frightening to themselves than other peoples are – they elude *definition* and are for that reason alone the despair of the French. It is characteristic of the Germans that the question 'what is German?' never dies out among them. Kotzebue certainly knew his Germans well enough: 'we are known' they cried to him jubilantly – but *Sand* too thought she knew them. Jean Paul knew what he was doing when he declared himself incensed by Fichte's mendacious but patriotic flatteries and exaggerations – but it is likely that Goethe thought otherwise of the Germans than Jean Paul did, even though he agreed with him about Fichte.

What Goethe really thought of the Germans? – But there were many things round him about which he never expressed himself clearly and his whole life long he knew how to maintain a subtle silence – he had no doubt good reason. What is certain is that it was not 'the Wars of Liberation' which made him look up more cheerfully, any more than it was the French Revolution – the event on account of which he *rethought* his *Faust*, indeed the whole problem of 'man', was the appearance of Napoleon. There exist statements by Goethe in which, as if he was from another country, he condemns with impatient severity that which the Germans take pride in: the celebrated German *Gemüt* he once defined as 'indulgence of others' weaknesses, and one's own'. Was he wrong? – it is characteristic of the Germans that one is seldom wholly wrong about them. The German soul has corridors and interconnecting corridors in it, there are caves, hiding-places, dungeons in it; its disorder possesses much of the fascination of the mysterious; the German is acquainted with the hidden paths to chaos. And as everything loves its symbol, the German loves clouds and all that is obscure, becoming, crepuscular, damp and dismal: the uncertain, unformed, shifting, growing of every kind he feels to be 'profound'. The German himself *is* not, he is *becoming*, he is 'developing'. 'Development' is thus the truly German discovery and lucky shot in the great domain of philosophical formulas – a ruling concept which, in concert with German beer and German music, is at work at the Germanization of all Europe. Foreigners are astonished and drawn by the enigmas which the contradictory nature at the bottom of the German soul propounds to them (which Hegel reduced to a system and Richard Wagner finally set to music). 'Good-natured and malicious' – such a juxtaposition, nonsensical in respect of any other people, is unfortunately too often justified in Germany: you have only to live among Swabians for a while! The ponderousness of the German scholar, his social insipidity, gets on frightfully well with an inner rope-walking and easy boldness before which all the gods have learned fear. If you want the 'German soul' demonstrated *ad oculos*, you have only to look into German taste, into German arts and customs: what boorish indifference to 'taste'! How the noblest and the commonest here stand side by side! How disorderly and wealthy this whole psychical household is! The German *drags* his soul, he drags everything he experiences. He digests his events badly, he is never 'done' with them; German profundity is often only a sluggish 'digestion'. And just as all chronic invalids, all dyspeptics, have an inclination for comfort, so the German loves 'openness' and 'uprightness': how *comfortable* it is to be open and upright! – Perhaps it is the most dangerous and successful disguise the German knows how to use today, this confiding, accommodating, cards-on-the-table German *honesty*: it is his real Mephistophelean art, with its aid he can 'still go far'! The German lets himself go, and as he does so he gazes out with true blue empty German eyes – and other countries at once confound him with his dressing-gown! – I meant to say: whatever 'German profundity' may be – and when we are quite by ourselves we shall perhaps permit ourselves to laugh at it? – we would do well to hold its appearance and good name in respect henceforth too and not to sell former old reputation as the profound nation too cheaply for Prussian 'dash' and Berlin wit and sand. It is clever for a people to be considered, to *get* itself considered, profound, clumsy, good-natured, honest, not clever: it might even be – profound! Finally: one ought not to be ashamed of one's own name –it is not for nothing one is called *das 'tiusche' Volk, das Täusche-Volk* . . .

245

The 'good old days' are gone, in Mozart they sang themselves out – how fortunate are *we* that his rococo still speaks to us, that his 'good company', his tender enthusiasm, his child-like delight in *chinoiserie* and ornament, his politeness of the heart, his longing for the graceful, the enamoured, the dancing, the tearful, his faith in the south may still appeal to some *residue* in us! Alas, some day it will all be gone – but who can doubt that understanding and taste for Beethoven will be gone first! – for Beethoven was only the closing cadence of a transition of style and stylistic breach and not, as Mozart was, the closing cadence of a great centuries-old European taste. Beethoven is the intermediary between an old mellow soul that is constantly crumbling and a future over-young soul that is constantly *arriving*; upon his music there lies that twilight of eternal loss and eternal extravagant hope – the same light in which Europe lay bathed when it dreamed with Rousseau, when it danced around the Revolution's Tree of Liberty and finally almost worshipped before Napoleon. But how quickly *this* feeling is now fading away, how hard it is today even to *know* of this feeling – how strange to our ears sounds the language of Rousseau, Schiller, Shelley, Byron, in whom *together* the same European destiny that in Beethoven knew how to sing found its way into words! – Whatever German music came afterwards belongs to romanticism, that is to say to a movement which was, historically speaking, even brieter, even more fleeting, even more superficial than that great interlude, that transition of Europe from Rousseau to Napoleon and to the rise of democracy. Weber: but what are *Freischütz* and *Oberon* to *us* today! Or Marschner's *Hans Heiling* and *Vampyr*! Or even Wagner's *Tannhäuser*! It is dead, if not yet forgotten, music. All this music of romanticism was, moreover, insufficiently noble, insufficiently musical, to maintain itself anywhere but in the theatre and before the mob; it was from the very first second-rate music to which genuine musicians paid little regard. It was otherwise with Felix Mendelssohn, that halcyon master who was, on account of his lighter, purer, happier soul, speedily honoured and just as speedily forgotten: as the beautiful *intermezzo* of German music. But as for Schumann, who took things seriously and was also taken seriously from the first – he was the last to found a school –: do we not now think it a piece of good fortune, a relief, a liberation that this Schumann-romanticism has been overcome? Schumann, fleeing into the 'Saxon Switzerland' of his soul, his nature half Werther, half Jean Paul, not at all like Beethoven, not at all Byronic! – his music for *Manfred* is a mistake and misunderstanding to the point of injustice – Schumann, with his taste which was fundamentally a *petty* taste (that is to say a dangerous inclination, doubly dangerous among Germans, for quiet lyricism and drunkenness of feeling), continually going aside, shyly withdrawing and retiring, a noble effeminate delighting in nothing but anonymous weal and woe, a kind of girl and *noli me tangere* from the first: this Schumann was already a merely *German* event in music, no longer a European event, as Beethoven was, as to an even greater extent Mozart had been – in him German music was threatened with its greatest danger, that of losing *the voice for the soul of Europe* and sinking into a merely national affair.

246

– What a torment books written in German are for him who has a *third* ear! How disgustedly he stands beside the slowly turning swamp of sounds without resonance, of rhythms that do not dance, which the Germans call a 'book'! Not to mention the German who *reads* books! How lazily, how reluctantly, how badly he reads! How many Germans know, or think they ought to know, that there is *art* in every good sentence – art that must be grasped if the sentence is to be understood! A misunderstanding of its tempo, for example: and the sentence itself is misunderstood! That one must be in no doubt about the syllables that determine the rhythm, that one should feel the disruption of a too-severe symmetry as intentional and as something attractive, that one should lend a refined and patient ear to every *staccato*, every *rubato*, that one should divine the meaning in the sequence of vowels and diphthongs and how delicately and richly they can colour and recolour one another through the order in which they come: who among book-reading Germans has sufficient goodwill to acknowledge such demands and duties and to listen to so much art and intention in language? In the end one simply 'has no ear for it': and so the greatest contrasts in style go unheard and the subtlest artistry is *squandered* as if on the deaf. – These were my thoughts when I noticed how two masters of the art of prose were clumsily and unsuspectingly confused with one another: one from whom words fall cold and hesitantly as from the roof of a damp cavern – he calculates on the heavy dullness of their sound and echo – and another who handles his language like a supple blade and feels from his arm down to his toes the perilous delight of the quivering, over-sharp steel that wants to bite, hiss, cut. –

247

How little German style has to do with sound and the ears is shown by the fact that precisely our good musicians write badly. The German does not read aloud, does not read for the ear, but merely with his eyes: he has put his ears away in the drawer. In antiquity, when a man read – which he did very seldom – he read to himself aloud, and indeed in a loud voice; it was a matter for surprise if someone read quietly, and people secretly asked themselves why he did so. In a loud voice: that is to say, with all the crescendos, inflections, variations of tone and changes of tempo in which the ancient *public* world took pleasure. In those days the rules of written style were the same as those of spoken style; and these rules depended in part on the astonishing development, the refined requirements of ear and larynx, in part on the strength, endurance and power of ancient lungs. A period is, in the sense in which the ancients understood it, above all a physiological whole, inasmuch as it is composed by a *single* breath. Periods such as appear with Demosthenes or Cicero, rising twice and sinking twice and all within a *single* breath: these are delights for men of *antiquity*, who knew from their own schooling how to value the virtue in them, the rarity and difficulty of the delivery of such a period – *we* have really no right to the *grand* period, we moderns, we who are short of breath in every sense! For these ancients were one and all themselves dilettantes in rhetoric, consequently connoisseurs, consequently critics – and so they drove their orators to extremes; in the same way as, in the last century, when all Italians and Italiennes knew how to sing, virtuosity in singing (and therewith also the art of melody –) attained its height with them. In Germany, however, there was (until very recently, when a kind of platform eloquence began shyly and heavily to flap its young wings) really but *one* species of public and *fairly* artistic oratory: that from the pulpit. The preacher was the only one in Germany who knew what a syllable, what a word weighs, how a sentence strikes, rises, falls, runs, runs to an end, he alone had a conscience in his ears, often enough a bad conscience: for there is no lack of reasons why it is precisely the German who rarely achieves proficiency in oratory, or almost always achieves it too late. The masterpiece of German prose is therefore, as is to be expected, the masterpiece of its great preacher: the *Bible* has been the best German book hitherto. Compared with Luther's Bible almost everything else is merely 'literature' – a thing that has not grown up in Germany and therefore has not taken and does not take root in German hearts: as the Bible has done.

248

There are two kinds of genius: the kind which above all begets and wants to beget, and the kind which likes to be fructified and to give birth. And likewise there are among peoples of genius those upon whom has fallen the woman's problem of pregnancy and the secret task of forming, maturing, perfecting – the Greeks, for example, were a people of this kind, and so were the French –; and others who have to fructify and become the cause of new orders of life – like the Jews, the Romans and, to ask it in all modesty, the Germans? – peoples tormented and enraptured by unknown fevers and irresistibly driven outside themselves, enamoured of and lusting after foreign races (after those which 'want to be fructified') and at the same time hungry for dominion, like everything which knows itself full of generative power and consequently 'by the grace of God'. These two kinds of genius seek one another, as man and woman do; but they also misunderstand one another – as man and woman do.

249

Every people has its own tartuffery and calls it its virtues. – The best that one is one does not know – one cannot know.

250

What Europe owes to the Jews? – Many things, good and bad, and above all one thing that is at once of the best and the worst: the grand style in morality, the dreadfulness and majesty of infinite demands, infinite significances, the whole romanticism and sublimity of moral questionabilities – and consequently precisely the most attractive, insidious and choicest part of those iridescences and seductions to life with whose afterglow the sky of our European culture, its evening sky, is now aflame – and perhaps burning itself up. We artists among the spectators and philosophers are – grateful to the Jews for this.

251

If a people is suffering and *wants* to suffer from nationalistic nervous fever and political ambition, it must be expected that all sorts of clouds and disturbances – in short, little attacks of stupidity – will pass over its spirit into the bargain: among present-day Germans, for example, now the anti-French stupidity, now the anti-Jewish, now the anti-Polish, now the Christian-romantic, now the Wagnerian, now the Teutonic, now the Prussian (just look at those miserable historians, those Sybels and Treitschkes, with their thickly bandaged heads –), and whatever else these little obfuscations of the German spirit and conscience may be called. May it be forgiven me that I too, during a daring brief sojourn in a highly infected area, did not remain wholly free of the disease and began, like the rest of the world, to entertain ideas about things that were none of my business: first symptom of the political infection. About the Jews, for example: listen. – I have never met a German who was favourably inclined towards the Jews; and however unconditionally all cautious and politic men may have repudiated real anti-Jewism, even this caution and policy is not directed against this class of feeling itself but only against its dangerous immoderation, and especially against the distasteful and shameful way in which this immoderate feeling is expressed – one must not deceive oneself about that. That Germany has an ample *sufficiency* of Jews, that the German stomach, German blood has difficulty (and will continue to have difficulty for a long time to come) in absorbing even this quantum of 'Jew' – as the Italians, the French, the English have absorbed them through possessing a stronger digestion –: this is the clear declaration and language of a universal instinct to which one must pay heed, in accordance with which one must act. 'Let in no more Jews! And close especially the doors to the East (also to Austria)!' – thus commands the instinct of a people whose type is still weak and undetermined, so that it could easily be effaced, easily extinguished by a stronger race. The Jews, however, are beyond all doubt the strongest, toughest and purest race at present living in Europe; they know how to prevail even under the worst conditions (better even than under favourable ones), by means of virtues which one would like to stamp as vices – thanks above all to a resolute faith which does not need to be ashamed before 'modern ideas'; they change, *when* they change, only in the way in which the Russian Empire makes its conquests – an empire that has time and is not of yesterday –: namely, according to the principle 'as slowly as possible'! A thinker who has the future of Europe on his conscience will, in all the designs he makes for this future, take the Jews into account as he will take the Russians, as the immediately surest and most probable factors in the great game and struggle of forces. That which is called a 'nation' in Europe today and is actually more of a *res facta* than *nata* (indeed sometimes positively resembles a *res ficta et picta* –) is in any case something growing, young, easily disruptable, not yet a race, let alone such an *aere perennius* as the Jewish type is: these 'nations' should certainly avoid all hot-headed rivalry and hostility very carefully! That the Jews *could*, if they wanted – or if they were compelled, as the anti-Semites seem to want – even now predominate, indeed quite literally rule over Europe, is certain; that they are *not* planning and working towards that is equally certain. In the meantime they are, rather, wanting and wishing, even with some importunity, to

be absorbed and assimilated by and into Europe, they are
longing to be finally settled, permitted, respected somewhere
and to put an end to the nomadic life, to the 'Wandering Jew' –;
one ought to pay heed to this inclination and impulse (which
is perhaps even a sign that the Jewish instincts are becoming
milder) and go out to meet it: for which it would perhaps be a
good idea to eject the anti-Semitic ranters from the country.
Go out to meet it with all caution, with selectivity; much as
the English nobility do. It is plain that the stronger and
already more firmly formed types of the new Germanism
could enter into relations with them with the least hesitation;
the aristocratic officer of the March, for example: it would be interesting in many ways to see whether the genius of money and
patience (and above all a little mind and spirituality, of which
there is a plentiful lack in the persons above mentioned –)
could not be added and bred into the hereditary art of
commanding and obeying, in both of which the above-
mentioned land is today classic. But here it is fitting that I
should break off my cheerful Germanomaniac address: for
already I am touching on what is to me *serious*, on the
'European problem' as I understand it, on the breeding of a
new ruling caste for Europe. –

252

They are no philosophical race – these English: Bacon signifies
an *attack* on the philosophical spirit in general, Hobbes,
Hume and Locke a debasement and devaluation of the concept
'philosopher' for more than a century. It was *against* Hume
that Kant rose up; it was Locke of whom Schelling *had a right*
to say: '*je méprise Locke*'; in their struggle against the English-
mechanistic stultification of the world, Hegel and Schopenhauer were (with Goethe) of one accord: those two hostile
brother geniuses who strove apart towards the antithetical
poles of the German spirit and in doing so wronged one
another as only brothers wrong one another. – What is
lacking in England and always has been lacking was realized
well enough by that semi-actor and rhetorician, the tasteless

muddlehead Carlyle, who tried to conceal behind passionate grimaces what he knew about himself: namely what was *lacking* in Carlyle – real *power* of spirituality, real *depth* of spiritual insight, in short philosophy. – It is characteristic of such an unphilosophical race that they should cling firmly to Christianity: they *need* its discipline if they are to become 'moral' and humane. The Englishman, gloomier, more sensual, stronger of will and more brutal than the German – is for just that reason, as the more vulgar of the two, also more pious than the German: he is in greater *need* of Christianity. To finer nostrils even this English Christianity possesses a true English by-scent of the spleen and alcoholic excess against which it is with good reason employed as an antidote – the subtler poison against the coarser: and indeed a subtle poisoning is in the case of coarse peoples already a certain progress, a step towards spiritualization. English coarseness and peasant seriousness still finds its most tolerable disguise in Christian gestures and in praying and psalm-singing: more correctly, it is best interpreted and given a new meaning by those things; and as for those drunken and dissolute cattle who formerly learned to grunt morally under the constraint of Methodism and more recently as the 'Salvation Army', a spasm of penitence may really be the highest achievement of 'humanity' to which they can be raised: that much may fairly be conceded. But what offends in even the most humane Englishman is, to speak metaphorically (and not metaphorically), his lack of music: he has in the movements of his soul and body no rhythm and dance, indeed not even the desire for rhythm and dance, for 'music'. Listen to him speak; watch the most beautiful Englishwomen *walk* – in no land on earth are there more beautiful doves and swans – finally: listen to them sing! But I ask too much . . .

253

There are truths which are recognized best by mediocre minds because they are most suited to them, there are truths which possess charm and seductive powers only for mediocre spirits

– one is brought up against this perhaps disagreeable proposition just at the moment because the spirit of respectable but mediocre Englishmen – I name Darwin, John Stuart Mill and Herbert Spencer – is starting to gain ascendancy in the mid-region of European taste. Who indeed would doubt that it is useful for *such* spirits to dominate for a while? It would be a mistake to regard exalted spirits who fly off on their own as especially well adapted to identifying, assembling and making deductions from a host of little common facts – as exceptions they are, rather, from the first in no very favourable position with respect to the 'rules'. After all, they have more to do than merely know something new – namely to *be* something new, to *signify* something new, to *represent* new values! The gulf between knowing and being able is perhaps wider, also more uncanny, than one thinks: the man who is able in the grand style, the creator, might possibly have to be ignorant – while, on the other hand, for scientific discoveries such as Darwin's a certain narrowness, aridity and industrious conscientiousness, something English in short, may not be an unfavourable disposition. – Finally, let us not forget that the English, with their profound averageness, have once before brought about a collective depression of the European spirit: that which is called 'modern ideas' or 'the ideas of the eighteenth century' or even 'French ideas' – that is to say, that which the *German* spirit has risen against in profound disgust – was of English origin, there can be no doubt about that. The French have been only the apes and actors of these ideas, also their finest soldiers, also unhappily their first and most thorough *victims*: for through the damnable Anglomania of 'modern ideas' the *âme française* has finally grown so thin and emaciated that today one recalls her sixteenth and seventeenth centuries, her profound passionate strength, her noble inventiveness, almost with disbelief. But one must hang on with one's teeth to this proposition of historical equity and defend it against the prejudice of the day: European *noblesse* – of feeling, of taste, of custom, in short *noblesse* in every exalted sense of the word – is the work and invention of *France*, European vulgarity, the plebeianism of modern ideas, that of – *England*.–

254

Even now France is still the seat of Europe's most spiritual and refined culture and the leading school of taste: but one has to know how to find this 'France of taste'. He who belongs to it keeps himself well hidden – it may be only a small number in whom it lives and moves, and they, perhaps, men whose legs are not of the strongest, some of them fatalists, gloomy, sick, some of them spoilt and artificial, such men as have an *ambition* to hide themselves. One thing they all have in common: they shut their ears to the raving stupidity and the noisy yapping of the democratic *bourgeois*. Indeed, it is a coarse and stupid France that trundles in the foreground today – it recently celebrated, at Victor Hugo's funeral, a veritable orgy of tastelessness and at the same time self-admiration. Something else too they have in common: a great will to resist spiritual Germanization – and an even greater inability to do so! Perhaps Schopenhauer has now become more at home and indigenous in this France of the spirit, which is also a France of pessimism, than he ever was in Germany; not to speak of Heinrich Heine, who has long since entered into the flesh and blood of the more refined and demanding lyric poets of Paris, or of Hegel, who today, in the shape of Taine – that is to say, in that of the *first* of living historians – exercises an almost tyrannical influence. As for Richard Wagner, however: the more French music learns to shape itself according to the actual needs of the *âme moderne*, the more will it 'Wagnerize', that one can safely predict – it is doing so sufficiently already! There are nevertheless three things which, despite all voluntary and involuntary Germanization and vulgarization of taste, the French can still today exhibit with pride as their inheritance and possession and as an indelible mark of their ancient cultural superiority in Europe. Firstly, the capacity for artistic passions, for devotion to 'form', for which, together with a thousand others, the term *l'art pour l'art* has been devised – it has been present in France for three hundred years and, thanks to their respect for the 'small number', has again and again made possible a kind of literary chamber music not to be found anywhere else in Europe –. The second thing by which the French can argue their superiority to the rest of Europe is their ancient, manifold, *moralistic* culture, by virtue of which one finds on average even in little *romanciers* of the newspapers and chance *boulevardiers de Paris* a psychological sensitivity and curiosity of which in Germany, for example, they have no conception (not to speak of having the thing itself!). The Germans lack the couple of centuries of moralistic labour needed for this, a labour which, as aforesaid, France did not spare itself; he who calls the Germans 'naïve' on that account commends them for a fault. (As antithesis to German inexperience and innocence *in voluptate psychologica*, which is not too distantly related to the boringness of German company - and as the most successful expression of a genuine French curiosity and inventiveness in this domain of delicate thrills, one should observe Henri Beyle, that remarkable anticipator and forerunner who ran with a Napoleonic tempo through *his* Europe, through several centuries of the European soul, as a detector and discoverer of his soul – it needed two generations to *overtake* him, to divine once more some of the riddles which tormented and delighted him, this strange Epicurean and question-mark who was France's last great psychologist –.) There is yet a third claim to superiority: in the French nature there exists a half-achieved synthesis of north and south which makes them understand many things and urges them to do many things which an Englishman will never understand. Their temperament, periodically turning towards the south and away from the south, in which the Provençal and Ligurian blood from time to time foams over, preserves them from dreary northern grey-on-grey and sunless concept-ghoulishness and anaemia – the disease of our *German* taste against whose excess one has at just this moment very resolutely prescribed blood and iron, that is to say 'grand politics' (in accordance with a dangerous therapeutic which has certainly taught me how to wait but has not yet taught me how to hope –). Even now there exists in France an understanding in advance and welcome for those rarer and rarely contented men who are too comprehensive to find their satisfaction in any kind of patriotism and know how to love the south in the north and the north in the south – for the born Midlanders, the 'good Europeans'. – It was for them that *Bizet* made music, that last genius to perceive a new beauty and a new seduction – who has discovered a region of the *south in music*.

255

Against German music I feel all sorts of precautions should be taken. Suppose one loves the south as I love it, as a great school of convalescence, for all the diseases of senses and spirit, as a tremendous abundance of sun and transfiguration by sun, spreading itself over an autonomous existence which believes in itself: well, such a person will learn to be somewhat on guard against German music because, by spoiling his taste again, it will also spoil his health again. Such a southerner, not by descent but by *faith*, must, if he dreams of the future of music, also dream of the redemption of music from the north and have in his ears the prelude to a deeper, mightier, perhaps wickeder and more mysterious music, a supra-German music which does not fade, turn yellow, turn pale at the sight of the blue voluptuous sea and the luminous sky of the Mediterranean, as all German music does; a supra-European music which holds its own even before the brown sunsets of the desert, whose soul is kindred to the palm-tree and knows how to roam and be at home among great beautiful solitary beasts of prey. . . . I could imagine a music whose rarest magic would consist in this, that it no longer knew anything of good and evil, except that perhaps some sailor's homesickness, some golden shadow and delicate weakness would now and then flit across it: an art that would see fleeing towards it from a great distance the colours of a declining, now almost incomprehensible *moral* world, and would be hospitable and deep enough to receive such late fugitives. –

256

Thanks to the morbid estrangement which the lunacy of nationality has produced and continues to produce between the peoples of Europe, thanks likewise to the shortsighted and hasty-handed politicians who are with its aid on top today and have not the slightest notion to what extent the politics of disintegration they pursue must necessarily be only an interlude – thanks to all this, and to much else that is altogether unmentionable today, the most unambiguous signs are now being overlooked, or arbitrarily and lyingly mis-interpreted, which declare that *Europe wants to become one*. In all the more profound and comprehensive men of this century the general tendency of the mysterious workings of their souls has really been to prepare the way to this new *synthesis* and to anticipate experimentally the European of the future: only in their foregrounds, or in hours of weakness, in old age perhaps, were they among the 'men of the fatherland' – they were only taking a rest from themselves when they became 'patriots'. I think of men such as Napoleon, Goethe, Beethoven, Stendhal, Heinrich Heine, Schopenhauer; I must not be blamed if I also include Richard Wagner among them: one should not let oneself be misled about him by his own misunderstandings – geniuses of his sort seldom have the right to understand themselves – and even less, to be sure, by the unseemly noise with which he is opposed and resisted today in France: the fact none the less remains that *French late romanticism* of the forties and Richard Wagner belong most closely and intimately together. They are related, fundamentally related, in all the heights and depths of their needs: it is Europe, the *one* Europe, whose soul forces its way longingly up and out through their manifold and impetuous art – whither? into a new light? towards a new sun? But who could express precisely what all these masters of new means of speech themselves did not know how to express clearly? What is certain is that they were tormented by the same storm and stress, that they *sought* in the same way, these last great seekers! One and all domi-nated by literature up to their eyes and ears – the first artists formed and cultivated by world literature – most of them even writers and poets themselves and mediators and minglers of the arts and senses (as a musician Wagner belongs among painters, as a poet among musicians, as an artist as such

189

among actors); one and all fanatics for *expression* 'at any cost' – I call particular attention to Delacroix, Wagner's closest relation – one and all great discoverers in the realm of the sublime, also of the ugly and horrible, even greater discoverers in effects, in display, in the art of the shop window, one and all talents far beyond their genius – virtuosos through and through, with uncanny access to everything that seduces, lures, constrains, overwhelms, born enemies of logic and straight lines, constantly hankering after the strange, the exotic, the monstrous, the crooked, the self-contradictory; as human beings Tantaluses of the will, plebeians risen in the world who knew themselves incapable, in their lives and in their works, of a noble tempo, a *lento* – think of Balzac, for instance – unbridled workers, almost destroying themselves through work; antinomians, fomenters of moral disorder, ambitious, insatiable men without balance or enjoyment; one and all collapsing and sinking at last before the Christian Cross (and with every right: for who among them would have been profound or primary enough for a philosophy of *anti-Christ*?) – on the whole an audacious-daring, splendidly violent, high-flying type of higher men who bore others up with them and whose lot it was to teach their century – and it is the century of the *mob*! – the concept 'higher man'. . . . Let the German friends of Richard Wagner deliberate whether there is in Wagnerian art anything simply German, or whether it is not precisely its distinction that it derives from *supra-German* sources and impulses: in considering which it should not be underestimated how indispensable Paris was for the cultivation of his type, how the depth of his instinct drew him precisely thither at the most decisive time, and how his whole manner of appearance and self-apostolate could perfect itself only by his seeing its French socialist model. Perhaps a subtler comparison will reveal that, to the credit of Richard Wagner's German nature, he fashioned stronger, more daring, more severe and more elevated things than a nineteenth-century Frenchman could have done – thanks to the circumstance that we Germans are still closer to barbarism than the French –; perhaps the most remarkable thing Wagner created is even inaccessible, inimitable to the entire, so late Latin race for ever and not only for the present: the figure of Siegfried, that *very free* human being who may indeed be much too free, too hard, too cheerful, too healthy, too *anti-Catholic* for the taste of peoples of an ancient, mellow culture. He may even have been a sin against romanticism, this anti-Romantic Siegfried: well, Wagner amply atoned for this sin in his old, melancholy days when – anticipating a taste which has since become political – he began, with the religious vehemence characteristic of him, if not to walk at any rate to preach *the road to Rome*. – That these last words shall not be misunderstood I shall call to my aid a few powerful rhymes which will reveal what I mean to less refined ears too – what I *object* to in 'late Wagner' and his *Parsifal* music:

> – Is this still German? –
> From German heart this sultry ululating?
> Of German body this self-lacerating?
> German, this altar-priest prostration,
> This incense-perfumed stimulation?
> German this reeling, stumbling, tumbling,
> This muddy booming bim-bam-bumbling,
> This nunnish ogling, Ave-hour-bell chiming,
> This false-ecstatic higher-than-heaven climbing?
> – Is this still German? –
> Reflect! And then your answer frame: –
> For what you hear is *Rome – Rome's faith in all but name!*

Part Nine: What is Noble?

257

Every elevation of the type 'man' has hitherto been the work of an aristocratic society — and so it will always be: a society which believes in a long scale of orders of rank and differences of worth between man and man and needs slavery in some sense or other. Without the *pathos of distance* such as develops from the incarnate differences of classes, from the ruling caste's constant looking out and looking down on subjects and instruments and from its equally constant exercise of obedience and command, its holding down and holding at a distance, that other, more mysterious pathos could not have developed either, that longing for an ever-increasing widening of distance within the soul itself, the formation of ever higher, rarer, more remote, tenser, more comprehensive states, in short precisely the elevation of the type 'man', the continual 'self-overcoming of man', to take a moral formula in a supra-moral sense. As to how an aristocratic society (that is to say, the precondition for this elevation of the type 'man') origi-nates, one ought not to yield to any humanitarian illusions: truth is hard. Let us admit to ourselves unflinchingly how every higher culture on earth has hitherto *begun*! Men of a still natural nature, barbarians in every fearful sense of the word, men of prey still in possession of an unbroken strength of will and lust for power, threw themselves upon weaker, more civilized, more peaceful, perhaps trading or cattle-raising races, or upon old mellow cultures, the last vital forces in which were even then flickering out in a glittering firework display of spirit and corruption. The noble caste was in the beginning always the barbarian caste: their superiority lay, not in their physical strength, but primarily in their psychical — they were *more complete* human beings (which, on every level, also means as much as 'more complete beasts' —).

258

Corruption as the indication that anarchy threatens within the instincts, and that the foundation of the emotions which is called 'life' has been shaken: corruption is something fundamentally different according to which life-form it appears in. When, for example, an aristocracy such as that of France at the start of the Revolution throws away its privileges with a sublime disgust and sacrifices itself to an excess of moral feeling, then that is corruption – it was really only the closing act of that corruption which had been going on for centuries by virtue of which it had step by step abdicated its prerogatives of government and demoted itself to a *function* of the monarchy (in the end to no more than its decoration and show-piece). The essential thing in a good and healthy aristocracy is, however, that it does *not* feel itself to be a function (of the monarchy or of the commonwealth) but as their *meaning* and supreme justification – that it therefore accepts with a good conscience the sacrifice of innumerable men who *for its sake* have to be suppressed and reduced to imperfect men, to slaves and instruments. Its fundamental faith must be that society should *not* exist for the sake of society but only as foundation and scaffolding upon which a select species of being is able to raise itself to its higher task and in general to a higher *existence*: like those sun-seeking climbing plants of Java – they are named *sipo matador* – which clasp an oak-tree with their tendrils so long and often that at last, high above it but supported by it, they can unfold their crowns in the open light and display their happiness. –

259

To refrain from mutual injury, mutual violence, mutual exploitation, to equate one's own will with that of another: this may in a certain rough sense become good manners between individuals if the conditions for it are present (namely if their strength and value standards are in fact similar and they both belong to *one* body). As soon as there is a desire to take this principle further, however, and if possible even as the *fundamental principle of society*, it at once reveals itself for what it is: as the will to the *denial* of life, as the principle of dissolution and decay. One has to think this matter thoroughly through to the bottom and resist all sentimental weakness: life itself is *essentially* appropriation, injury, overpowering of the strange and weaker, suppression, severity, imposition of one's own forms, incorporation and, at the least and mildest, exploitation – but why should one always have to employ precisely those words which have from of old been stamped with a slanderous intention? Even that body within which, as was previously assumed, individuals treat one another as equals – this happens in every healthy aristocracy – must, if it is a living and not a decaying body, itself do all that to other bodies which the individuals within it refrain from doing to one another: it will have to be the will to power incarnate, it will want to grow, expand, draw to itself, gain ascendancy – not out of any morality or immorality, but because it *lives*, and because life *is* will to power. On no point, however, is the common European consciousness more reluctant to learn than it is here; everywhere one enthuses, even under scientific disguises, about coming states of society in which there will be 'no more exploitation' – that sounds to my ears like promising a life in which there will be no organic functions. 'Exploitation' does not pertain to a corrupt or imperfect or primitive society: it pertains to the *essence* of the living thing as a fundamental organic function, it is a consequence of the intrinsic will to power which is precisely the will of life. – Granted this is a novelty as a theory – as a reality it is the *primordial fact* of all history: let us be at least that honest with ourselves! –

260

In a tour of the many finer and coarser moralities which have ruled or still rule on earth I found certain traits regularly recurring together and bound up with one another: until at length two basic types were revealed and a basic distinction emerged. There is *master morality* and *slave morality* – I add at once that in all higher and mixed cultures attempts at mediation between the two are apparent and more frequently confusion and mutual misunderstanding between them, indeed sometimes their harsh juxtaposition – even within the same man, within *one* soul. The moral value-distinctions have arisen either among a ruling order which was pleasurably conscious of its distinction from the ruled – or among the ruled, the slaves and dependants of every degree. In the former case, when it is the rulers who determine the concept 'good', it is the exalted, proud states of soul which are considered distinguishing and determine the order of rank. The noble human being separates from himself those natures in which the opposite of such exalted proud states find expression: he despises them. It should be noted at once that in this first type of morality the antithesis 'good' and 'bad' means the same thing as 'noble' and 'despicable' – the antithesis 'good' and *'evil'* originates elsewhere. The cowardly, the timid, the petty, and those who think only of narrow utility are despised; as are the mistrustful with their constricted glance, those who abase themselves, the dog-like type of man who lets himself be mistreated, the fawning flatterer, above all the liar – it is a fundamental belief of all aristocrats that the common people are liars. 'We who are truthful' – thus did the nobility of ancient Greece designate themselves. It is immediately obvious that designations of moral value were everywhere first applied to *human beings*, and only later and derivatively to *actions*: which is why it is a grave error when moral historians start from such questions as 'why has the compassionate action been praised?' The noble type of man feels *himself* to be the determiner of values, he does not need to be approved of, he judges 'what harms me is harmful in itself', he knows himself to be that which in general first accords honour to things, he *creates values*. Everything he knows to be part of himself, he honours: such a morality is self-glorification. In the foreground stands the feeling of plenitude, of power which seeks to overflow, the happiness of high tension, the consciousness of a wealth which would like to give away and bestow – the noble human being too aids the unfortunate but not, or almost not, from pity, but more from an urge begotten by superfluity of power. The noble human being honours in himself the man of power, also the man who has power over himself, who understands how to speak and how to keep silent, who enjoys practising severity and harshness upon himself and feels reverence for all that is severe and harsh. 'A hard heart has Wotan set in my breast', it says in an old Scandinavian saga: a just expression coming from the soul of a proud Viking. A man of this type is actually proud that he is *not* made for pity: which is why the hero of the saga adds as a warning: 'he whose heart is not hard in youth will never have a hard heart'. Brave and noble men who think that are at the farthest remove from that morality which sees the mark of the moral precisely in pity or in acting for others or in *désintéressement*; belief in oneself, pride in oneself, a fundamental hostility and irony for 'selflessness' belong just as definitely to noble morality as does a mild contempt for and caution against sympathy and the 'warm heart'. – It is the powerful who *understand* how to honour, that is their art, their realm of invention. Deep reverence for age and the traditional – all law rests on this twofold reverence – belief in and prejudice in favour of ancestors and against descendants, is typical of the morality of the powerful; and when, conversely, men of 'modern ideas' believe almost instinctively in 'progress' and 'the future' and show an increasing lack of respect for age, this reveals clearly enough the ignoble origin of these 'ideas'. A morality of the rulers is, however, most alien and painful to contemporary taste in the severity of its principle that one has duties only towards one's equals; that towards beings of a lower rank, towards everything alien, one may act as one wishes or 'as the heart dictates' and in any case 'beyond good and evil' – : it is here that pity and the like can have a place. The capacity for and the duty of protracted gratitude and protracted revenge – both only among one's equals – subtlety in requittal, a refined conception of friendship, a certain need to have enemies (as conduit systems, as it were, for the emotions of envy, quarrelsomeness, arrogance – fundamentally so as to be able to be a good *friend*): all these are typical marks of noble morality which, as previously indicated, is not the morality of 'modern ideas' and is therefore hard to enter into today, also hard to unearth and uncover. – It is otherwise with the second type of morality, *slave morality*. Suppose the abused, oppressed, suffering, unfree, those uncertain of themselves and weary should moralize: what would their moral evaluations have in common? Probably a pessimistic mistrust of the entire situation of man will find expression, perhaps a condemnation of man together with his situation. The slave is suspicious of the virtues of the powerful: he is sceptical and mistrustful, *keenly* mistrustful, of everything 'good' that is honoured among them – he would like to convince himself that happiness itself is not genuine among them. On the other hand, those qualities which serve to make easier the existence of the suffering will be brought into prominence and flooded with light: here it is that pity, the kind and helping hand, the warm heart, patience, industriousness, humility, friendliness come into honour – for here these are the most useful qualities and virtually the only means of enduring the burden of existence. Slave morality is essentially the morality of utility. Here is the source of the famous antithesis 'good' and '*evil*' – power and danger were felt to exist in evil, a certain dreadfulness, subtlety and strength which could not admit of contempt. Thus, according to slave morality the 'evil' inspire fear; according to master morality it is precisely the 'good' who inspire fear and want to inspire it, while the 'bad' man is judged contemptible. The antithesis reaches its height when, consistently with slave morality, a breath of disdain finally also comes to be attached to the 'good' of this morality – it may be a slight and benevolent disdain – because within the slaves' way of thinking the good man has in any event to be a *harmless* man: he is good-natured, easy to deceive, perhaps a bit stupid, *un bonhomme*. Wherever slave morality comes to predominate, language exhibits a tendency to bring the words 'good' and 'stupid' closer to each other. – A final fundamental distinction: the longing for *freedom*, the instinct for the happiness and the refinements of the feeling of freedom, belong just as necessarily to slave morality and morals as the art of reverence and devotion and the enthusiasm for them are the regular symptom of an aristocratic mode of thinking and valuating. – This makes it clear without further ado why love *as passion* – it is our European speciality – absolutely must be of aristocratic origin: it was, as is well known, invented by the poet-knights of Provence, those splendid, inventive men of the '*gai saber*' to whom Europe owes so much and, indeed, almost itself. –

261

Among the things which a noble human being perhaps finds hardest to understand is vanity: he will be tempted to deny its existence where a different type of human being will think it palpably evident. For him the problem is to imagine creatures who try to awaken a good opinion of themselves which they themselves do not hold – and thus do not 'deserve' either – and yet subsequently come to *believe* this good opinion themselves. This seems to him in part so tasteless and lacking in self-respect and in part so baroquely irrational that he would prefer to consider vanity exceptional and in most cases where it is spoken of he doubts its existence. He will say, for example: 'I can rate my value incorrectly and yet demand that others too should recognize my value exactly as I rate it – but that is not vanity (but self-conceit, or, more usually, what is called "humility" or "modesty").' Or he will say: 'I can, for many reasons, take pleasure in the good opinion of others, perhaps because I love and honour them and take pleasure in all their pleasures, perhaps because their good opinion sustains me in my faith in my own good opinion, perhaps because the good opinion of others, even when I do not share it, is still useful to me or promises to be useful – but none of this is vanity.' The noble human being requires the assistance of history if he is to see that, from time immemorial, in all strata which were in any way dependent the common man *was* only that which he *counted as* – in no way accustomed to positing values himself, he also accorded himself no other value than that which his master accorded him (it is the intrinsic *right of*

masters to create values). It can be conceived as the consequence of a tremendous atavism that even now the ordinary
man still always *waits* for an opinion about himself and then
instinctively submits to it: but this happens not merely in the
case of a 'good' opinion, but also in that of a bad and unfair
one (consider, for instance, the greater part of the self-esti-
mates and self-underestimates which believing women acquire
from their father-confessors and the believing Christian
acquires from his Church). Now it is a fact that, in accordance
with the slow rise of the democratic order of things (and its
cause, the mixing of the blood of masters and slaves), the
originally noble and rare impulse to ascribe a value to oneself
on one's own account and to 'think well' of oneself will be
increasingly encouraged and spread wider and wider: but it
has at all times an older, more widespread and more thoroughly ingrained inclination against it – and in the phenomenon of 'vanity' this older inclination masters the younger.
The vain man takes pleasure in *every* good opinion he hears
about himself (quite apart from any point of view of utility
and likewise regardless of truth or falsehood), just as he
suffers from every bad opinion: for he submits to both, he
feels subject to them from that oldest instinct of subjection
which breaks out in him. – It is 'the slave' in the vain man's
blood, a remnant of the craftiness of the slave – and how
much 'slave' still remains in woman, for example! – which
seeks to *seduce* him to good opinions about himself; it is
likewise the slave who immediately afterwards falls down
before these opinions as if he himself had not called them
forth. – And to say it again: vanity is an atavism.

262

A *species* arises, a type becomes fixed and strong, through
protracted struggle against essentially constant *unfavourable*
conditions. Conversely, one knows from the experience of
breeders that species which receive plentiful nourishment and
an excess of care and protection soon tend very strongly to
produce variations of their type and are rich in marvels and

monstrosities (also in monstrous vices). Now look for once at an aristocratic community, Venice, say, or an ancient Greek *polis*, as a voluntary or involuntary contrivance for the purpose of *breeding*: there there are human beings living together and thrown on their own resources who want their species to prevail usually because they *have* to prevail or run the terrible risk of being exterminated. Here those favourable conditions, that excess, that protection which favours variations, is lacking; the species needs itself as species, as something that can prevail and purchase durability in its continual struggle against its neighbours or against the oppressed in revolt or threatening revolt, precisely by virtue of its hardness, uniformity, simplicity of form. The most manifold experience teaches it which qualities it has principally to thank that, in spite of all gods and men, it still exists and has always been victorious: these qualities it calls virtues, these virtues alone does it breed and cultivate. It does so with severity, indeed it wants severity; every aristocratic morality is intolerant, in the education of the young, in the measures it takes with respect to women, in marriage customs, in the relations between young and old, in the penal laws (which are directed only at variants) – it counts intolerance itself among the virtues under the name 'justice'. A type with few but very marked traits, a species of stern, warlike, prudently silent, determined and taciturn men (and, as such, men of the finest feeling for the charm and *nuances* of society), is in this way firmly fixed beyond the changes of generations; continual struggle against ever-constant *unfavourable* conditions is, as aforesaid, that which fixes and hardens a type. In the end, however, there arises one day an easier state of affairs and the tremendous tension relaxes; perhaps there are no longer any enemies among their neighbours, and the means of life, even for the enjoyment of life, are there in plenty. With one stroke the bond and constraint of the ancient discipline is broken: it is no longer felt to be a necessity, a condition of existence – if it were to persist it could be only as a form of *luxury*, as an archaizing *taste*. Variation, whether as deviation (into the higher, rarer, more refined) or as degeneration and monstrosity, is suddenly on the scene in the greatest splendour and abundance, the individual dares to be individual and stand out. At these turning-points of history there appear side by side and often entangled and entwined together a glorious, manifold, jungle-like growth and up-stirring, a kind of *tropical* tempo in competition in growing, and a tremendous perishing and self-destruction, thanks to the savage egoisms which, turning on one another and as it were exploding, wrestle together 'for sun and light' and no longer know how to draw any limitation, any restraint, any forbearance from the morality reigning hitherto. It was this morality which stored up such enormous energy, which bent the bow in such a threatening manner – now it is 'spent', now it is becoming 'outlived'. The dangerous and uncanny point is reached where the grander, more manifold, more comprehensive life *lives beyond* the old morality; the 'individual' stands there, reduced to his own law-giving, to his own arts and stratagems for self-preservation, self-enhancement, self-redemption. Nothing but new whys and wherewithalls, no longer any common formulas, misunderstanding in alliance with disrespect, decay, corruption and the highest desires horribly tangled together, the genius of the race overflowing out of every cornucopia of good and bad, spring and autumn falling fatally together, full of novel charms and veils such as pertain to youthful, still unexhausted, still unwearied corruption. Danger is again present, the mother of morality, great danger, only this time it comes from the individual, from neighbour and friend, from the street, from one's own child, from one's own heart, from the most personal and secret recesses of wish and will: what will the moral philosophers who come up in this age now have to preach? They discover, these acute observers and idlers, that the end is fast approaching, that everything around them is corrupt and corrupting, that nothing can last beyond the day after tomorrow, *one* species of man excepted, the incurably *mediocre*. The mediocre alone have the prospect of continuing on and propagating themselves – they are the men of the future, the sole survivors; 'be like them! become mediocre!' is henceforth the only morality that has any meaning left, that still finds ears to

hear it. – But it is difficult to preach, this morality of mediocrity! – for it can never admit what it is and what it wants! it
has to speak of moderation and dignity and duty and love of
one's neighbour – it will scarcely be able to *conceal its irony*! –

263

There is an *instinct for rank* which is more than anything else
already the sign of a high rank; there is a *delight* in the nuances
of reverence, which reveals a noble origin and noble habits.
The refinement, goodness and loftiness of a soul is put to a
perilous test whenever something passes before it that is of
the first rank but not yet protected from importunate clumsiness and claws by the awe of authority: something that goes
its way unsignalized, undiscovered, tempting, perhaps arbitrarily obscured and disguised, like a living touchstone. He
whose task and practice it is to explore the soul will avail
himself of precisely this art in many forms in order to determine the ultimate value of a soul, the unalterable innate order
of rank to which it belongs: he will test it for its *instinct of
reverence*. *Différence engendre haine*: the commonness of some
natures suddenly spurts up like dirty water whenever some
sacred vessel, some precious object from a closed shrine, some
book with the marks of a great destiny is carried by; and on
the other hand there is an involuntary falling silent, a hesitation of the eye, a cessation of all gestures, which reveal that a
soul *feels* the proximity of something most worthy of respect.
The way in which reverence for the *Bible* has hitherto been
generally maintained in Europe is perhaps the best piece of
discipline and refinement of manners that Europe owes to
Christianity: such books of profundity and ultimate significance require for their protection an external tyranny of
authority, in order that they may achieve those millennia of
continued existence which are needed if they are to be exhausted
and unriddled. Much has been gained when the feeling has at
last been instilled into the masses (into the shallow-pates and
greedy-guts of every sort) that there are things they must not
touch; that there are holy experiences before which they have

to take off their shoes and keep their unclean hands away – it is almost their highest advance towards humanity. Conversely, there is perhaps nothing about the so-called cultured, the believers in 'modern ideas', that arouses so much disgust as their lack of shame, the self-satisfied insolence of eye and hand with which they touch, lick and fumble with everything; and it is possible that more *relative* nobility of taste and reverential tact is to be discovered today among the people, among the lower orders and especially among peasants, than among the newspaper-reading *demi-monde* of the spirit, the cultured.

264

That which his ancestors most liked to do and most constantly did cannot be erased from a man's soul: whether, for instance, they were diligent savers and the accessories of a desk and cash-box, modest and bourgeois in their desires, modest also in their virtues; or whether they lived accustomed to command-ing from morn to night, fond of rough amusements and perhaps of even rougher duties and responsibilities; or whether, finally, they at some time or other sacrificed ancient privileges of birth and possessions in order to live entirely for their faith – for their 'god' – as men of an inexorable and tender conscience which blushes at all half-measures. It is quite impossible that a man should *not* have in his body the qualities and preferences of his parents and forefathers: what-ever appearances may say to the contrary. This constitutes the problem of race. If one knows something about the parents, it is permissible to draw a conclusion about the child: any sort of untoward intemperance, any sort of narrow enviousness, a clumsy obstinate self-assertiveness – these three things to-gether have at all times constituted the characteristics of the plebeian type – qualities of this sort must be transferred to the child as surely as bad blood; and the best education and culture will succeed only in *deceiving* with regard to such an inheritance. – And what else is the objective of education and culture today? In our very democratic, that is to say plebeian age, 'education' and 'culture' *have* to be in essence the art of deceiving – of deceiving with regard to origins, to the inherited plebeian in soul and body. An educator who today preached truthfulness above all and continually cried to his pupils 'Be true! Be natural! Give yourselves out for what you are!' – even such a virtuous and simple ass would after a time learn to reach for that *furca* of Horace to *naturam expellere*: with what success? 'The plebeian' *usque recurret*. –

265

At the risk of annoying innocent ears I set it down that egoism pertains to the essence of the noble soul, I mean the immovable faith that to a being such as 'we are' other beings have to be subordinate by their nature, and sacrifice themselves to us. The noble soul accepts this fact of its egoism without any question-mark, also without feeling any severity, constraint, caprice in it, but rather as something that may be grounded in the primal law of things: – if it sought a name for it, it would say 'it is justice itself'. Under certain circumstances which make it hesitate at first, it will admit that there are others with rights equal to its own; as soon as it is clear as to this question of rank, it moves among these its equals and equal-in-rights with the same sure modesty and tender reverence as it applies to itself – in accordance with an innate celestial mechanism which all stars understand. This refinement and self-limitation in traffic with its equals is one *more* aspect of its egoism – every star is such an egoist – : it honours *itself* in them and in the rights it concedes them, it is in no doubt that the exchange of honours and rights, as the *essence* of social intercourse, is likewise part of the natural condition of things. The noble soul gives as it takes, out of the passionate and sensitive instinct of requital which lies in its depths. The concept 'favour' has no meaning or good odour *inter pares*; there may be a sublime way of letting gifts from above as it were befall one and drinking them up thirstily like drops: but for this sort of behaviour the noble soul has no aptitude. Its egoism hinders it here: it does not like to look 'up' at all – it prefers to look either *in front*, horizontally and slowly, or down – *it knows it is at a height.* –

266

'One can truly respect only him who does not *look out* for himself.' – Goethe to Rat Schlosser.

267

The Chinese have a proverb which mothers even teach their children: *siao-sin*: 'Make your heart *small*!' This is the characteristic basic tendency in late civilizations: I do not doubt that the first thing an ancient Greek would remark in us Europeans of today would also be self-diminution – through that alone we should be 'contrary to his taste'. –

268

What ultimately is commonness? – Words are sounds designating concepts; concepts, however, are more or less definite images designating frequently recurring and associated sensations, groups of sensations. To understand one another it is not sufficient to employ the same words; we have also to employ the same words to designate the same species of inner experiences, we must ultimately have our experience *in common*. That is why the members of *one* people understand one another better than do members of differing peoples even when they use the same language; or rather, when human beings have lived together for a long time under similar conditions (of climate, soil, danger, needs, work), there *arises* from this a group who 'understand one another', a people. In every soul in this group an equivalent number of frequently recurring experiences has gained the upper hand over those which come more rarely: it is on the basis of these that people understand one another, quickly and ever more quickly – the history of language is the history of a process of abbreviation –; it is on the basis of this quick understanding that they unite together, closely and ever more closely. The greater the danger, the greater is the need to reach agreement quickly and easily as to what has to be done; not to misunderstand one another in situations of danger is an absolute necessity in human relations. One makes this same test even in the case of friendships or love-affairs: nothing of that sort can last once it is discovered that when one party uses words he connects them with feelings, intentions, perceptions, desires, fears different from those the other party connects them with. (Fear of the 'eternal misunderstanding': that is the benevolent genius who so often keeps persons of differing sex from over-hasty attachments to which senses and heart prompt them – and *not* some Schopenhaueran 'genius of the species' – !) Exactly which groups of sensations are awakened, begin to speak, issue commands most quickly within a soul, is decisive for the whole order of rank of its values and ultimately determines its table of desiderata. A human being's evaluations betray something of the *structure* of his soul and where it sees its conditions of life, its real needs. Now supposing that need has at all times brought together only such human beings as could indicate similar requirements, similar experiences by means of similar signs, it follows that on the whole the easy *communicability* of need, that is to say ultimately the experiencing of only average and *common* experiences, must have been the most powerful of all the powerful forces which have disposed of mankind hitherto. The more similar, more ordinary human beings have had and still have the advantage, the more select, subtle, rare and harder to understand are liable to remain alone, succumb to accidents in their isolation and seldom propagate themselves. Tremendous counter-forces have to be called upon to cross this natural, all too natural *progressus in simile*, the continuing development of mankind into the similar, ordinary, average, herdlike – into the *common*!

269

The more a psychologist – a born, an unavoidable psychologist and reader of souls – turns his attention to the more select cases and human beings, the greater grows the danger of his suffocating from pity: he *needs* hardness and cheerfulness more than other men. For the corruption, the ruination of higher human beings, of more strangely constituted souls, is the rule: it is dreadful to have such a rule always before one's eyes. The manifold torment of the psychologist who has discovered this ruination, who discovers this whole inner 'wretchedness' of the higher human being, this eternal 'too late!' in every sense, first once and then *almost* always throughout the whole of history – may perhaps one day make him turn against his whole lot and drive him to attempt self-destruction – to his own 'ruination'. One will perceive in almost every psychologist a telltale preference for and pleasure in associating with everyday and well-ordered people: this betrays that he is in constant need of a cure, that he requires a kind of flight and forgetting, away from that which his insights and incisions, his 'trade', has laid upon his conscience. It is characteristic of him that he is afraid of his memory. He is easily silenced by the judgement of others: he listens with a straight face when people venerate, admire, love, transfigure where he has *seen* – or he conceals even his silence by expressly agreeing with some superficial opinion. Perhaps the paradox of his situation is so ghastly that precisely where he has learned great pity together with great contempt the mob, the cultured, the enthusiasts learn great veneration – veneration for 'great men' and prodigies on whose account they bless the fatherland, the earth, the dignity of mankind and themselves, in whose direction they point the young and on whose model they educate them. . . . And who knows whether what has happened hitherto in all great cases has not always been the same thing: that the mob worshipped a god – and that the 'god' was only a poor sacrificial beast! Success has always been the biggest liar – and the 'work' itself a kind of success; the great statesman, the conqueror, the discoverer is disguised by his creations to the point of unrecognizability: the 'work', that of the artist or the philosopher, invents him who created it, is supposed to have created it; 'great men', as they are venerated, are bad little fictions invented afterwards;

in the world of historical values false coinage *is the rule*. Great
poets, for example, such as Byron, Musset, Poe, Leopardi,
Kleist, Gogol (I do not dare to name greater names, but I
mean them) – as they are and perhaps have to be: men of
moments, enthusiastic, sensual, childish, sudden and frivolous
in trust and mistrust; with souls in which some fracture is
usually trying to hide; often taking revenge with their works
for an inner defilement, often seeking with their exaggerations
forgetfulness of an all too faithful memory, often lost in the
mud and almost in love with it, until they become like will-o'-
the-wisps around swamps and *pretend* to be stars – the people
may then call them idealists – often struggling against a
protracted disgust, a recurring spectre of unbelief which
freezes them and compels them to languish for *gloria* and to
devour 'belief in themselves' out of the hands of intoxicated
adulators – what a *torment* these great artists and higher
human beings in general are for him who has once divined
what they are! It is so very understandable that they should so
easily receive precisely from woman – who is clairvoyante in
the world of suffering and unfortunately also eager to help
and save far beyond her power to do so – those outbursts of
boundless, most devoted *pity* which the mob, above all the
venerating mob, fails to understand and loads with inquisitive
and self-satisfied interpretations. This pity habitually deceives
itself about its strength; woman would like to believe that
love can do *everything* – it is her characteristic *faith*. Alas, he
who knows the heart divines how poor, stupid, helpless,
arrogant, blundering, more prone to destroy than save is even
the best and deepest love! – It is possible that within the holy
disguise and fable of Jesus' life there lies concealed one of the
most painful cases of the martyrdom of *knowledge about love*:
the martyrdom of the most innocent and longing heart which
never had sufficient of human love, which *demanded* love, to
be loved and nothing else, demanded it with hardness, with
madness, with fearful outbursts against those who denied it
love; the story of a poor soul unsated and insatiable in love
who had to invent hell so as to send there those who did not
want to love him – and who, having become knowledgeable

about human love, finally had to invent a god who is wholly love, wholly *ability* to love – who has mercy on human love because it is so very paltry and ignorant! He whose feelings are like this, he who *knows* about love to this extent – *seeks* death. – But why reflect on such painful things? As long as one does not have to. –

270

The spiritual haughtiness and disgust of every human being who has suffered deeply – *how* deeply human beings can suffer almost determines their order of rank – the harrowing certainty, with which he is wholly permeated and coloured, that by virtue of his suffering he *knows more* than even the cleverest and wisest can know, that he is familiar with, and was once 'at home' in, many distant, terrible worlds of which '*you* know nothing!' . . . this spiritual, silent haughtiness of the sufferer, this pride of the elect of knowledge, of the 'initiated', of the almost sacrificed, finds all forms of disguise necessary to protect itself against contact with importunate and pitying hands and in general against everything which is not its equal in suffering. Profound suffering ennobles; it separates. One of the most subtle forms of disguise is Epicureanism and a certain ostentatious bravery of taste which takes suffering frivolously and arms itself against everything sorrowful and profound. There are 'cheerful people' who employ cheerfulness because they are misunderstood on account of it – they *want* to be misunderstood. There are 'men of science' who employ science because it produces a cheerful appearance and because scientificality gives the impression a person is superficial – they *want* to give a false impression. There are free insolent spirits who would like to conceal and deny that they are broken, proud, incurable hearts (the cynicism of Hamlet – the case of Galiani); and sometimes folly itself is the mask for an unhappy, all too certain knowledge. – From which it follows that it is part of a more refined humanity to have reverence 'for the mask' and not to practise psychology and inquisitiveness in the wrong place.

271

That which divides two people most profoundly is a differing sense and degree of cleanliness. Of what good is all uprightness and mutual usefulness, of what good is mutual good will: the fact still remains – they 'cannot bear each other's odour!' The highest instinct of cleanliness places him who is affected with it in the strangest and most perilous isolation, as a saint: for precisely this is saintliness – the highest spiritualization of the said instinct. To know an indescribable pleasure in bathing, to feel an ardour and thirst which constantly drives the soul out of night into morning, and out of gloom and 'gloominess' into brightness, into the glittering, profound, refined – : such an inclination is *distinguishing* – it is a noble inclination – but it also *separates*. – The saint's pity is pity for the *dirt* of the human, all too human. And there are degrees and heights at which he feels pity itself as defilement, as dirt . . .

272

Signs of nobility: never to think of degrading our duties into duties for everybody; not to want to relinquish or share our own responsibilities; to count our privileges and the exercising of them among our *duties*.

273

A human being who strives for something great regards everybody he meets on his way either as a means or as a delay and hindrance – or as a temporary resting-place. The lofty *goodness* towards his fellow men which is proper to him becomes possible only when he has reached his height and he rules. Impatience and his consciousness that until that time he is condemned to comedy – for even war is a comedy and a concealment, just as every means conceals the end – spoil all his association with others: this kind of man knows solitude and what is most poisonous in it.

274

The problem of those who wait – It requires luck and much that is incalculable if a higher human being in whom there slumbers the solution of a problem is to act – 'break out' one might say – at the right time. Usually it does *not* happen, and in every corner of the earth there are people waiting who hardly know to what extent they are waiting but even less that they are waiting in vain. Sometimes the awakening call, that chance event which gives 'permission' to act, comes but too late – when the best part of youth and the strength to act has already been used up in sitting still; and how many a man has discovered to his horror when he 'rose up' that his limbs had gone to sleep and his spirit was already too heavy! 'It is too late' – he has said to himself, having lost faith in himself and henceforth for ever useless. Could it be that, in the realm of genius, 'Raphael without hands' is, taking the phrase in its widest sense, not the exception but the rule? – Perhaps genius is not so very rare: perhaps what is rare is the five hundred *hands* needed to tyrannize over the *kairos*, 'the right time' – to take chance by the forelock!

275

He who does not *want* to see what is elevated in a man looks all the more keenly for what is low and foreground in him – and thereby gives himself away.

276

In every kind of injury and loss the lower and coarser soul is better off than the nobler: the dangers facing the latter are bound to be greater, the probability that it will come to grief and perish is, considering the multiplicity of the conditions of its life, enormous. – When a lizard loses a finger that finger grows again: not so in the case of man. –

277

– Annoying! The same old story! When one has finished one's house one realizes that while doing so one has learnt unawares something one absolutely *had* to know before one – began to build. The everlasting pitiful 'too late!' – The melancholy of everything *finished*! . . .

278

– Wanderer, who are you? I see you go your way without scorn, without love, with unfathomable eyes; moist and sad as a sounding-lead that has returned to the light unsated from every deep – what was it looking for down there? – with a breast that does not sigh, with a lip that hides its disgust, with a hand which now reaches out but slowly: who are you? what have you done? Repose here: this place is hospitable to everyone – refresh yourself! And whoever you may be: what would you like now? What will refresh you? You have only to name it: whatever I have I offer you! – 'Refreshment? Refreshment? O inquisitive man, what are you saying! But please give me –' What? What? Say it – 'One more mask! A second mask!' . . .

279

Men of profound sorrow give themselves away when they are happy: they have a way of grasping happiness as if they wanted to crush and smother it, from jealousy – alas, they know too well that it will flee away.

280

'Bad! Bad! What? Is he not going – backwards?' – Yes! But you ill understand him if you complain about it. He goes backwards as everyone goes backwards who wants to take a big jump. –

281

'Will they believe me? but I insist they believe me: I have always thought little of and about myself, only in very rare instances have I done so, only when compelled, always without wanting "to go in for it", liable to digress from "myself", never with any faith in the outcome, thanks to an unconquerable mistrust of the *possibility* of self-knowledge which has led me so far as to sense a *contradictio in adjecto* even in the concept "immediate knowledge" which theoreticians permit themselves – this whole fact is almost the most certain thing I know about myself. There must be a kind of aversion in me to *believing* anything definite about myself. – Is there perhaps a riddle concealed here? Probably; but fortunately one not for my own teeth. – Does it perhaps betray the species to which I belong? – But not to me: which suits me well enough. –'

282

'But whatever has happened to you?' – 'I don't know,' he said, hesitating; 'perhaps the Harpies flew over my table.' – It sometimes happens today that a mild, moderate, reserved man suddenly breaks out into a rage, smashes the plates, throws the table over, screams, raves, insults everybody – and ends by going off ashamed, furious with himself – where? why? To starve all alone? To choke on his recollections? – He who has the desires of an elevated, fastidious soul, and rarely finds his table laid and his food ready, will be in great danger at all times: but today the danger he is in has become extraordinary. Thrown into a noisy and plebeian age with which he has no wish to eat out of the same dish, he can easily perish of hunger and thirst, or, if he does eventually 'set to' – of a sudden nausea. – We have all no doubt eaten at tables where we did not belong; and precisely the most spiritual of us who are most difficult to feed know that dangerous dyspepsia which comes from a sudden insight and disappointment about our food and table-companions – the *after-dinner nausea*.

283

Supposing one wants to praise at all, it is a refined and at the same time noble piece of self-control to praise only where one does *not* agree – for in the other case one would be praising oneself, which is contrary to good taste – but it is a sort of self-control which offers a nice instigation and occasion for constantly being *misunderstood*. If one is to be able to afford this real luxury of taste and morality one has to live, not among blockheads of the spirit, but rather among people in whom misunderstandings and blunders are still amusing because of their subtlety – or one will have to pay dearly for it! – 'He praises me: *therefore* he thinks I am right' – this asinine conclusion spoils half the life of us hermits, for it makes asses come along to be our friends and neighbours.

284

To live with a tremendous and proud self-possession; always beyond –. To have and not have one's emotions, one's for and against, at will, to condescend to have them for a few hours; to *seat* oneself on them as on horses, often as on asses – for one has to know how to employ their stupidity as well as their fire. To keep one's three hundred foregrounds; also one's dark glasses: for there are instances where no one may look into our eyes, still less into our 'grounds'. And to choose for company that cheerful and roguish vice, politeness. And to remain master of one's four virtues, courage, insight, sympathy, solitude. For solitude is with us a virtue: it is a sublime urge and inclination for cleanliness which divines that all contact between man and man – 'in society' – must inevitably be unclean. All community makes somehow, somewhere, sometime – 'common'

285

The greatest events and thoughts – but the greatest thoughts are the greatest events – are comprehended last: the generations which are their contemporaries do not *experience* such events – they live past them. What happens here is similar to what happens in the realm of the stars. The light of the furthest stars comes to men last; and before it has arrived man *denies* that there are – stars there. 'How many centuries does a spirit need to be comprehended?' – that too is a standard, with that too there is created an order of rank and etiquette such as is needed: for spirit and star. –

286

'Here is the prospect free, the spirit exalted.' – But there is an opposite kind of man who is also on the heights and for whom the prospect is also free – but who looks *down*.

287

– What is noble? What does the word 'noble' mean to us today? What, beneath this heavy, overcast sky of the beginning rule of the rabble which makes everything leaden and opaque, betrays and makes evident the noble human being? – It is not his actions which reveal him – actions are always ambiguous, always unfathomable –; neither is it his 'works'. One finds today among artists and scholars sufficient who reveal by their works that they are driven on by a profound desire for the noble: but precisely this need *for* the noble is fundamentally different from the needs of the noble soul itself, and in fact an eloquent and dangerous sign of its lack. It is not the works, it is the *faith* which is decisive here, which determines the order of rank here, to employ an old religious formula in a new and deeper sense: some fundamental certainty which a noble soul possesses in regard to itself, something which may not be sought or found and perhaps may not be lost either. – *The noble soul has reverence for itself.* –

288

There are people unavoidably possessed of spirit, let them twist and turn how they may and hold their hands before their treacherous eyes (– as if the hand were not also a traitor! –): in the end it always comes out that they have something they are hiding, namely spirit. One of the subtlest ways of deceiving, for as long as possible at any rate, and of successfully posing as more stupid than one is – which in everyday life is often as desirable as an umbrella – is called *enthusiasm*: plus what belongs with it, for example virtue. For, as Galiani, who ought to know, said – : *vertu est enthousiasme*.

289

One always hears in the writings of a hermit something of the echo of the desert, something of the whisper and shy vigilance of solitude; in his strongest words, even in his cry, there still resounds a new and more dangerous kind of silence and concealment. He who has sat alone with his soul day and night, year in year out, in confidential discord and discourse, and in his cave – it may be a labyrinth, but it may be a gold-mine – become a cave-bear or treasure-hunter or a treasure-guardian and dragon, finds that his concepts themselves at last acquire a characteristic twilight colour, a smell of the depths and of must, something incommunicable and reluctant which blows cold on every passer-by. The hermit does not believe that a philosopher – supposing that a philosopher has always been first of all a hermit – has ever expressed his real and final opinions in books: does one not write books precisely to conceal what lies within us? – indeed, he will doubt whether a philosopher *could* have 'final and real' opinions at all, whether behind each of his caves there does not and must not lie another, deeper cave – a stranger, more comprehensive world beyond the surface, an abyss behind every ground, beneath every 'foundation'. Every philosophy is a foreground philos-ophy – that is a hermit's judgement: 'there is something arbitrary in the fact that *he* stopped, looked back, looked around here, that he stopped digging and laid his spade aside *here* – there is also something suspicious about it.' Every philosophy also *conceals* a philosophy; every opinion is also a hiding-place, every word also a mask.

290

Every profound thinker is more afraid of being understood than of being misunderstood. The latter may perhaps wound his vanity; but the former will wound his heart, his sympathy, which says always: 'alas, why do *you* want to have as hard a time of it as I had?'

291

Man, a manifold, mendacious, artificial and untransparent animal, uncanny to the other animals less on account of his strength than on account of his cunning and cleverness, invented the good conscience so as to enjoy his soul for once as *simple*; and the whole of morality is a protracted audacious forgery by virtue of which alone it becomes possible to feel pleasure at the sight of the soul. From this point of view there is perhaps much more in the concept 'art' than is generally believed.

292

A philosopher: a man who constantly experiences, sees, hears, suspects, hopes, dreams extraordinary things; who is struck by his own thoughts as if from without, as if from above and below, as by *his* kind of events and thunder-claps; who is himself perhaps a storm and pregnant with new lightnings; a fateful man around whom snarling, quarrelling, discord and uncanniness is always going on. A philosopher: alas, a creature which often runs away from itself, is often afraid of itself – but which is too inquisitive not to keep 'coming to itself' again . . .

293

A man who says: 'I like this, I take it for my own and mean to protect it and defend it against everyone'; a man who can do something, carry out a decision, remain true to an idea, hold on to a woman, punish and put down insolence; a man who has his anger and his sword and to whom the weak, suffering, oppressed, and the animals too are glad to submit and belong by nature, in short a man who is by nature a *master* – when such a man has pity, well! *that* pity has value! But of what account is the pity of those who suffer! Or, worse, of those who *preach* pity! There exists almost everywhere in Europe today a morbid sensitivity and susceptibility to pain, likewise a repellent intemperance in lamentation, a tenderization which, with the aid of religion and odds and ends of philosophy, would like to deck itself out as something higher – there exists a downright cult of suffering. The *unmanliness* of that which is in such fanatic circles baptized 'pity' is, I think, the first thing which leaps to the eye. – This latest species of bad taste must be resolutely and radically excommunicated; and I would like to see the good amulet *'gai saber'* worn around neck and hearts so as to ward it off – 'gay science', to make the matter plain.

294

The Olympian vice – In spite of that philosopher who, being a real Englishman, sought to bring laughter into disrepute among all thinking minds – 'laughter is a bad infirmity of human nature which every thinking man will endeavour to overcome' (Hobbes) – I would go so far as to venture an order of rank among philosophers according to the rank of their laughter – rising to those capable of *golden* laughter. And if gods too philosophize, as many an inference has driven me to suppose – I do not doubt that while doing so they also know how to laugh in a new and superhuman way – and at the expense of all serious things! Gods are fond of mockery: it seems they cannot refrain from laughter even when sacraments are in progress.

295

The genius of the heart as it is possessed by that great hidden one, the tempter god and born pied piper of consciences

whose voice knows how to descend into the underworld of
every soul, who says no word and gives no glance in which
there lies no touch of enticement, to whose mastery belongs
knowing how to seem – not what he is but what to those who
follow him is one constraint *more* to press ever closer to him,
to follow him ever more inwardly and thoroughly – the genius
of the heart who makes everything loud and self-satisfied fall
silent and teaches it to listen, who smooths rough souls and
gives them a new desire to savour – the desire to lie still as a
mirror, that the deep sky may mirror itself in them – ; the
genius of the heart who teaches the stupid and hasty hand to
hesitate and grasp more delicately; who divines the hidden
and forgotten treasure, the drop of goodness and sweet spirituality under thick and opaque ice, and is a divining-rod for
every grain of gold which has lain long in the prison of much
mud and sand; the genius of the heart from whose touch
everyone goes away richer, not favoured and surprised, not as
if blessed and oppressed with the goods of others, but richer
in himself, newer to himself than before, broken open, blown
upon and sounded out by a thawing wind, more uncertain
perhaps, more delicate, more fragile, more broken, but full of
hopes that as yet have no names, full of new will and current,
full of new ill will and counter-current ... but what am I
doing, my friends? Of whom am I speaking to you? Have I so
far forgot myself that I have not even told you his name?
Unless you have already yourselves divined who this questionable god and spirit is who wants to be *praised* in such a
fashion. For as happens to everyone who has always been on
the move and in foreign lands from his childhood up, so
many a strange and not undangerous spirit has crossed my
path too, but above all he of whom I was just speaking, and
he again and again, no less a personage in fact than the god
Dionysus, that great ambiguous and tempter god to whom, as
you know, once I brought in all secrecy and reverence my
first-born – being, as it seems to me, the last to have brought
him a *sacrifice*: for I have found no one who could have
understood what I was then doing. Meanwhile, I have learned
much, all too much more about the philosophy of this god

and, as I have said, from mouth to mouth – I, the last disciple and initiate of the god Dionysus: and perhaps I might at last begin to give you, my friends, a little taste of this philosophy, in so far as I am permitted to? In a hushed voice, as is only proper: for it involves much that is secret, new, unfamiliar, strange, uncanny. The very fact that Dionysus is a philosopher, and that gods too therefore philosophize, seems a by no means harmless novelty and one calculated to excite suspicion precisely among philosophers – among you, my friends, it will meet with a friendlier reception, unless it comes too late and not at the right time: for, as I have discovered, you no longer like to believe in God and gods now. Perhaps I shall also have to go further in the frankness of my story than may always be agreeable to the strict habits of your ears? Certainly the above-named god went further, very much further, in conversations of this sort, and was always many steps ahead of me. . . . Indeed, if it were permitted to follow the human custom of applying to him beautiful, solemn titles of pomp and virtue, I would have to extol his courage as investigator and discoverer, his daring honesty, truthfulness and love of wisdom. But such a god has nothing to do with all this venerable lumber and pomp. 'Keep that,' he would say, 'for yourself and your like and for anyone else who needs it! I – have no reason to cover my nakedness!' – One will see that this species of divinity and philosopher is perhaps lacking in shame? – Thus he once said: 'Under certain circumstances I love mankind' – alluding to Ariadne, who was present – : 'Man is to me an agreeable, brave, ingenious animal without equal on earth, he knows how to make his way through every labyrinth. I like him: I often ponder how I might advance him and make him stronger, more evil and more profound than he is.' – 'Stronger, more evil and more profound?' I asked in alarm. 'Yes,' he repeated, 'stronger, more evil and more profound; also more beautiful' – and as he said that the tempter god smiled his halcyon smile, as though he had just paid a charming compliment. Here one will also see that this divinity is lacking not only in shame – ; and there is in general good reason to suppose that in several respects the gods could all benefit from instruction by us human beings. We human beings are – more humane . . .

296

Alas, and yet what *are* you, my written and painted thoughts! It is not long ago that you were still so many-coloured, young and malicious, so full of thorns and hidden spices you made me sneeze and laugh – and now? You have already taken off your novelty and some of you, I fear, are on the point of becoming truths: they already look so immortal, so pathetically righteous, so boring! And has it ever been otherwise? For what things do we write and paint, we mandarins with Chinese brushes, we immortalizers of things which *let* themselves be written, what alone are we capable of painting? Alas, only that which is about to wither and is beginning to lose its fragrance! Alas, only storms departing exhausted and feelings grown old and yellow! Alas, only birds strayed and grown weary in flight who now let themselves be caught in the hand – in *our* hand! We immortalize that which cannot live and fly much longer, weary and mellow things alone! And it is only your *afternoon*, my written and painted thoughts, for which alone I have the colours, many colours perhaps, many many-coloured tendernesses and fifty yellows and browns and greens and reds: – but no one will divine from these how you looked in your morning, you sudden sparks and wonders of my solitude, you my old beloved – *wicked* thoughts!

From High Mountains: Epode

Oh life's midday! Oh festival! Oh garden of summer! I wait in restless ecstasy, I stand and watch and wait – where are you, friends? It is you I await, in readiness day and night. Come now! It is time you were here!

Was it not for you the glacier today exchanged its grey for roses? The brook seeks you; and wind and clouds press higher in the blue, longingly they crowd aloft to look for you.

For you have I prepared my table in the highest height – who lives so near the stars as I, or who so near the depths of the abyss? My empire – has an empire ever reached so far? And my honey – who has tasted the sweetness of it?

– And there you *are*, friends! – But, alas, am *I* not he you came to visit? You hesitate, you stare – no, be angry, rather! Is it no longer – I? Are hand, step, face transformed? And *what* I am, to you friends – I am not?

Am I another? A stranger to myself? Sprung from myself? A wrestler who subdued himself too often? Turned his own strength against himself too often, checked and wounded by his own victory?

Did I seek where the wind bites keenest, learn to live where no one lives, in the desert where only the polar bear lives, unlearn to pray and curse, unlearn man and god, become a ghost flitting across the glaciers?

– Old friends! how pale you look, how full of love and terror! No – be gone! Be not angry! Here – *you* could not be at home: here in this far domain of ice and rocks – here you must be a huntsman, and like the Alpine goat.

A *wicked* huntsman is what I have become! – See how bent my bow! He who drew that bow, surely he was the mightiest of men – : but the arrow, alas – ah, *no* arrow is dangerous as *that* arrow is dangerous – away! be gone! For your own preservation! . . .

You turn away? – O heart, you have borne up well, your hopes stayed strong: now keep your door open to *new* friends! Let the old go! Let memories go! If once you were young, now – you are younger!

What once united us, the bond of *one* hope – who still can read the signs love once inscribed therein, now faint and faded? It is like a parchment – discoloured, scorched – from which the hand *shrinks back.*

No longer friends, but – what shall I call them? – they are the ghosts of friends which at my heart and window knock at night, which gaze on me and say: '*were* we once friends?' – oh faded word, once fragrant as the rose!

Oh longing of youth, which did not know itself! Those *I* longed for, those I deemed changed into kin of mine – that they have *aged* is what has banished them: only he who changes remains akin to me.

Oh life's midday! Oh second youth! Oh garden of summer! I wait in restless ecstasy, I stand and watch and wait – it is friends I await, in readiness day and night, *new* friends. Come now! It is time you were here!

This song is done – desire's sweet cry died on the lips: a sorcerer did it, the timely friend, the midday friend – no! ask not who he is – at midday it happened, at midday one became two . . .

Now, sure of victory together, we celebrate the feast of feasts: friend *Zarathustra* has come, the guest of guests! Now the world is laughing, the dread curtain is rent, the wedding day has come for light and darkness . . .

COMMENTARY

The dates of Nietzsche's main works referred to in the following commentary are:

1872 *The Birth of Tragedy* (3rd edn 1886)
1873 *David Strauss* (*Untimely Meditations* I)
1874 *On the Use and Disadvantage of History for Life* (*Untimely Meditations* II)
      Schopenhauer as Educator (*Untimely Meditations* III)
1876 *Richard Wagner in Bayreuth* (*Untimely Meditations* IV)
1878 *Human, All Too Human* (2nd edn 1886)
1879 *Assorted Opinions and Maxims* (1st supplement to *Human, All Too Human*. 2nd edn 1886)
1880 *The Wanderer and his Shadow* (2nd supplement to *Human, All Too Human*. 2nd edn 1886)
1881 *Dawn* (2nd edn 1887)
1882 *The Gay Science* (2nd edn 1887)
1883 *Thus Spoke Zarathustra* I and II
1884 *Thus Spoke Zarathustra* III
1885 *Thus Spoke Zarathustra* IV (published 1892)
1886 *Beyond Good and Evil*
1887 *On the Genealogy of Morals*
1888 *The Wagner Case*
      Twilight of the Idols (published 1889)
      The Anti-Christ (published 1895)
      Ecce Homo (published 1908)
      Nietzsche contra Wagner (published 1895)
      Dithyrambs of Dionysus (published 1892)

The Will to Power is a collection of notes written between 1883 and 1888: published 1901, much expanded edn 1905.

Preface. *dogmatists . . . dogmatism . . . dogmatizing . . . dogmatic*: the *Shorter Oxford Dictionary* defines 'dogmatic' (in the philosophical sense) as 'proceeding upon *a priori* principles accepted as true', and 'dogmatism' as 'a system of philosophy based upon principles dictated by reasoning alone; opposite of *scepticism*. More generally, a way of thinking based upon principles which have not been tested by reflection'.

Vedanta: the Veda is the body of Hindu scripture, the Vedanta the religious and philosophical teaching derived from it.

good Europeans: a coinage of Nietzsche's, probably as an antithesis to 'good German' (first used in *Human, All Too Human* 475).

free spirits: freien Geister. '*Geister*' is the plural of '*Geist*', a word whose meaning and overtones cannot be fully transmitted in a single English word: it means mind, intellect, the intelligence, the thinking faculty, the 'spirit' as opposed to the 'body' (and thus, in the right context, 'ghost'), and broadly speaking everything contained in the concept 'the human spirit'. In the present translation I have consistently rendered *Geist* as 'spirit', but the reader should remember that the word as used in German is strongly biased towards equating 'spirit' and 'mind', so that the idea of intelligence is bound up with it. A 'free spirit' is thus something comparable with a 'free-thinker', although Nietzsche very strongly repudiates any equating of the two (see Section 44).

target: the primary meaning of *Ziel*, the word used here, is 'goal, aim, objective', but it is also used for a 'target' or 'butt'; the primary meaning is, of course, intended, but the metaphor from archery prevents us from using it.

2. *de omnibus dubitandum*: everything is to be doubted (Descartes).

foreground valuations: *Vordergrunds-Schätzungen*. 'Foreground' a Nietzschean idiom meaning 'surface, superficial'; balanced by 'background', meaning 'fundamental, real'.

3. *niaiserie*: foolishness. *man . . . the 'measure of things'*: a dictum of Protagoras: 'Man is the measure of things, of the things that are that they are, of the things that are not that they are not.'

4. *synthetic judgements a priori*: 'judgement' is Kant's term for

a proposition; a synthetic judgement is a proposition whose predicate is not contained in its subject and the contrary of which is not a self-contradiction; an *a priori* judgement is a proposition which is independent of experience; a synthetic *a priori* judgement is a proposition whose contrary is not a self-contradiction and which is independent of experience. 'Every event has a cause' is a synthetic *a priori* judgement: synthetic because its predicate 'cause' is not contained in its subject 'event', *a priori* because it is not verifiable by experience. Kant maintained that the propositions of mathematics, science and morality are all synthetic *a priori* and his concern was to discover how they are *possible*. (For Nietzsche's criticism of his answer, see Section 11.)

5. *'categorical imperative'*: 'Act as if the maxim of your action were to become through your will a general natural law' is one of the definitions of the 'categorical imperative' in Kant's *Metaphysic of Morals*.

'the love of his *wisdom'*: 'philosophy' means 'love of wisdom'.

7. Nietzsche's respect for Epicurus was by 1886 in decline, and he later called him 'a typical decadent' (*Anti-Christ* 30), but in earlier years he had held him in the highest regard – see *Human, All Too Human* 68, *Assorted Opinions and Maxims* 408, *The Wanderer and his Shadow* 7, 192, 227, 295, *Dawn* 72, *The Gay Science* 45.

Dionysus: tyrant of Syracuse at whose court Plato spent some years.

8. *adventavit, etc.*: the ass came along, beautiful and strong.

9. *causa prima*: first cause (usually = God).

11. *table of categories*: the concepts which are *a priori* Kant called 'categories'.

by means of a faculty: Vermöge eines Vermögens – the tautology is more evident in the original.

niaiserie allemande: German foolishness.

College of Tübingen: a theological seminary in Swabia.

'finding' and 'inventing': 'finden' und 'erfinden'.

quia est in eo, etc.: because there is in it a sleep-inducing faculty whose property it is to make the senses drowsy.

inverted commas: Gänsefüsschen, literally 'goose-feet'.

COMMENTARY

12. *the Pole Boscovich*: Ruggiero Giuseppi Boscovich (1711–87), mathematician and physicist; actually a Croatian.

inventing ... finding: Erfinden ... Finden.

13. For his opposition to explanation in terms of purpose, see e.g. *Dawn* 130, *Gay Science* 360, *Twilight of the Idols* VI 8, *Will to Power* 260, 526, 552, 574, 602, 666, 671; for his opposition to mechanistic explanations, see e.g. Section 21, and *Will to Power* 551, 617, 634, 635, 660, 689, 1066.

15. Phenomena 'in the sense of idealist philosophy' are the product of the mind which perceives them.

reductio ad absurdum: reduction to the absurd.

causa sui: the cause of itself (usually = God).

16. *contradictio in adjecto*: contradiction in terms (literally a contradiction between the adjective and the noun it qualifies).

19. *L'effet, c'est moi*: I am the effect.

21. *'la religion de la souffrance humaine'*: the religion of human suffering.

22. *'Ni dieu, ni maître'*: neither God nor master.

23. *sacrifizio dell'intelletto*: sacrifice of the intellect.

26. *Abbé Galiani*: Ferdinando Galiani (1728–87), Italian writer and economist.

27. *gangasrotogati*: correctly *gāngāsrotagati* = as the Ganges flows (i.e. fast). *kurmagati*: correctly *kūrmagati* = as the tortoise moves (i.e. slowly). *mandeikagati*: correctly *mandūkagati*. (These corrections and definitions are taken from Walter Kaufmann's edition of *Beyond Good and Evil*.)

28. *in moribus et artibus*: in morals and arts. *Bayle*: Pierre Bayle (1647–1706), philosopher, author of the *Dictionnaire Historique et Critique* (1692), one of the most famous works of seventeenth-century philosophy.

petit fait: little fact.

31. As a supplement to this acute piece of psychological analysis, compare *On the Use and Disadvantage of History* 10, *Human, All Too Human* 539, *Assorted Opinions and Maxims* 161, 285, 289.

34. *advocatus dei*: God's advocate.

35. *'il ne cherche le vrai', etc.*: he seeks the true only so as to do the good.

38. For more on the French Revolution, see e.g. Sections 46, 191, 239, 244, 245, 258, and *Human, All Too Human* 463, *Dawn* 534, *Gay Science* 350, *Genealogy of Morals* I 16, *Twilight* IX 48, *Anti-Christ* 11, *Will to Power* 60, 90, 94, 184, 864, 877.

39. *'Pour être bon philosophe'*, etc.: 'To be a good philosopher it is necessary to be dry, clear, without illusion. A banker who has made a fortune has something of the character needed for making discoveries in philosophy, that is to say for seeing clearly into that which is.'

42. *attempters ... attempt: ... temptation: Versucher ... Versuch ... Versuchung*. *'Versucher'* also means 'experimenter', *'Versuch'* experiment. The point is that these coming philosophers' will not be dogmatists. Compare *Gay Science* 51: 'Give me any kind of sceptical proposal to which I am permitted to reply: "Let's try it! [*Versuchen wir's!*]" But I want to hear nothing more of any thing or any question which does not permit of experimentation ...' The play upon *Versuch* and *Versuchung* is very frequent in Nietzsche's work.

45. *knowledge and conscience: Wissen und Gewissen.*
homines religiosi: religious men.

46. In 1888 Nietzsche planned a book to be called *The Revaluation of All Values*. (*The Anti-Christ* was originally intended as the first part of it.) His employment of the identical phrase (*Umwertung aller ... Werte*) to describe the effect of Christianity on the ancient world illumines the nature of his own 'revaluation' and 'anti-Christianity': what he proposed was not an inversion of values but the undoing of a previous inversion.

absurdissimum: extreme of absurdity.

47. In the phrase 'the religious nature' (*das religiöse Wesen*), 'nature' is not quite satisfactory as a translation of *'Wesen'*, but I have used it because the phrase is also the title of this Part of the book. *'Wesen'* is a word with many meanings: here the foreground meaning seems to be 'ado', 'to-do' – the 'ado about religion'.

Kundry: the female character in Wagner's *Parsifal*.
type vécu: a type that has existed.

48. *Auguste Comte*: French philosopher (1798–1857). *Sainte-*

Beuve: Charles-Augustin Sainte-Beuve (1804–69), French literary critic and historian.

Ernest Renan: French rationalist (1823–92).

'Disons donc hardiment', etc.: 'Therefore let us venture to say that religion is a product of the normal man, that man is nearest to the truth when he is most religious and most assured of an eternal destiny . . . It is when he is good that he wants virtue to correspond to an eternal order, it is when he contemplates things in a disinterested way that he finds death revolting and absurd. How can we not suppose it is in these moments that man sees best?'

49. For another, much more detailed discussion of 'what is noble in Greek religiosity', see *Human, All Too Human* 111.

50. *Madame de Guyon*: Jeanne-Marie Bouvier de la Motte-Guyon (1648–1717), French mystic and Quietist.

51. Nietzsche's principal excursus on asceticism and the ascetic saint is in *On the Genealogy of Morals* III (a sixty-page essay called 'What is the Meaning of Ascetic Ideals?').

52. Compare *Dawn* 84 and the *Genealogy of Morals* III 22.

53. On atheism as a question of honesty, see *Gay Science* 357 and the *Genealogy of Morals* II 27.

55. For more on cruelty, see Sections 229 and 230; and compare *Human, All Too Human* 101, *Dawn* 18, *Genealogy of Morals* II.

da capo: again from the beginning – a reference to the eternal recurrence, for which see *Gay Science* 341 and *Zarathustra* III 2, 13, 15, 16, and IV 19.

56. *circulus vitiosus deus*: a vicious circle as God, or God as a vicious circle.

57. *old man . . . 'old man'*: the first 'man' is *Mann*, the second *Mensch*, i.e. mankind, the human race.

59. Compare *Human, All Too Human* 4, which begins: 'It is probable that the objects of the religious, moral and aesthetic sensations belong . . . only to the surface of things . . .'

60. Compare Section 198, and *Zarathustra* I 16.

61. On the conception of the philosopher as 'the man of the most comprehensive responsibility who has the conscience for the collective evolution of mankind', compare *Human, All Too Human* 25:

Since the belief that a God directs the fate of the world has disappeared ... mankind itself must set up oecumenical goals embracing the entire earth ... if mankind is not to destroy itself through conscious possession of such universal rule, it must first of all attain to an unprecedented *knowledge of the preconditions of culture* as a scientific standard for oecumenical goals. Herein lies the tremendous task facing the great spirits of the coming century.

62. Compare Section 46 and the note to that section; and see also *Twilight* VII 2, and *Anti-Christ* 2–7.

64. Section 344 of *The Gay Science* (in Book Five, added to the second edition of 1887) is the best commentary on this aphorism.

65a. In the original edition numbered 65, like the section preceding it; the 'a' added in the standard edition. (Similarly for Section 73a.)

66. Compare *Twilight* IX 46.

68. Describes a phenomenon now called, after Freud, 'repression'.

105. *pia fraus*: pious fraud.

122. *politeness of the heart*: a phrase from Goethe's *Elective Affinities* (II 5): 'There is a politeness of the heart; it is related to love. It gives rise to the most comfortable politeness of outward behaviour.'

142. '*Dans le véritable amour*', etc.: 'In true love it is the soul which envelops the body.'

147. *buona femmina, etc.*: good women and bad women need beating. *Sacchetti*: Franco Sacchetti (*c.* 1330–1400), Florentine poet and novelist.

186. *Fundamental Problems of Ethics*: Schopenhauer's *Die beiden Grundprobleme der Ethic* (*The Two Fundamental Problems of Ethics*) was published in 1841. The passage quoted comes from 'On the Basis of Morals', the second of the two long essays of which the book consists. 'Actually' and 'actual' are emphasized by Nietzsche, not in the original.

neminem laede, etc: harm no one, rather help everyone as much as you are able.

188. *laisser aller*: letting go.

189. 'Sublimated itself' is, in the original, '*sich sublimiert*'. It

is interesting that Nietzsche should employ precisely the word
'*sublimieren*', instead of such synonyms of it as '*selbst-aufheben*'
or '*selbst-überwinden*', which he employs in other contexts,
when referring to the sublimation of sexuality. For an example
of his use of the phrase 'sublimated (*sublimierte*) sexuality', see
Assorted Opinions and Maxims 95.

190. *prosthe Platōn, etc.*: Plato in front, Plato behind, chimaera in the middle. The phrase is based on the description of
the chimaera in the *Iliad*: 'Lion in front, serpent behind, goat
in the middle'.

191. On the relationship between instinct and reason in
Socrates, see especially *Twilight* II.

192. *arcubalista*: crossbow. *Armbrust*: also crossbow – but
the elements of which the word is composed mean 'arm' and
'breast': '*Armbrust*' is clearly a mere imitation of sounds
without regard to their meaning.

193. *Quidquid luce fuit, etc.*: That which happens in the light
persists in the dark.

195. The thesis of this section is greatly elaborated in the
Genealogy of Morals I, *Twilight* VII and the *Anti-Christ passim*.
For Nietzsche's opinions on ancient and contemporary Jewry,
see also Sections 248, 250 and 251, and *Human* 475, *Dawn* 38,
205, 377, *Gay Science* 135, 136, 248, 361.

197. For Nietzsche on Cesare Borgia, see also *Twilight* IX
37, *Anti-Christ* 46, 61, *Ecce Homo* III 1, *Will to Power* 871, and
his letter to Brandes of 20 November 1888.

198. *Hafiz and Goethe*: Hafiz (Mahommed Shams-ud-din,
died 1389) is reputedly the greatest Persian poet, compared
with whom our own adopted Omar is a tinkling bell, and this
status-relationship is repeated in that between Goethe's *West-
östlicher Divan* (inspired by Hafiz) and Fitzgerald's *Rubáiyát*.
But the voice within the tavern was as clearly audible to Hafiz
as it was to Omar, and he obeyed it just as readily. (It is
presumably the direct prohibition of alcohol in the Koran
which made of these poets, not merely heavy drinkers, but
vehement *advocates* of drunkenness.) Goethe was also, and
even by the liberal standards of his age and class, a very heavy
drinker – but he could hold his drink and the suggestion

(perhaps not wholly serious) that he was a drunkard derives from Nietzsche's own enforced abstemiousness.

licentia morum: moral licence.

199. For Nietzsche on Napoleon, see also Sections 244 and 256, and compare *The Birth of Tragedy* 18, *Human* 164, *Dawn* 109, 245, 298, 549, *The Gay Science* 23, 282, 362, the *Genealogy* I 16, *Twilight* IX 44, 45, 48, 49, *Will to Power* 27, 104, 544, 751, 829, 877, 975, 1017, 1018, 1026.

201. For further reflections on the role of fear in human culture and morality, see Section 229, and *Human* 169, *Wanderer and his Shadow* 50, *Dawn* 26, 57, 104, 142, 173, 174, 220, 241, 250, 309, 310, 538, 551, *Gay Science* 355, *Genealogy* II 19, *Will to Power* 576; and for a contrasting point of view, *Zarathustra* IV 15.

res publica: commonwealth.

202–3. These two sections are a restatement in more directly political terms of the assertions which find 'poetic' expression in *Zarathustra*: see especially I Prologue, II 7 and 18, III 5 and 12 (2).

204. In this Part of the book 'scholar' and 'man of science' are used indifferently to mean the practitioners of the learned professions as opposed to the philosopher in Nietzsche's conception of him. (See especially Sections 205, 206, 207 and 211.)

montrer ses plaies: display of one's wounds.

most cultured and conceited: gebildetsten und eingebildetsten.

otium: leisure.

Eugen Dühring (1833–1921), *Eduard von Hartmann* (1842–1906), German philosophers.

207. *ipsissimosity*: 'very ownness', from *ipsissima* = very own.

caput mortuum: dross.

'*Je ne méprise presque rien*': I despise almost nothing.

Gewaltmensch: I leave this word in German because, like a few other German substantives (e.g. *Schadenfreude, Delikatessen, Festschrift*), it precisely designates something for which no single English word exists. '*Gewalt*' means primarily the power to dominate other people, and is connected with *walten* = to rule, but it also contains the idea of violence or brutality. A *'Gewaltmensch'* is thus a 'strong man' who dominates by violence; the *usage* of the word, however, has given it a definitely medieval sound – so that its true English definition would be 'a man like William the Conqueror or Edward I'.

208. *bonae voluntatis*: of good will.

l'art pour l'art: art for art's sake.

209. *'dogmatic slumber'*: alludes to Kant's statement that Hume had awoken him from his 'dogmatic slumber'.

210. *Chinaman of Königsberg*: Kant.

211–13. For further examples of Nietzsche's conception of the philosopher, see *Schopenhauer as Educator* 3, 5, 7, *Gay Science* Preface 3, 289, 343, 381, *Genealogy* I note, III 7, 8.

218. *bêtise bourgeoise*: bourgeois stupidity.

'homo bonae voluntatis': man of good will.

222. *suffers ... 'suffer with his fellows': leidet ... 'mit leidet'. Mitleiden* = to pity (suffer with).

223. Nietzsche's most extended critique of the nineteenth century's unprecedented sense of and preoccupation with history is his essay *On the Use and Disadvantage of History for Life*.

224. For further remarks on Homer, see *Homer and Classical Philology* (1869), 'Homer's Contest' (*Five Prefaces to Five Unwritten Books*, 1872), *Birth of Tragedy* 3, 5, *Human* 45, 125, 159, 211, 262, *Assorted Opinions and Maxims* 189, 212, 219, 220, *Wanderer and his Shadow* 113, 140, *Gay Science* 302, *Genealogy* III 4, 25; and on Shakespeare, *Birth of Tragedy* 7 (Hamlet), *Richard Wagner in Bayreuth* 3, *Human* 61 (Othello), 125, 162, 176, 221, *Assorted Opinions* 162, *Dawn* 76, 240 (Macbeth), 549, *Gay Science* 98 (Julius Caesar), 167 (Hamlet), *Ecce Homo* II 4, *Will to Power* 848, 996.

227. *'nitimur in vetitum'*: we strive after the forbidden (Ovid).

228. *Helvétius*: Claude Adrien Helvétius (1715–71), encyclopedist, atheist, materialist.

ce senateur Pococurante: *'pococurante'* means easy-going.

comfort ... fashion: in English in the original.

229. *'milk of pious thoughts'*: from Schiller's *Wilhelm Tell*.

232. *'the eternal-boring in woman'*: alludes to 'the eternal-

womanly', a phrase in the closing chorus of Goethe's *Faust* (quoted in Section 236).

mulier . . . ecclesia: let woman be silent in church. *mulier . . . politicis*: let woman be silent in matters of politics. *mulier . . . muliere*: let woman be silent about woman.

235. *'mon ami', etc.*: My friend, never permit yourself anything but follies which will give you a great deal of pleasure.

236. *'ella guardava suso', etc.*: she looked upward and I at her.

237. *Few words, much meaning*: *Kurze Rede, langer Sinn* – an inversion of Schiller's phrase *'der langen Rede kurzer Sinn'* (*Die Piccolomini*) = the concise meaning of the long speech.

240. Wagner is referred to in almost all Nietzsche's books, and often he is being referred to when he is not actually named (often he appears as 'the artist'). The most extended discussion is to be found in *The Birth of Tragedy* 16–25, *Richard Wagner in Bayreuth*, *Zarathustra* IV (where Wagner is 'the Sorcerer'), *The Wagner Case*, and *Nietzsche contra Wagner*.

241. The statesman referred to is, of course, Bismarck. Compare the words with which the first paragraph of *David Strauss* ends:

> Of all the evil consequences which have followed the recent war with France perhaps the worst is a widespread if not universal error . . . that German culture too was victorious in the struggle . . . This delusion . . . is capable of turning our victory into a complete defeat: *into the defeat if not the extirpation of the German spirit* [Geist] *for the benefit of the 'German Reich'*.

This was written in 1873; in 1888 Nietzsche wrote:

> Nowadays the Germans are bored with intellect [*Geist*], the Germans mistrust intellect, politics devours all seriousness for really intellectual [*geistige*] things – *Deutschland, Deutschland über alles* was, I fear, the end of German philosophy . . . (*Twilight* VIII 1)

His attitude towards the *Reich* was consistent throughout: the *Reich* was destructive of what was best in Germany and demanded of the Germans that which they were least fitted for.

244. *'two souls, alas', etc.*: from Goethe's *Faust*, Part I Scene 2.

COMMENTARY

Kotzebue: August Friedrich Ferdinand von Kotzebue (1761–1819), one of the most popular dramatists of his day.

Sand: Karl Ludwig Sand (1795–1820), the student who murdered Kotzebue.

Gemüt: warm-heartedness, 'soul'; more familiar in the form *'Gemütlichkeit'* = good-fellow plus beer.

ad oculos: visibly to the eyes.

Berlin wit and sand: the region around Berlin is notoriously arid and sandy. The word here translated 'wit' (*Witz*) does not imply any great degree of refinement. Jokiness, smartness, even 'cockney humour' might render it better. The whole phrase is probably meant to be derogatory.

das 'tiusche' Volk, das Täusche-Volk: *täuschen* = to deceive. This is a piece of joke-etymology: *'täusche'* is derived from *'tiusche'*, and, by implication, *'deutsch'* from *'täusche'*. The joke is effective because 'deutsch' does (according to the usual account) derive from *'tiusche'* (in Old High German *diutisc* = of the people, national), as does 'Teuton' and 'Dutch'.

245. *'Saxon Switzerland'*: mountainous region near Dresden.

noli me tangere: do not touch me.

251. *Sybels and Treitschkes*: Heinrich von Sybel (1817–95) and Heinrich von Treitschke (1834–96), German historians.

anti-Jewism: Antisemiterei. res facta . . . nata: something made . . . born. *res ficta et picta*: something invented and unreal. *aere perennius*: more enduring than bronze (Horace).

the March: i.e. the March of Brandenburg, the area around Berlin.

252. *'je méprise Locke'*: I despise Locke.

253. *âme française*: French soul.

254. *Victor Hugo's funeral*: May 1885.

in voluptate psychologica: in taking pleasure in psychology.

Henri Beyle: better known by the pen-name Stendhal.

blood and iron: a phrase of Bismarck's meaning, of course, 'war'.

Bizet: for Nietzsche Bizet was the antithesis of Wagner, and it is in that role that he appears in *The Wagner Case* (see especially the Foreword and Sections 1–3).

257. The ideas expressed in this section are developed at length in the *Genealogy* I and II.

260. The coinages *Herren-Moral* and *Sklaven-Moral* make their first appearance in this section. The conception of a 'twofold prehistory of good and evil' was first promulgated in *Human* 45, and its implications are further discussed and elaborated in the *Genealogy* I.

'*gai saber*': gay science, meaning the art of the Provençal troubadours. Nietzsche had adopted the phrase as the title of his *Die fröhliche Wissenschaft* which, so that there should be no doubt as to what that German phrase was intended to translate, he subtitled '*la gaya scienza*'.

263. For another attack on 'the cultured', see *Zarathustra* II 14.

Différence engendre haine: Difference engenders hate.

264. *furca . . . naturam expellere . . . usque recurret*: alludes to Horace's 'Try to drive out nature with a pitchfork, it always returns.'

265. *inter pares*: among equals.

269. For another, more detailed analysis of Jesus, see *Anti-Christ* 28–37 and 39.

271. Compare with the last two sentences the main argument and action of *Zarathustra* IV.

274. '*Raphael without hands*': alludes to the words of the painter Conti in Lessing's *Emilia Galotti*: 'or do you think, Prince, that Raphael would not still have been the greatest genius of painting if he had unfortunately been born without hands?'

275. Compare Section 26.

284. *four virtues*: 'sympathy' = *Mitgefühl*, not *Mitleid* (pity), and might perhaps be better rendered 'empathy'. There is another list of four virtues in *Dawn* 556 (honesty, bravery, magnanimity, politeness). Politeness has now become a 'roguish vice'.

285. Compare *Zarathustra* II 18 and 22.

286. '*Here is the prospect free*', *etc.*: from the closing scene of Goethe's *Faust* II. The whole movement of this scene is upwards: one group after another is left below as the 'immortal part' of Faust is borne higher and higher.

289. *abyss . . . ground . . . 'foundation'*: *Abgrund . . . Grunde . . . 'Begründung'*.

290. *sympathy*: *Mitgefühl*.

293. *'gay science', to make the matter plain*: *'fröhliche Wissenschaft', um es den Deutschen zu verdeutlichen*. The last clause means: to elucidate it for the Germans. Plays upon *'deutsch'* and *'deutlich'* (clear) occur elsewhere in Nietzsche – he humorously (and seriously) supposes them to be opposites.

294. For examples of Nietzsche on laughter, see *Human* 553, *Wanderer* 173, *Gay Science* 1, 200, *Zarathustra* I 7, II 13, IV 13 (16–20), *Will to Power* 990.

'laughter is a bad infirmity', etc: quoted in German and translated back.

295. The quotation of the first part of this section in *Ecce Homo* (III 6), prefaced by the admonition that no one is to try to guess who is being described, suggests that Nietzsche is here describing himself.

Epode. A poem in fifteen stanzas, with a somewhat complicated rhyme scheme and strongly marked rhythm. Two kinds of metrical translation would, of course, be possible: one which preserved the existing rhyme scheme and rhythm and one which rewrote the poem in a new metre. But neither would, in this case, be appropriate: the former would be the more faithful to Nietzsche's intentions, but the result would be a very ugly and hard-to-read *poem* because of the distortion and contortion of language necessary for preserving something of the meaning; the latter would certainly result in a better poem but would deviate so far from the author's intentions as to be a falsification of them. Nietzsche's normal form of communication was prose, and he wrote a quantity of prose, notably but not only in *Zarathustra*, of the kind usually called 'poetic': he found no difficulty in employing in prose the more highly emotional or rhapsodic language which was in the nineteenth century the hallmark of the vocabulary of poetry, and there is little in his poems which would seem out of place in his 'poetic' prose. In a poem such as the present one, therefore, that which is distinctive is not the vocabulary or the thought but precisely the rhyme-scheme and strongly marked rhythm. (This is more immediately obvious in the case of 'To the Mistral', the poem with which *The Gay Science* closes: based on a somewhat similar scheme to 'From High Mountains', the poem's whole significance resides in its fast-running rhythm – a very successful imitation of speed and energy.) I have therefore thought it best to provide a prose translation which is, I hope, readable as a 'prose poem', and to indicate the shape of the original poem here. I reproduce the opening and closing stanzas.

> O Lebens Mittag! Feierliche Zeit!
>   O Sommergarten!
> Unruhig Glück im Stehn und Spähn und Warten: –
> Der Freunde harr' ich, Tag und Nacht bereit,
> Wo bleibt ihr, Freunde? Kommt! 's ist Zeit! 's ist Zeit!
>
> *
>
> Nun feiern wir, vereinten Siegs gewiss,
>   Das Fest der Feste:
> Freund *Zarathustra* kam, der Gast der Gäste!
> Nun lacht die Welt, der grause Vorhang riss,
> Die Hochzeit kam für Licht und Finsternis . . .

CHRONOLOGY

1844   15 October. Friedrich Wilhelm Nietzsche born in the parsonage at Röcken, near Lützen, Germany, the first of three children of Karl Ludwig, the village pastor, and Fraziska Nietzsche, daughter of the pastor of a nearby village.

1849   27 July. Nietzsche's father dies.

1850   The Nietzsche family moves to Naumberg, in Thuringia, in April. Arthur Schopenhauer publishes *Essays, Aphorisms and Maxims*.

1856   Birth of Freud.

1858   The family moves to No. 18 Weingarten. Nietzsche wins a place at the prestigious Pforta grammar school.

1860   Forms a literary society, 'Germania', with two Naumberg friends. Jacob Burckhardt publishes *The Civilization of the Renaissance in Italy*.

1864   Enters Bonn University as a student of theology and philology.

1865   At Easter, Nietzsche abandons the study of theology having lost his Christian belief. Leaves Bonn for Leipzig, following his former tutor of philology, Friedrich Ritschl. Begins to read Schopenhauer.

1867   First publication, 'Zur Geschichte der Theognideischen Spruchsammlung' (The History of the Theognidia Collection) in the *Rheinische Museum für Philiogie*. Begins military service.

1868   Discharged from the army. Meets Richard Wagner.

1869   Appointed to the chair of classical philology at Basle University having been recommended by Ritschl. Awarded a doctorate by Leipzig. Regular visitor at Wagners' home in Tribschen.

1870   Delivers public lectures on 'The Greek Music Drama' and 'Socrates and Tragedy'. Serves as a medical orderly with the Prussian army where he is taken ill with diphtheria.

1871   Applies unsuccessfully for the chair of philology at Basle. His health deteriorates. Takes leave to recover and works on *The Birth of Tragedy*.

1872   *The Birth of Tragedy* published (January). Public lectures 'On the Future of our Educational Institutions'.

1873   *Untimely Meditations I: David Strauss* published.

1874   *Untimely Meditations II: On the Use and Disadvantage of History for*

Life and *III: Schopenh...s Educator* published.

1875 Meets Peter Gast, w...o become his earliest 'disciple'. Suffers from ill-health leadi... ...eneral collapse at Christmas.

1876 Granted a long absence... Basle due to continuing ill-health. Proposes marriage to ... ...le Trampedach but is rejected. *Untimely Meditations IV: Richard Wagner in Bayreuth* published. Travels to Italy.

1878 *Human, All Too Human* published. His friendship with the Wagners comes to an end.

1879 *Assorted Opinions and Maxims* publis...d. Retires on a pension from Basle due to sickness.

1880 *The Wanderer and his Shadow* and *Human, All Too Human* II published.

1881 *Dawn* published.

1882 *The Gay Science* published. Proposes to Lou Andreas Salomé and is rejected.

1883 13 February. Wagner dies in Venice. *Thus Spoke Zarathustra* I and II published.

1884 *Thus Spoke Zarathustra* III published.

1885 *Zarathustra* IV privately printed.

1886 *Beyond Good and Evil* published.

1887 *On the Genealogy of Morals* published.

1888 *The Wagner Case* published. First review of his work as a whole published in the Bern *Bund*. Experiences some improvement in health but this is short-lived.

1889 Suffers mental collapse in Turin and is admitted to a psychiatric clinic at the University of Jena. *Twilight of the Idols* published and *Nietzsche contra Wagner* privately printed.

1890 Nietzsche returns to his mother's home.

1891 *Dithyrambs of Dionysus* published.

1894 *The Anti-Christ* published. The 'Nietzsche Archive' founded by his sister, Elisabeth.

1895 *Nietzsche contra Wagner* published.

1897 20 April. Nietzsche's mother dies; and Elisabeth moves Nietzsche to Weimar.

1900 25 August. Nietzsche dies. Freud publishes *Interpretation of Dreams*.

1901 Publication of *The Will to Power*, papers selected by Elisabeth and Peter Gast.

1908 *Ecce Homo* published.